Advances in Experiential
Social Processes

Volume 1

Advances in Experiential Social Processes

Volume 1

Edited by

Cary L. Cooper

*University of Manchester Institute of Science and Technology
England*

and

Clayton P. Alderfer

*Yale University
U.S.A.*

JOHN WILEY & SONS

Chichester · New York · Brisbane · Toronto

Library of Congress Cataloging in Publication Data:
Main entry under title:

Advances in experiential social processes.

   Includes index.
   1. Group relations training—Addresses, essays,
lectures.   2. Interpersonal relations—Addresses, essays,
lectures.   3. Experience—Addresses, essays, lectures.
I. Cooper, Cary L. II. Alderfer, Clayton P.
HM134.A38   158′.2   77-22060

ISBN 0 471 99546 0

Photosetting by Thomson Press (India) Limited, New Delhi,
and printed in Great Britain by The Pitman Press. Bath. Avon.

List of Contributors

CLAYTON P. ALDERFER   *Professor of Organization Behaviour, Yale University, U.S.A.*

LEE BOLMAN   *Lecturer in Education, Harvard University, U.S.A.*

L. DAVID BROWN   *Professor of Organization Behaviour, Case Western Reserve University, U.S.A.*

CARY L. COOPER   *Professor of Management Educational Methods, University of Manchester Institute of Science and Technology, England.*

ROBERT E. KAPLAN   *Professor of Organization Behaviour, Case Western Reserve University, U.S.A.*

EDWARD KLEIN   *Professor of Psychology, University of Cincinnati, U.S.A.*

SVEN LENNUNG   *Professor of Education, Lunds University, Sweden*

NED LEVINE   *Senior Research Fellow, Institute of Social Science Research, University of California, Los Angeles, U.S.A.*

RONALD LIPPITT   *Independent Consultant and Professor Emeritus of the University of Michigan, Ann Arbor, Michigan, U.S.A.*

ALVIN R. MAHRER   *Professor of Psychology, University of Ottawa, Canada*

EVA SCHINDLER-RAINMAN   *Independent Consultant, Ann Arbor, Michigan, U.S.A.*

RICHARD A. SCHMUCK   *Director, Center for Educational Policy and Management, University of Oregon, U.S.A.*

GORDON A. WALTER   *Professor of Business Administration, University of British Columbia, Canada*

Contents

General Introduction to Series

It has been nearly three decades since the first sensitivity training groups were developed as an innovative educational technique in social and human relations training. Since that time, the sensitivity training or T-group has spawned a wide range of experiential methods, which have had an enormous growth in a variety of settings (Cooper, 1973). Personal growth groups, life and career planning, laboratory education, management development, organization development, and community interventions all represent vehicles which have been heavily influenced, if not themselves created, by advances in experiential social processes. New developments in this multifaceted field are often scattered through a variety of academic journals and books in a number of different disciplines (e.g., psychology, sociology, management, education, etc.). It was felt that what was needed was a series of books which could provide a focal point for bringing together and summarizing what has been learned in this growing and diversifying field. This volume represents the first in such a series and it is our intention to produce further volumes on a regular basis containing articles which either review a field of application, describe a technique, summarize design developments, integrate research, or take some tack which systematizes and advances the field of experiential learning.

In the first volume of the **Advances in Experiential Social Processes** series, our intention is to take a 'broad brushstroke' approach to the field of experiential learning. That is, to provide a series of papers highlighting experiential social processes that range from a focus on individual, group, intergroup, to organizational, and ultimately community, issues and problems.

We start the book with two overview chapters; first, one that provides a classification schema of experiential social processes, as seen by a European scholar in the field; and second, one that examines the *values* implicit in experiential learning approaches and how they affect the learning process. These introductory chapters should provide us with an anchor of these learning experiences in terms of their role in the wider educational process and their underlying value assumptions. Then the book develops progressively from individual-based to community-based experiential applications, theories, problem-areas, etc. For example, Dr Mahrer's original and highly intriguing chapter on experiential psychotherapies highlights a number of important individually based learning and re-educative strategies, while Dr Kaplan's work on 'open interaction' focuses more on group-based phenomena (such as T-groups). Dr Brown's chapter on intergroup relations and Drs Schindler-Rainman and Lippitt's concentrate on improving the quality of total community life, to mention only a few.

Throughout this book we have asked our contributors to be thoughtful and innovative in their style of presentation and to attempt to communicate to a broad audience which includes academicians, practitioners and informed participants. If they have a point of view, make it clear. If they are summarizing, make it fair, and if they are conjecturing, state their premises. If their writing is personal, be personal; if objective, be objective. Wherever possible, provide readers with a data base to reflect on—this could mean anecdotes as well as research findings. On balance, we asked our contributors to inform our readers of the exciting developments in the field of experiential social processes, to reflect the current state of the art as well as to help push forward the frontiers of 'involved learning' a bit further.

Reference

Cooper, C. L. (1973) *Group Training for Individual and Organizational Development.* Basel, S. Karger.

Chapter 1

Implicit Values in Experiential Learning Groups: Their Functional and Dysfunctional Consequences

Cary L. Cooper

University of Manchester Institute of Science and Technology, England

and

Ned Levine

University of California, Los Angeles U.S.A.

Experiential learning groups have been available as a method of social skill training for nearly 30 years (Bradford, Gibb and Benne, 1964; Cooper 1972), (we will from time to time refer to the experiential activities as T-groups, as a shorthand phrase). In that time, they have blossomed into a wide range of different applications with different populations (Siroka, Siroka, and Schloss, 1971; Blumberg and Golembiewski, 1976). They have also been subsumed under a host of different labels—T groups, sensitivity groups, encounter groups, *Gestalt* therapy groups, Esalen groups, personal growth groups, sometimes indicating a different orientation, but more often not (Mills, 1976). Nonetheless, there has been a common core of values which has cut through these groups and made them a distinct type of group experience (Levine and Cooper, 1976). They have been one of the major educational innovations of the last 30 years and they have affected substantially the development of other educational techniques over that period. Our purpose in this chapter is to discuss explicitly the values inherent in experiential learning groups, the value conflicts that emerge frequently in such groups and the manner in which an understanding of the underlying assumptions and values under which practitioners are operating can help in the planning of a more internally consistent and effective group experience.

Values in groups

In the last few years, there have been a number of criticisms levelled against these group-learning techniques, many of which raise serious questions about goals and values involved (Bach, 1967; Lakin, 1969; Back, 1972). While some of these criticisms have been wide off the mark, others have struck at the core of assumptions and values upon which this movement has legitimated itself. Group practitioners have been accused of being anti-scientific, unconcerned with the problems of society, of not showing an awareness for ethical issues, and of not making careful selection of prospective participants. The strength of the criticisms, it appears, paralleled the growth of the group movement. As it expanded into different areas, allowing more and more persons to participate in various group experiences, the criticisms levelled against it however, often made the criticisms more scathing by retreating occasionally into Messianic positions ('We are creating a new way'), more often into self-fulfilling justifications ('You have to go through this experience to understand it'), and quite commonly into conceptually sloppy and mystifying rationales for their purpose.

Very rarely did the 'group people' systematically try to study the group phenomenon that they had created and to subject it to the type of evaluation that most other educational approaches are eventually forced to accept. The research, naturally, did show that participants in group situations could change under certain circumstances (Cooper and Mangham, 1971). People could learn to be more open with others (Rubin, 1967), more sensitive to social situations (Bass, 1962), more understanding of how other people see them (Burke and Bennis, 1961), have more insight into human behaviour (Argyris, 1965), more aware of their own feelings (French, Sherwood, and Bradford, 1966), and more adaptable and flexible in social situations (Cooper, 1972). In short, experiential learning groups could be meaningful experiences for people *under certain circumstances*. The key here, however, is 'under certain circumstances', for there is sufficient research to show that the trainer, the group context, the personalities of the members are all critical dimensions in determining whether a group experience is valuable or not (Cooper, Levine, and Kobayashi, 1976; Cooper, 1977). There is a great deal of research evidence showing that group experiences can be neutral in their effect (Cooper and Mangham, 1971) and some even shows that such experiences could be harmful under certain circumstances (Cooper, 1975; Smith, 1975).

I. Groups as technology

Experiential learning groups, just like any other educational or programmatic techniques, have to be evaluated continuously in order to improve their effectiveness as a technique. Consciousness of the process grows slowly as mistakes are made, as criticisms are levelled, and as a growing level of sophistication about selectivity of participants and methods is obtained. The effect of all of this is to provide practitioners with a greater insight into the whys and wherefores of the technique. If we want to put this more abstractly, we can say that any educational technique has a set of assumptions and a set of values inherent in it. The assumptions take the form of operating rules, whereby the practitioners need guidelines to respond to their participants, and the values emerge in the form of desired ends or goals for which the technique is aimed (Levine, 1971; 1972). It may take a while before practitioners can verbalize explicitly the values and assumptions upon which they operate, but eventually with experience this emerges. There are, of course, alternative values and assumptions possible, and they have their own techniques associated with them. But this is in the nature of all technologies. Technologies always have particular values, goals and assumptions, and the manner in which choice between technologies is made is at this theoretical level, rather than as a technical decision.

This might seem relatively straightforward, and somewhat pedantic at that, if we did not realize that practitioners of experiential learning group techniques have been extremely guilty of not facing up to the assumptions and values inherent in the type of groups they operate; and at times these practitioners have even gone to the other extreme and insisted that they operate according to 'no values and assumptions'! (Clark, 1962). The experiential learning group was, after all, conceived of in the context of allowing a free interchange of communication, of focusing on 'emergent' problems in a group (the 'here and now') rather than on external 'structural' problems, on being open to all kinds of different feelings, on acknowledging the impact of people as they occur, and on learning to be flexible and adaptive in relating to others. Their whole focus has been on spontaneity and creativity, rather than on structured cognition. People go to groups to 'discover things', to be surprised, to be active, to try out different behaviours, to experience intense emotions (to be angry, to fall in love, to be free, to be childlike and happy again); they do not go to groups to be lectured to, to learn formal material(s), to have to 'work hard', to have to accomplish things, to have to behave in structured ways. Experiential learning groups are 'fun' and are not supposed to be 'hard work'. They are innovative and creative, not formalized. They have their own 'experiential logic', not a mathematical, nor a social conventional, nor even an 'ideal behaviour' logic.

Such feelings often underlie participation in group experiences by practitioners and members alike. It is, however, one thing to say that experiential learning groups do not have structured activities, and another to pretend that they do not have 'structure' to them—a set of assumptions, values and goals. For it is our contention here that such groups are highly structured, that the practitioners and members both act in accordance with this structure, and, more importantly, that their awareness of the inherent structure can allow a greater degree of planning of the part of practitioners. Making more explicit assumptions, goals and values is the first step towards planning how this process is to be effectively handled. The more explicit one is about the process, the clearer one can be about how to plan it, the more open one can be about mistakes in the design, the quicker a rectification will occur, and the more effective the technique will become in the long run. In short, what we are saying is that experiential learning groups form a technology just like any other technology, and thus the same rules and logic can be applied towards improving this technology as any other.

4

II. Experiential learning groups as value systems

In an earlier article (Levine and Cooper, 1976), we attempted to define some of the expressed common goals that are often stated in experiential learning groups and some of the underlying social conditions that have created this movement. Basically, we argued that a T-group is a type of group in which there is a commitment towards involvement, towards relating the groups to its outside environment. These four or five values, as a composite, form roughly a type of group that can be distinguished from other types of groups. This does not mean that all experiential learning groups are the same (they certainly are not) nor that there are not differences in style, goals, purposes between groups. Rather, virtually all of the experiential group movement has accepted these values in their general form, as well as adding new ones depending on the context.

The T-groups and the common values expressed by them, however, must be seen as a product of four societal conditions which created the demands for this type of group. The T-group movement emerged as a function of an Anglo-American dominance in social science after the Second World War, as a product of an advanced capitalist economy in which there was a concern for improving administrative and organizational skills, as a function of a young age structure due to the high birth rates after the war, and as an expression of middle-class needs. The experiential learning group or T-group was the child of post Second World War Anglo-American society (Levine and Cooper, 1976). Experiential learning groups emerged as a sought-after technology. The state of society at the time they emerged was one dominated by large organizations (both private and public), which had complicated problems of planning, organizing, producing, and distributing their product (Galbraith, 1967). A whole range of new managerial and administrative problems emerged in this context, and the interests of group-training people, who were beginning to discover a number of principles of small group behaviour, were aimed in this direction. The demand for these applications came primarily from these large organizations, for without them the group movement would never have grown and developed like it did.

Also, people were concerned about their sense of 'being' in this new advanced, corporate society. The increasing bureaucratic organization of America and Europe after the war created new roles for people (Reisman, 1950). There were strong pressures towards improving one's living standard, and the means for doing this were suddenly more available for a higher proportion of the society than was the case previously. There were less strong, but developing, pressures towards social equality, which started to show themselves in the late 1950s (Civil Rights movement, equal opportunity, etc.). There was a negative side to this, of course. New roles created confusion over expected behaviour, and people started to question how they are supposed to act (Erikson, 1950). In the 1950s and especially during the 1960s, there was suddenly a widespread concern in American–European society over finding a sensible style of relating to other people. This concern was shown by the increase in books and films on behaviour, psychology, therapy, and liberation, on seeking out new ways of 'relating to one's body', on 'discovering ourselves', and so forth. Participants, and trainers, were attending the groups partly to obtain skills in relating to large organizations, but also towards discovering hidden aspects of themselves and new ways of behaving towards others. The problem was perceived at an individual level—discovering oneself, developing one's personal resources, eliminating neurotic behavioural patterns—but the stimulus for such a problem was rooted in the society, and the values implicit in this behaviour were social (Erikson, 1956).

This brings us up against one of the most important implicit assumptions of the whole experiential learning group movement, namely that change is to be sought through 'individuals' rather than through 'collectivities' (Bradford, Gibb, and Benne, 1964). The new large organizations that have emerged slowly throughout this century, and which blossomed after the Second World War, were assumed to be permanant, 'fixed' entities. Change, if it had to occur, had to be through 'individuals'. Thus, people are brought to groups to learn about behaviour, to learn about their behaviour in social situations, to learn how to be more flexible, etc. When we make such a commitment towards 'individual education', we are implicitly accepting the *status quo* of the society. Society is all right; individuals must change. There is nothing wrong, of course, with working with individuals; the whole education system is set up on similar premises, after all; but there is an aspect of this that we must accept if we are to properly understand the values and assumptions inherent in an experiential group process. This is namely that education always has a strong socializing component—a normative dimension; education teaches knowledge and skills, but it also teaches attitudes, values, and roles which are part of a social formation. And, that, therefore, we are learning to fit into a social system in learning these. Even the knowledge and skill components are social to a large extent. Knowledge is not created abstractly, but by specific individuals working within specific institutions, existing in specific places, etc. Similarly with skills; skills must be acted out in certain places and on certain materials and in certain relationships with specific people. We live in a real social world, not an abstract one, so that education is always social in form.

This emphasis on the individual, however, brings up an important complication, which is that individual change must be consistent with the given organizations within which a person works or lives. Many people involved in group work, especially those concerned with organizational development, soon discovered the limits of the group approach when they attempted to push participants to express behaviours that were inconsistent with the norms in which these individuals worked (Harrison, 1972). A potential conflict between the values pursued in a T-group and the values existing in a social organization emerges because the limits for change of the organization are so narrow. Most large organizations are economic-based; they either produce something, distribute that produce, or else give services and collect their income from other producing organizations (e.g., the government). Economic relationships tend to be relatively stable ones, for people have too much to lose by changing these frequently. Thus, economic organizations are essentially conservative. The T-group, on the other hand, argues for flexibility on the part of participants, on openness to new experiences, on confronting people who are not communicating, and generally on individual change. What happens, then, when an individual working within an organization tries to change his behaviour? If that change is inconsistent with the existing norms, the chances are that he will have to accept the norms or else become a deviant in that situation.

All of this is a way of saying that experiential learning groups are specific groups which occur in a specific social context. To talk about such groups as if they are removed from that context, as if the goals and values that they express are 'universal' ones (free of social sanctions), as if people can act any way they want without impunity, is to create a myth about groups, and a very antisocial one at that—which is incapable of being enacted on in any real society. Unstructured groups, which allow total freedom to individuals to act and express anything they want, cannot produce any permanant change in individuals; the groups can only exist by themselves, and as soon as the group disbands the reality of the behaviour disbands.

Sources of values

Values become important to experiential learning groups because they affect the way people behave and they affect what people learn in the groups. Therefore, we will have to explore these values in more depth—what values are important, how these are expressed in the group, and how a trainer or facilitator can incorporate value-analysis in setting up and planning the design of experiential learning group experiences.

Values which affect T-groups can have five different sources.

(1) They can come from the society at large, and be general values.
(2) They can come from the organizational context of the group.
(3) They can come from the trainer.
(4) They can come from the members themselves.
(5) They can emerge in the process of the interaction.

Let us take each of these in turn.

I. Societal values

Societal values come from the society at large. Sometimes these values are made explicit; other times they are not. But they are always *potential*—they emerge if someone violates them. For example, there are social conventions that are normally followed in groups, such as the wearing of clothes. This convention is so accepted and commonly understood that it deserves little comment in a group, except when it is explicitly violated as in the case of nude marathon groups (Appley and Winter, 1973).

Aside from these normal conventions, there are a number of social values which are important in affecting the behaviour of members in an experiential group. The most obvious are the perceived status characteristics of the members. All societies acknowledge age and sex differences, and they usually also acknowledge class, ethnic, racial, educational, and sometimes religious differences. Most groups have to work through these differences, and yet they have not been properly discussed by 'group people'. Older persons command more respect by virtue of their age. Sometimes this is made explicit by members, especially if it proves to be a problem, but often it is not. Similarly, sex differences are usually acknowledged, sometimes worked on, but often played down. Sex differences usually create a double-edged problem for groups. On the one hand, there are the usual assumptions about sex-role differences. In some (e.g., managerial groups), women are not expected to play an equal role with men especially as it relates to power and decision-making, but are encouraged to play social–emotional or integrative roles. But more often than not, this role typing is questioned, usually by women, and the group is pushed to handle the issue. The social value of sex roles emerges here because that value is itself undergoing a change in the society, and new roles for men and women are being created. Thus, what one often observes inside a group is the acting out of this role transition in mirror form. The submissive/social–emotional female is transformed into the assertive/aggressive female trying to overcome this passive role, while the aggressive/dominant male is transformed into a more passive/accepting male trying to overcome guilt feelings about being dominant. The T-group does no more than highlight the social conflict outside by creating a microcosm inside.

The other side of the sex difference problem, however, is the question of sexuality. Men and women are naturally attracted to each other, and the relative freedom of the T-group and the strong pressure on expression of feelings quickly brings such feelings out. How this is expressed, however, varies according to the type of sex-role model accepted by the group. In 'Male Chauvinistic' groups, women are usually in the minority anyway, so the traditional role of men competing to 'capture' the women is played out in a symbolic way. By the nature of the situation, however, this game must end in negating sexual advances, so that sex-role equality emerges as a means of controlling sexuality (see Freud, 1918, for an analogous model). In other cases, however, when the participants generally accept more egalitarian and less stereotyped sex roles, and in situations where women are in the majority, the groups may shy away from expressing such feelings. Usually group pressures are such as to discourage the overt expression of sexuality in the public area.

Groups often handle these two types of issues, at least superficially. But other status-issues usually do not emerge, if only because T-groups are run with such a homogeneous population. Class differences rarely occur because of the over-dominant middle-class orientation of the groups, nor do ethnic or racial differences, which often interrelate with class differences (see Rubin, 1967; Olmosk and Graverson, 1972; Smith and Wilson, 1975 for examples of groups run along these lines). Religious differences often do not occur because these are becoming less important, especially in the more developed countries.

To the extent that these differences do not appear, however, they tend to reinforce particular class values and fail to confront these with broader, more egalitarian social values. If participants are never exposed to class or racial differences because working-class and various racial minority group persons rarely come to T-groups, then members of groups—white, middle-class people—are never exposed to other perceptions of the society and have difficulty in grasping or understanding the position of more exploited people.

In addition, the intimate, involved atmosphere of the T-group creates strong pressures towards minimizing social conflict when it appears. Groups quickly agree that 'women are equal to men', 'blacks' have been discriminated against and ought to be 'integrated', 'workers are human just like everyone else and ought to receive their fair share of the social wealth', and then go on to deny such differences. In doing this, however, groups are playing down the existence of these social conflicts, which actually do exist in the society (and are taking sides in doing so). They are saying 'we are all white middle-class at roots', a myth which is so blatantly wrong as to be obvious. In this sense participants are not learning anything useful, and in fact, are actually helping to perpetuate the problem.

Another type of social value which emerges in T-groups, often in a very disguised form, is the notion of the 'well-adjusted Man'. Groups make assumptions about psychological 'normality' and then expect participants to conform to these assumptions (Szasz, 1961; Laing, 1965). Participants are assumed to be healthy, emotionally well-adjusted individuals (normative people), as distinct from 'sick', pathological individuals seeking help (for example, as in therapy groups). People who do not act in these 'normal' ways are considered 'deviant', 'undersocialized', 'disturbed', or a whole host of other labels which can be applied. Now, quite clearly, 'normality' is a set of normative behaviours which varies by society, by social class, by subculture, and there may be differences in the interpretation of members over what is acceptable behaviour and what is not. Young people tolerate sexuality, aggression, drugs, the expression of positive feelings far more easily than do older, pre-Second World War persons. On the other hand, materialistic motives, competition, power-seeking are far more acceptable norms to express for the older than for the younger generation. Nonetheless, in spite of these subcultural differences, there is still a great deal of overlap and communality on what is considered 'normal' behaviour. In particular, participants will become very disturbed when confronted by bizarre behaviour on the part of one member. If they cannot attribute the behaviour to events which occurred inside the group, or to role-playing, then the members become very uncomfortable and feel an inadequacy to deal with the situation. Participants are expected to act within normal limits, and if someone goes outside these limits no one knows how to handle the situation. Sometimes, of course, the individual is actually play-acting, and other times the individual may be threatening the group (e.g. as if he or she was saying 'I'm going to get you people. I'm going to throw a schizophrenic episode at you and see how you handle it. I'm going to freak out'), but this type of behaviour is always disturbing to the members. It is hard to give rules-of-thumb on what to do in such a situation if one is a group leader, but we have often found that confronting the situation in just these terms has often alleviated the tension. We point out to the group that the members are making assumptions about normality, and that person X is challenging those assumptions. Often this has allowed the group to redefine the situation and perhaps reintegrate person X back into the group. For example, this person may have been acting this way because he or she felt excluded from the group. Of the behaviour may have occurred because the person could not handle the trust being shown, or, more likely, the person may be acting this way just because there is a lack of trust in the group and this is the manner in which this individual can express that. Pointing out the implicit norms of normality can be a fruitful way of opening up members towards greater flexibility and innovative behaviour by a group, especially those used to rigid hierarchies.

II. Organizational or contextual values

A second source of values for experiential learning groups, and possibly the least recognized by trainers, is the organizational context. Groups always develop and operate in a specific environment. Starting with the recruitment into the group, through assembling the group at a time and place, to the actual interaction of the members there is always a specific context which surrounds the group. In some cases, this context may be explicit (e.g., managers from a single company, members of a course structure), but more often than not it is implicit. Yet even where the context does not seem to be the overriding issue in a group, there are many contextual assumptions and values. The most basic one is the idea of 'relevance'. The behaviour in the group, and the learning to be achieved, must be 'relevant'. Relevance, of course, has a specific meaning, one defined by the contextual environment. For an OD group, relevance is behaviour and learning that will help individuals adapt to their specific work environment. For a more individualistic group, relevance is behaviour-oriented towards self-knowledge, and attitudes and beliefs related to a specific social group. Seeking intimacy is relevant for groups in which intimacy is valued. Showing aggression may be relevant for social groups which value aggression. Showing aggression may be bad, for other social groups which play down competition and aggression. Psychological states are very circumscribed by societal and situational norms. Even the most universalistic of human expressions, such as love, intimacy, trust, acknowledgement, positive regard are meaningful at certain times and places. For a manager attending an OD group, exploring his deeper feelings of intimacy and love for his wife will be irrelevant for the organizational purpose which he joined the group in the first place.

But relevance has other meanings than just the situational appropriateness of various behaviours. It also has the idea of loyalty attached to it. In order for behaviour to be relevant for a setting, one must belong to a group in which that behaviour is expressed. This point has not been properly grasped by many group facilitators who have insisted on pushing certain behaviours as if they were universal and relevant for every group and every situation. 'Be more open' is like the Eleventh Commandment in many group leaders' eyes. But why? Is it always appropriate to be open? What about when a person meets an enemy? Should he be open then? What happens to a poor black person when he is confronted with a hostile white policeman wanting to know what he is doing? Should he be open? In fact, *can* he be open? Openness requires that the other person is willing to tolerate openness, and in some situations it is better to be a little bit paranoid if one is going to be adaptive to a situation.

Do not get us wrong. We are not advocating that people do not have to be open, that they should be defensive and manipulative, that they should mistrust their fellow men. We know the full value of openness and honesty, of expressing one's feelings (or knowing how to express one's feelings); these are all valuable states and the group movement has done much to encourage these social values. All we are saying is that the appropriateness of a behaviour pattern must be relevant to the context in which it occurs, and a trainer should pay attention to this (see Cooper, Levine, and Kobayashi, 1976). The establishment of trust and openness are two-way communications, after all, and pushing these values on only one side may not be enough. For example, managers often complain that they cannot communicate with their bosses, that either their bosses do not understand them or feel afraid that they will be superseded by their subordinate. Clearly the organizational setting in which such a perception occurs is a competitive one in which loyalty to the firm and self-promotion are delicately balanced in a semi-stable equilibrium. How can one expect one's boss to be open and accepting if he or she fears that his job may be lost if he does? In this case, 'openness', as a behavioural value, has to be modified so that it becomes relevant for the situation. Perhaps the manager would do well to test limits slowly and see if it is possible to open up the dialogue over a long period rather than prematurely exposing himself.

One of the most pressing problems of relevance in any group situation concerns the question of divided loyalties. If, in particular, the members happen to come from a single institution, there may be a split between a feeling of loyalty to the whole institution and a loyalty to one of its parts. This is more obvious with participants from a formal organization, especially a large one. Commitment to the particular subdivision that one belongs to (such as a production unit, or a sales unit inside a large company, or a particular academic department inside a university) often takes priority over a commitment towards the organization as a whole. This can be seen in terms of the necessities inherent in a job—that certain demands are required in order to satisfy the role requirements of the job—or it can be as a reaction to the particularism of another subdivision. For example, academic departments often feel maligned by university administrations for looking after themselves only. The behavioural consequences of such particularism should be fairly evident—the functioning of the whole may be disrupted by the particularism of the parts. In the above example, the academic department tries to hang on to as much money as possible in the annual budget allocated to it, even if it will not spend all its funds sensibly. There may be a long-standing history which has created mistrust between units, and it may be necessary to recreate trust before units will accept the goals of the whole organization first. Such a problem creates substantial material for any T-group wanting to look at such issues.

Even with groups that are not obviously from a single institution, the issue of particular versus holistic loyalty emerges. There is a conflict over more individual values being followed compared to more social ones. Within the group interaction itself, group members must negotiate a balance between allowing individuals to satisfy their own needs as opposed to creating a group structure that allows more interdependency. 'Giving to others', after all, means 'denying to oneself', in the short run at least. Groups may confront certain individuals with the idea that they are attempting to satisfy their own needs at the expense of others. Members may be accused of 'dominating the group', 'not listening to others', 'cutting out certain members', and so forth. As group trainers, we usually advocate a group-oriented approach on the grounds that once an effective, trustful, communicative group structure has been built, then individuals can more easily satisfy their own individual needs. But still this does not solve the issue; different groups achieve more group-oriented structures than others. In fact, the different approaches to experiential groups often breaks down on this issue. Personal expression-type groups are far more individualistic than the traditional T-group, and both are much less so than OD groups (Mills, 1976).

The issue of particularism appears, however, on an even more social level. To what extent do the members of the group see themselves as belonging to a broader collectivity? T-groups with students often show this dilemma (Levine, 1973). Especially in America and Great Britain, students tend to treat their experiences as students in isolation from the university context in which they participate. It is as if they were saying 'I am an individual trying to get along in the world. I can't be bothered with other peoples' needs. All I want to do is satisfy my own needs'. Sampson (1975) has called this 'self-contained individualism' and he sees this as emanating from a capitalistic economy that pits people against each other in a competitive manner. It is very hard for a person to see himself as part of a broader collectivity, especially when that collectivity is so loosely defined. Yet we do live in a society, and how we act does affect others in that society. Perhaps we have been too guilty of encouraging individualism at all costs, and not paying enough attention to one's role in the social world in which we live.

III. Trainer's values

There are a number of ways in which experiential group leaders can communicate values that can influence individual learning. First and foremost, values are highlighted and communicated by the intervention behaviour of the group facilitator, that is, his behaviour serves as a 'value model'. For example, a passive, interpretative authority-orientated trainer (in the Tavistock mode) is modelling and could be seen to be advocating 'emotional distance', 'patriarchial relationships', and 'low involvement and participation' (Cooper, 1976). In addition, an aggressive, dominant and highly active group leader could be positing control, confrontation, low social support, etc. On the other hand, an interactive or congruent one could be advocating a democratic process, collective decision-making and collective responsibility. It is terribly important for trainers to be aware that their behaviour reflects, communicates, and in many cases, models certain values which can influence immediate learning and subsequent behaviour of participants. Second, trainer values are also expressed in the design of the training experience; how structured or unstructured the sessions are, how the trainer's role is defined in the sessions, the nature of the role that the trainer adopts *vis-à-vis* the participants outside the group, the degree of involvement of the constiuents in the design of the programme, etc. This is to a large extent related to the motives of the group leaders, in the first place, in engaging in experiential group activity. Each trainer behaves in ways that create the conditions for both psychological success and failure, which is related to their own needs and psychological make-up (Argyris, 1965). The group facilitator can exploit his role in the pursuance of these needs, particularly in his desire to be liked or to exercise power. As Schein and Bennis (1965) have emphasized: 'the possibilities for unconscious gratification in the change-agent's role are enormous and because of their consequences (for the health of the client as well as the change-agent) they must be examined'. It is essential that training programmes be developed that focus on the trainer's motives and values and how these may enable or prevent participants from learning in their own way.

IV. Members values

A fourth source of values comes from the participants of experiential learning groups. Group member values take the form of 'needs' and 'desired goals'. Needs refer of various personal and interpersonal predispositions and 'desired goals' as to what is expected to be obtained from participating in a group (e.g., specific help to solve an organizational problem, learning to assert oneself better, learning to communicate better, learning to be more open to one's feelings, etc.) The 'desired goals' may be implicit and not recognized at the start of an experiential group by the member—he/she may discover them as the group unfolds. The needs, desired goals, and implicit goals will play a very important part in the development of group climate, the effectiveness of the group experience, etc. More importantly, where we have trouble with member values is when they come into conflict with trainer values. Trainers have a way of imposing their own values on the participants; in fact, this frequently stems from the lack of awareness of trainee needs or from an overwhelming need to express their own values. Group members may go along with this imposition, but will resent it later if they do not satisfy their own needs through the intervention (for example, the trainer wants to push an encounter exercise, while members want to integrate or conceptualize the experiences thus far acquired). We must distinguish here between situations when the trainer can perceive some needs that the group will discover and, thus, he/she structures the group in order to demonstrate them versus situation where the trainer is trying to use the group to satisfy his own needs, irrespective of what the members want.

Nevertheless, the understanding of member values are critical to the success of the group experience—unfortunately these are not always conscientiously considered.

V. Emergent values

A fifth source of values involves values which are discovered during the process of the interaction, which were neither planned by the trainer nor defined by the members; they are, so to speak, 'spontaneously' discovered. One of the best illustrations of these values are conclusions the group may reach as a consequence of actions that have developed during the interaction. For example, at large group sessions, there is often a fragmentation that takes place partly because of the large size and partly because of a lack of integration. A subgroup of this larger group may decide to 'act out' on their own, and the consequence of this will be further fragmentation. Such behaviour may come back to haunt the subgroup as a chain of events it triggered off that soon affects the initial fragmentation (i.e., subgroup *A* breaks off, subgroup *B* then follows, then subgroup *C* fragments, and soon there is no large group any more). The members may come to the conclusion that action on the part of a subgroup fundamentally threatens the overall cohesiveness of the large group, unless it has been discussed and agreed on by the larger collectivity. Thus, a value emerges—the need for macro-planning as a consequence of the interaction.

Other examples can be given of emergent values, for they constitute one of the major learning experiences in T-groups. People discover principles because they can view the consequences of certain actions. A person who controls his feelings and does not communicate with others may learn that by doing so other people will not trust him. If he can see the consequences of his actions, then he may take an important value from the group. A dominant member may learn that he/she is not trusted or followed, again because other members will not accept his/her leadership when he/she is mistrusted. We learn very much through the consequences of our actions, if we are lucky enough to see them, and one of the important purposes of a T-group is to provide this type of learning.

Value conflicts

So far we have discussed values as if they emerge naturally in the group and are quite compatible with each other. Quite clearly this is wrong and it is more likely that there are values which are in direct conflict with one another, as well as a normal competition between alternative values for priorities in the group. If we think of the group as a sort of market-place to values, then we can better understand some of the interaction that is occurring. The trainer and the members are competing to push their own values, and it may take time before the group achieves a consensus over which values take higher priorities.

Conflicting values occur periodically in groups, and in the normal course of social life. Conflict over external values—political, economic, religious—may enter into the interaction, as they do outside the group. But there may also be a conflict over values which relate directly to the behaviour of the members. Some members or trainers place greater value on the satisfaction of individual needs within the group, while others emphasize more social needs. This is not just a question of competing values, but one of fundamental emphasis. Is it better to express one's feelings towards someone or is it better to be sensitive to the needs of others? There are times when these are conflicting values which are not reducible to a common theme. As trainers, we like to believe that the open expression of feelings will necessarily lead to better interaction between members, but it does not always follow. Sometimes the expression of feelings will push the group in a certain, individualistic direction, and it becomes difficult, if not impossible, to get the group moving in a more social direction. There are certain critical periods in a group's life when there is a fluidity of direction. At these points, a trainer has a lot of influence and can push the group in a number of different directions; this has been even simulated in experiments of group-training style (Cooper, 1969). If the trainer is more individually oriented, the group will go in that particular direction, whereas if the trainer is more socially oriented, the group will move accordingly. The choice of values is between conflicting ones, not congruent values. Usually trainers decide on some kind of trade-off between these two values, but in all cases this involves a conscious choice.

Some other conflicts which occur frequently in OD groups are an emphasis on adapting towards the institutional framework of the organization versus emphasizing fundamental change in the organization. Do we encourage people to be flexible and adaptable when they return to their organization or do we want them to be more radical in their approach? At times, social class conflicts also have a great bearing on the way OD groups are run. Whom do we encourage the members to identify with? The management? The total organization? The workers? To the extent that such conflicts do not emerge within the organization, this will not be an issue, but most organizations periodically do go through 'class conflicts', especially at wage negotiation time, and a T-group caught in the middle of this will be divided by this issue. Which side will the trainer opt for in encouraging the group to move in a certain direction? Or let us take another example. Frequently, large private industrial corporations pursue economic goals which may at times conflict with larger societal goals. For example, an industrial company may wish to expand its production which increases pollution in the environment and thus may bring harm to the society. How does the trainer handle this issue, especially when the trainer is usually an organizational outsider, while being a member of the society? Does the trainer pretend that the issue does not exist, and tries to avoid it inside the group? If so, the trainer is taking sides—with the company against the society! Or does the trainer confront the group with his own values? It takes a lot of courage to confront a group such as that, considering that one may not be invited back to run any more groups. Yet a trainer is forced to choose one of two conflicting social values at this point by his behaviour.

These are extreme examples, but they do illustrate the value limits within which we work as trainers. We are not valueless people, but thinking, feeling, acting people who have a place in a social world. At times we will be periodically called upon the express our values, and to implement them into action, and a T-group is a very likely place where this might happen, given the open, fluid, permissive milieu.

More often than not, however, trainers and members will be forced to choose between competing values in defining priorities. Very often this occurs in the recruitment process. A group which is advertised as 'Encounter Group', 'Gestalt Therapy Group', 'Self-Actualizing', or 'Personal Growth Group' will convey a very different set of priorities that one which is advertised as 'Group Dynamics Group', 'Sensitivity Group', 'T-Group', or 'OD Group'. Regardless of what the trainer had in mind [and research has shown that labels are not particularly good guides to trainers' values (Mills, 1976)], the first type of group will conjure up in the mind of the potential participant an image of very individualistic goals, whereas the second type of group will convey a promise of more 'groupy' activities. Participants will select themselves partly on the basis of these images, and some of the goals for the group will be defined already.

But even within the group interaction, there will be a need to choose between competing values: between emphasizing the expression of feelings in contrast to emphasizing perceptions of each other; between emphasizing our senses (such as touch, hearing, seeing) compared to emphasizing our intellect (that is, better understanding of the dynamics); between emphasizing more activity in contrast to emphasizing more awareness and sensitivity; between emphasizing role behaviour and role awareness in contrast to emphasizing the breaking-out of roles; between emphasizing orderly and rational planning compared to emphasizing spontaneity and adaptive/decision-making. We are continually faced with choices where we have to order our priorities. We have to say that some behaviours or ideas are more important than others, and we have to structure our behaviour accordingly. And not only are trainers doing this, but members are doing it as well in their interaction. The main difference, however, is that the trainer is the most important person in the group, at least in the sense that the trainer structures the group, takes responsibility for its planning and execution, continually intervenes in order to point the group in certain directions, and has to acknowledge any outcomes of the group. If the members are satisfied, then the trainer receives praise. If the members are not, then blame is attributed accordingly.

Values and planning

The point we have been trying to make throughout this chapter is that an experiential learning group can be designed with more explicit and conscious decision-making processes. Values are being selected and chosen and brought into the group, or rejected resulting in the group seeking an outcome for its efforts. Any group has an elaborate structure to it, comprising the assumptions, goals and values of the society reflected in the trainer and the members. The trainer, furthermore, is given the responsibility and power to plan and guide the group in a certain direction, and therefore he or she must choose between alternative values. The more explicit the group leader can be about the values involved, the more effective the group experience will be by virtue of the 'means having been adapted to fit the goal'.

Many trainers would reject this philosophy as being 'too intellectual' or 'too structured' and would prefer instead a philosophy that is 'more open' or 'more accepting of what happens'. 'Whatever happens, happens!' might be a convenient label for such a philosophy. There is a reluctance to acknowledge that group situations are structured with many values. But in adopting such a position, a trainer is accepting an extremely fatalistic philosophy, one that is denying that we have the ability to structure our own future. After all, one of the major values of T-groups is to show people that they can structure their prospects and behaviour to some extent, that they can influence other people, and that they can change their behaviour when necessary. Surely it is a little bit inconsistent, therefore, for a trainer to advocate active, purposeful behaviour on the part of the members of the group, but to adopt passive and aimless fatalism on the part of himself or herself?

In this section, therefore, we would like to discuss some possible planning techniques and the manner in which values might be incorporated into the group process. Planning, of course, takes different forms. It usually involves the trainer(s) sitting down with the organizers and conceptualizing why, how, where, and when the groups will take place. Then it usually involves the trainer sitting down before the group begins and planning an overall structure and schedule for the group, be it a residential, marathon, or weekly group. But planning also takes on an evaluative role as the trainers will take stock of the group situation periodically to check on the effectiveness of the design, to analyse barriers that have emerged in the groups, to incorporate new goals that may have emerged, and to organize interventions that might facilitate the process. Planning in this sense is really a flexible procedure whereby the initial goals are continually re-evaluated and adjusted in order to incorporate the unique characteristics of each group. Finally, planning has a *post hoc* nature whereby the trainers sit down after the group has finished and take stock of the outcome of the group experience. This type of activity is planning for future groups, to incorporate the lessons of the past. In this sense, research on group experiences is, or should be, part of planning as it can provide feedback on the process and outcome of groups.

I. *Decision-tree approach of planning*

How one plans, of course, varies from situation to situation, depending upon what kind of group is being run, how many trainers and groups there are, where the group is being run, what outcomes are anticipated and so forth. Nonetheless, there are certain guidelines that one can lay down, and we have put these into a decision-tree (see Figure 1).

The key to planning is to start with the outcome—the participants. We

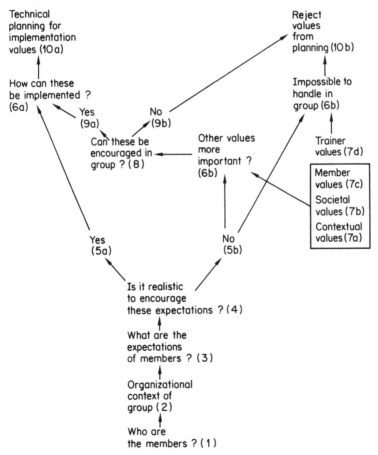

Figure 1 Decision tree of planning decisions on value premises

start with certain questions about the population (step 1). Who are they? Where do they come from? This then raises the next issue: what is the organizational context in which the group operates? We have to, at this stage, ask questions about the purpose of the group (step 2). Why is the group being held? Who has sponsored the group? Why have the participants volunteered to come? Answering these questions helps us define the third step, which is what are the expectations of the members? What do they want to learn from the group? This defines the members' goals in the group.

At this point, the trainers' skills become important because a technical assessment must be made of the feasibility of developing these goals (step 4). We have to ask, 'Is it realistic to push these expectations?' For the sake of simplicity we divide the answer to this question into two parts, 'yes' and 'no'. If the answer is 'yes', then our next stage is to think about how this can be done (step 6a); our focus at this point is a 'technical' one. But if the answer is 'no', then we have to assess why it is not realistic to push these goals (step 5b). Again, we can simplify the answer to this question into two branches: (1) that it is impossible to handle these goals in this context (step 6c), and (2) that other values might also be important to push for (step 6b). In the first instance, the trainer must assess whether the time and resources allotted is sufficient to carry out the task. Knowing the limits to a group experience is perhaps one of the most important skills a trainer can ever learn, because it means being realistic about what is possible. For example, many participants come to groups expecting to gain therapy from the group. A wise trainer must be sensitive to this issue because, first, there may be insufficient time to really handle this kind of issue, and, second, the trainer may not be qualified to go into such depth. It would be very harmful indeed to try to raise emotional issues in a group situation if there was not enough time or sufficient skills available to do this. We must be realistic about what we are capable of doing in a group, and it is better to reject such goals at the beginning than to create false expectations among the participants that we cannot fulfil.

The second branching to this question (step 6b) involves bringing in our judgement about which other values are important. We may agree to accept some of the expected goals of the participants, but add some more, or we may decide to override some of these expectations. In both cases, however, trainers need a rationale for doing so and should present this to the members in some way. There may be values that the members have not perceived which may be useful in the broader context in which they were recruited (e.g., certain skills that are useful for organizations—step 7a). There may be values that are relevant in the broader society which are not being assumed by the members (step 7b); in this case, the trainers are apt to find themselves confronting the members in some way in order to explicate this broader societal value. There may be values which will be useful for the individuals themselves, but for which they cannot clearly perceive at this point (step 7c). In this case, the trainers will be trying to illustrate certain principles or skills while trying to encourage members to explore some new directions. Finally, there may be values which are useful for the trainer (step 7d); the trainer needs to do certain things in order to satisfy his/her psyche. In this latter case, as should be clear from our earlier remarks, the trainer would do well to leave these values out of the situation and work on them somewhere else. For in accepting the role of trainer, the individual who works with groups accepts a professional responsibility to act in a service capacity; the trainer provides a service (and is paid for it accordingly).

In the first three of these juxtaposing of alternative values on top of the goals of the participants (or the trainer's perceptions of the goals of the participants, to be more precise), the trainer is responding with a broader perspective of the process. But in doing so, the trainer is confronting the members with an alternative framework, and this confrontation is the essence of technical planning. The confrontation dimension is important because it means that we somehow have to show participants a different way, a new approach. We do this all the time in other activities (for example, a teacher tries to orient a student towards some new dimensions), but there is always some resistance brought by this confrontation. We feel that trainers should be conscious of this confrontation and should try to make it public in some way, to explain to some way, to explain to the participants why it is that you are confronting them. This is one way in which making one's values explicit about a group situation can make it easier to integrate these values into the process.

Logically, the next step (step 8) involves testing these new values for feasibility, as we did in step 4, and then, depending on the answers (steps 9a, 9b), either rejecting the value as being impossible to build into the experience or else accepting it and concentrating on technically developing it (step 6a again). The final step in this process is the actual planning of techniques (step 10a). What we have done, therefore, is logically to prune our values so that we have some idea of what we are doing as we approach a group. Obviously, the better we know the situation of the participants, the better we know ourselves as trainers, and the more experience we have had as trainers, the clearer our planning will be and the more effective will be the outcome.

Some methods for exploring value themes

We would like to end this discussion by briefly introducing a few methods that would be appropriate for exploring value themes. We will not go into detail, but will outline the general form.

I. Creating conflicting values

Conflicting values are common in the real world outside experiential learning groups, but have not been explored very adequately by group trainers. The most basic method in developing conflict is to create a division in a membership. The criteria upon which the division is made then becomes critical in focusing the members' awareness on this issue. This division can be built into the formal design or it can be introduced at a latter stage. But the more formal the division, the more attention will be focused on the criteria of division.

Let us start with a division that already exists after a group has developed to a certain point. For example, the group may be dominated by a small subgroup while a larger subgroup is very uninvolved. One technique is to make this division explicit and have the 'quiet' subgroup form a discussion group with the 'noisy' subgroup watching them. A less obvious way is to force the group to divide itself. The trainer poses the problem of a division (e.g., 'Let's split into quartets for one hour in order to explore our perceptions of each other') and let the group divide itself. Such a division may bring out the underlying division, or it may backfire and create two 'feudal armies'—the 'noisy' members capturing a couple of 'quiet' ones each and forming groups around them. The technique used will depend upon what is more appropriate to the situation; the trainer can usually get a sense of what might work, but the basic logic is the same.

Other subgrouping techniques that have been used by trainers are to break into pairs, trios, quartets, or even quintets. But the smaller subgroupings will usually focus attention on individual issues and less on conflict issues. Two divisions serve best for focusing attention on conflict, and three on coalition formation, a point noted long ago by Simmel (1908).

Conflict can usually be explored more fruitfully by deliberately building it into a design at the beginning. The earlier example gives one possibility. Another basis for division would be to choose some theme around which a division could be made; this, of course, would depend on there being enough individuals to fulfil the conditions of the theme. So, for example, one could create two or three groups on the basis of class, religion, nationality, sex, course structure, age, income, or any other social indicator. Splitting the group along these lines forces the group to face up to this issue; often the members may initially resent the division, for it brings conflict into the open. But in the end such a division will pose a problem for the members which they must try to solve. Self-divisions, as illustrated above, are often good for focusing attention on implicit divisions in a community of members. Similarly, one might want to focus the attention of the conflict on the intragroup process, rather than on the intergroup process.

A technique which is useful for exploring social conflict in a more sociological context is the use of simulation. In this case, a whole role structure has to be elaborated on in order to focus awareness on this, and participants become actors playing a role, rather than people playing themselves. Simulations were first developed as a form of war-gaming, but they have developed over the years to include political, economic, social and even psychological conflict situations (Guetzkow, 1959; Levine, 1973: Kolb et al., 1974). The simulations can be full-blown ones (e.g., a decision-making exercise in a fictitious company; a student–administration conflict in an imaginary university) or they may be introduced as a part of a broader design (e.g., a production exercise within an OD laboratory). More details on simulations can be found in Kanderdine and Keys (1974), and Kibbee, Craft, and Nanus (1962).

II. Creating integrating values

The obverse of conflict is stability and integration, and there are a host of techniques available for creating these. In fact, much of the development of techniques in the group movement have concentrated on supporting these values (such as trust exercises, building better communication exercises, creating openness, etc.). But there are some common themes which run through these methods which distinguish them clearly from methods aimed at exploring conflict. First, divisions are discouraged, either by having only one group or by leaving the groups relatively autonomous if there is more than one group in an experiential design. Second, the method must encourage members that they will gain something by cooperating together, or lose something by not cooperating. Third, the method must encourage members to step out of social roles in their interaction, since social roles often have built-in conflicts, and if members continue to act out these social roles conflict will emerge. These methods are useful for developing skills for changing situations, or for developing behaviours not circumscribed by social roles. In this sense, they are appropriate for behaviour that constitutes most of our informal life: family, social life, informal communication, even some of our organized life.

The most important skills are methods designed to improve trust between people. Trust is a basic dimension of human life, and has many aspects: openness, honesty, dependability, predictability, love, protection, and acknowledgement. It is a dimension fundamental to all social interaction, even to role-defined behaviour (Erikson, 1950; Levine, 1971). But within formal roles, trust has an institutional component which is usually lacking in informal behaviour (i.e., one gains trust by effectively carrying out a role). The basic technique for creating trust in a group is to build a link between people. This can take many forms: establishing a talking relationship, establishing a physical relationship (for example, 'blindwalk', holding hands, other intimacies), creating a work-role relationship, creating an experiential relationship (i.e., experiencing something at the same time and place). The relationship thus established must be a predictable one; individuals must act according to expectations. The relationship does not have to be a very intimate one (though, of course, that may help), for many trust relationships are not intimate.

Putting trust somewhat mechanistically like this forces us to see it in a different light than the way we normally view it. For if a division and role behaviour constitute ingredients of conflict, while lack of division and role (and a predictable relationship) create trust, then it is clear that conflict and trust could alternate within the same person and could even affect the same relationship. In the basic 'division technique' outlined earlier, conflict is created between the divided groups while trust is created within the groups. As long as the members agree to play the roles involved, this polarity will exist. Conversely, if some members decide to break up the intergroup division by redefining the situation (for example, 'they are not really different from us'), this may bring the conflict back into a group because these members have violated the basic assumption holding the group together. Conflict and trust stand on a knife's edge equilibrium with one another and are very easily disrupted, as all couples know. Even with the same relationship, trust and conflict can alternate quickly. Take a couple as an example. The couple's intimacy holds the relationship together—they trust each other. If one or both of them suddenly starts reverting to formal roles usually external to the household (such as concentrating too much on work, 'staying out with the boys too late, getting too involved in the women's organization), then the potential for conflict is enormously increased, since the basic assumptions holding the pair together are violated; if there are children involved so that multiple linking assumptions exist, then the tension created by the role behaviour may be magnified more intensely.

'External' and 'internal' roles compete with one another for priority, making us both sociological and psychological creatures at the same time, though in a tenuous balance between the two. Changes in external roles may disrupt the internal equilibrium in a relationship, and the consequences may be so great that the result may be a splitting up of the group. This is why we observe that marriage and divorce patterns change with the ups-and-downs of the economy; economic growth creates higher aspirations and opportunities, thereby disrupting relationships; whereas stagnation creates dependency and stability (Levine, 1975).

There are other skills which are important for integrating groups. Communication is one such basic skill, so basic that we usually take it for granted. Communication involves keeping channels open so that information can be interchanged. Usually this involves talking and listening, but there are other methods. The great interest shown by the group movement in non-verbal communication attests to the desire to strengthen some 'not-very-used' channels. Written communication is another form which has not really been developed by the group movement. Writing is useful for communicating complicated, technical information, for communicating deeper feelings and thoughts, for communicating structured thinking, for making difficult requests in which face-saving is an important aspect of a relationship, for giving instructions, and so forth. These are important dimensions of social life, too, and perhaps the 'experiential movement' should pay more attention to this mode.

Symbolic communication is another form which is very undeveloped in the group movement. We are all aware that groups often create their own symbol system, a codified language which refers to specific events, people, and roles in the group. But we rarely think of using symbols in a more sociological sense as a mode for group communication. The United States, in fact, is a very bad place for developing symbolic communication, as there is a somewhat nihilistic rejection of symbolic forms. Probably this developed because the 'Americans' were from so many countries that they were required to drop many of their ethnic symbols in order to be accepted in this society. But the point is, such a mode of communication is very useful to develop, at least for other societies than the United States. Symbols have certain common elements: an agreed-upon meaning, belonging to a group or community of some sort, a sense of commitment of this group, a commitment to action on the part of the group in order to defend it, a commitment from members of the group for help in order to defend oneself, and certain level of trust which can be expected from members of the group. Communication of these symbols is often subtle; they can be stated verbally or non-verbally, but more than not, they involve a complex pattern relating the two, so that 'outsiders' cannot intervene as imposters. The communication is 'flashed' on suddenly by one person who then waits for an appropriate 'signal' back from the other. This interchange continues until it is accepted by both that they both belong to the group. The basis for symbolic communication are many, but they usually have a strong sociological dimension to them: ethnic communication, religious communication, political communication, social class communication, and so forth. But there are also some psychological dimensions to symbolic communication, too, usually involving an expression of certain linguistic forms. One can, with proper use of language, convey to others different types of self-definitions and motive structure (for examples 'I am a sensitive, turned-on person who is open to new experiences. Do you want to have a new experience together?'; 'I am a hippy–yippy, freaked-out social deviant looking for drugs. Do you happen to have any?'; 'I am a member of the ————, a semi-secret organization which promises help to all its members. Can you help me?'). Thus, symbolic communication is an important mode of expression for group loyalties and serves to communicate motives and needs as well. In this sense, there is a lot of material here for social learning in groups, of which the group movement has barely touched.

These examples illustrate the wide range of possible methods for defining integrating values, and how they are contrasted with conflict values. They all have the characteristic of defining a group boundary, of encouraging mutual satisfaction, and of discouraging the introduction of external roles.

III. Creating individual values

We will look briefly at one final form of values—individual values—and explore, somewhat generally, the form of method used to create these in a group situation. The previous two types of values were group-based values in that they assumed a relationship to a group, either antagonistic or supportive. Individual values, on the other hand, isolate the individual from a group by focusing on his or her unique characteristics. The methods developed for exploring individual values, therefore, will aim to isolate the individual from the group. Either the individual is selected to perform some task or to receive feedback from the group, or else the individual's behaviour is isolated from that of the other members and explored. This can be done in an informal or formal way.

Most groups spend some of their time looking at individuals in the group during the normal give-and-take of group interaction. At times there may be special exercises which can do this: role plays, *Gestalt* exercise, personal feedback exercises, acting out exercises, etc. But it is at this point that the value argument becomes important, because in focusing on individuals, many values are being expressed. These can be values that are considered necessary for mental health (such as increasing trust, openness, self-awareness), values that are necessary for interaction with others (such as interdependency, mutual reciprocity, increasing awareness of others) or values that are useful for oneself (such as increasing one's potency with others, improving one's ability to express oneself, increasing one's ability to accept feelings, increasing one's spontaneity). Some of these values may be consistent with social values that are being expressed, but others definitely may contradict social values. Some groups seem to take a very anti-social perspective, emphasizing individualism at all costs. It is as if they are saying, 'Save yourself. No one is going to help you at all in this world. And don't waste your time helping others'. The group process becomes, 'How am I, an individual, different from everyone else here?', a theme which already creates a division between people. This kind of group very often has a directive trainer who very actively guides the group process, a style made necessary, possibly, in order to prevent the potential conflict from coming out in such a group.

If we emphasize strong social values, then we create conflicts with other groups. If we emphasize strong individual values, then we create divisions within a group. If we try to make a trade-off between these two by emphasizing the group and the individual in interaction, then we may mollify conflict to some extent but also may create an unreal situation in which transfer of learning to the outside world is minimal. 'Happy' group situations are, after all, not necessarily realistic ones, and since one of our major purposes in running groups is to teach participants about social skills, emphasizing smoothness of social interaction may not necessarily be a good thing. Our feeling is that values are inherent in social life, whether they be social or individual values. They achieve their meaning in a social framework and are fought for within that framework. Without values, in fact, it would be impossible to give feedback to members in a group. We would not be able to say, 'Hey, look what you're doing!', because without accepting values, there would be no means of evaluating behaviour. Values are essential to our existence and we would do well to make these as explicit as possible.

Conclusion

We have tried in this chapter to focus attention on the nature of values in experiential learning groups, because we feel that group trainers have not properly acknowledged the importance of these in their group work. Trainers have tried to act as if they worked outside the real world, or were creating an alternative society to the one that already existed. And while this goal of isolating human behaviour from its natural social context may be a noble one, and filled with idealistic and humanitarian overtones, it is unrealistic. For we as trainers live in that society and are part of the same contradictions that confront everyone else. Values, after all, become important when there are alternatives available. They derive their meaning from conflict, not consensus, for if we all were to agree, there would be no reason to be concerned. Thus, it is the essential nature of social conflict which focuses attention on values as the conflict shifts to an ideological level.

T-groups were created as a consequence of a corporate society in an advanced state of conflict. At the time, they fulfilled the felt need to provide some new skills for administrators who would run these large corporations. The issues posed to big corporations spilled over into the broader society in the form of questions concerning appropriate behaviour and norms. This has been the case in the last 30 years. But history is a progressive force in which social forms create their own antagonisms and alternative models become available. The growth of large corporations in the United States and Europe created a shift from an entrepreneurial society to a bureaucratic one (Baron and Sweezy, 1966). Industry became capital-intensive, thereby producing a shift towards a more service-oriented labour force, and in addition reduced the chances for upward mobility of some groups (e.g., the blacks, and American Indians in the United States, and to a lesser extent the West Indians in Britain). These changes also polarized international relations with the poorer countries of the world. A polarization of values emerges from such as economic polarity, as the high standards of affluence being demanded within the developed countries were seen to be achieved at the expense of the lesser developed countries. 'I want to achieve a greater understanding of myself', as seen by one person, becomes 'you are achieving your greater understanding at my expense' by another. For it is an old cliché that freedom is a relative concept. Freedom cannot be 'absolute freedom' if it is given to some people and denied to others. And yet this is where many of our social values in the developed world have taken us. Extreme individualism shows a contempt for humanity when it becomes anti-social, when it encourages individuals to pay attention only to themselves. If that freedom is socially guaranteed so that all humanity benefits from it, then the satisfaction of individual needs will not be at the expense of others. Freedom, in order not to be sectarian, must be a social concept first, and not just an individual one.

Experiential groups are, of course, no place to handle the conflicts of the world. We cannot tell participants, 'Do not concern yourself with yourselves, but only with the poor unfortunates of this world!' Such a mandate would be absurd and silly, and would do more than make people feel mildly guilty for acknowledging their own needs. But in T-groups we can encourage a sensitivity to other people, if only to the other members of the group. For that sensitivity underlies a greater sense of social responsibility. Thus, in being

26

sensitive, we learn to adjust our behaviour to acknowledge the needs of other people, with the end-product being a kind of compromise to a broader commitment to social freedom, for it gives to the other person the right to exist and be happy. And if we all could act in such a way, would this not be a good thing for humanity, too?

References

Appley, D. G. and Winter A. R. (1973) *T-Groups and Therapy Groups in a Changing Society*. San Francisco: Jossey-Bass.

Argyris, C. (1965) 'Explorations in interpersonal competence.' *Journal of Applied Behavioral Science*, 1, 58–84.

Bach, G. R. (1967) 'Marathon group dynamics: I. Some functions of the professional group facilitator.' *Psychological Reports*, 20, 995–99.

Back, K. W. (1972) *Beyond Words*. New York: Russell Sage Foundation.

Baron, P. A. and Sweezy, P. M. (1966) *Monopoly Capital*. New York: Monthly Review Press.

Bass, B. (1962) 'Reactions to twelve angry men as a measure of sensitivity training.' *Journal of Applied Psychology*, 46, 120–24.

Blumberg, A. and Golembiewski, R. T. (1976) *Learning and Change in Groups*. Harmondsworth Middx: Penguin.

Bradford, L. P., Gibb, J. R. and Benne, K. D. (1964) 'Two educational innovations.' In L. P. Bradford, J. R. Gibb, and K. D. Benne (eds.), *T-group Theory and Laboratory Method*. New York: Wiley.

Burke, R. L. and Bennis, W. B. (1961) 'Changes in perception of self and others during human relations training.' *Human Relations*, 14, 165–82.

Clark, J. V. (1962) 'Some troublesome dichotomies in human relations training.' *Human Relations Training News*, 6, 3–6.

Cooper, C. L. (1969) 'Influence of the trainer in T-groups', *Human Relations*, 22, 515–30.

Cooper, C. L. (1972) *Group Training for Individual and Organizational Development*. Basel: S. Karger.

Cooper, C. L. (1975) *Theories of Group Processes*. New York: Wiley.

Cooper, C. L. (1976) *Developing Social Skills in Managers*. London: Macmillan.

Cooper, C. L. (1977) 'Adverse and Growthful Effects of Experiential Learning Groups.' *Human Relations*, 30, in press.

Cooper, C. L. and Mangham, I. L. (1971) *T-Groups: A Survey of Research*. London: Wiley.

Cooper, C. L., Levine, N. and Kobayashi, K. (1976) 'Developing one's potential: from west to east.' *Group and Organization Studies*, 1, 43–55.

Erikson, E. H. (1950) *Childhood and Society*. New York: Norton.

Erikson, E. H. (1956) 'The problem of ego identity.' *Journal of the American Psychoanalytic Association*, 4, 56–121.

French, J. R. P., Sherwood, J. J. and Bradford, D. (1966) 'Changes in self-identity in a management training conference.' *Journal of Applied Behavioral Science*, 2, 210–18.

Freud, S. (1918) *Totem and Taboo*. London: Routledge and Kegan Paul.

Galbraith, J. K. (1967) *The New Industrial State*. Boston: Houghton-Mifflin.

Guetzkow, H. (1959) 'A use of simulation in the study of international relations.' *Behavioral Science*, 4, 183–91.

Harrison, K. (1972) Chapter in Cooper, C. L. *Group Training for Individual and Organizational Development*. Basel: S. Karger.

Kanderdine, J. and Keys, G. (1974) 'A rationale for the evaluation of learning in simulation and games.' Paper presented to the National Gaming Council.

Kibbee, J., Craft, C. and Nanus, B. (1962) *Management Games*. New York: Rineholt.

Kolb, D., Rubin, I. M. and McIntyre, J. M. (1974) *Organizational Psychology*. Englewood Cliffs, N. J.: Prentice-Hall.

Laing, R. D. (1965) *The Divided Self*. Harmondsworth, Middx.: Penguin.

Lakin, M. (1969) 'Some ethical issues in sensitivity training.' *American Psychologist*, **24**, 923–29.

Levine, N. (1971) 'Emotional factors in group development.' *Human Relations*, **24**, 65–89.

Levine, N. (1973) 'Group training with students in higher education.' In C. L. Cooper (ed.), *Group Training for Individual and Organizational Development*, p. 40–67. Basel: S. Karger.

Levine, N. (1975) 'Divorce in Turkey.' Paper presented at the Second Turkish Demography Conference, Izmir, Turkey.

Levine, N. and Cooper, C. L. (1976) 'T-groups—twenty years on: a prophecy.' *Human Relations*, **29**, 1–23.

Mills, C. (1976) Chapter in C. L. Cooper, *Developing Social Skills in Managers*. London: Macmillan.

Olmosk, K. and Graverson, G. (1972) 'Group training for community relations. The community workshop.' In C. L. Cooper (ed.), *Group Training for Individual and Organizational Development*. Basel: S. Karger.

Rubin, I. (1967) 'The reduction of prejudice through laboratory training.' *Journal of Applied Behavioral Science*, **3**, 29–50.

Sampson, E. E. (1975) *Ego at the Threshold*. New York: Delta Books.

Schein, E. H. and Bennis, W. G. (1965) *Personal and Organizational Change through Group Methods*. New York: Wiley.

Simmel, G. (1908). *Conflict*. New York: Free Press of Glencoe.

Siroka, R. W., Siroka, E. K. and Schloss, G. (1971) *Sensitivity Training and Group Encounter: An Introduction*. New York: Grosset and Dunlap.

Smith, P. B. (1975) 'Are there adverse effects of sensitivity training.' *Journal of Human Psychology*, **15**, 29–47.

Smith, P. B. and Wilson, M. (1975) 'The use of group training methods in multiracial settings.' *New Community*, **4**, (2), 218–31.

Szasz, T. (1961) *The Myth of Mental Illness*. New York: Harper.

Chapter 2

A Classification of Experiential
Social Processes: A European Perspective

Sven-Åke Lennung

University of Lund, Sweden

During the last few years, there have been heated arguments regarding experiential group training methods. Doubts have been expressed as to whether these methods have had any effect on participants (Dunnette and Campbell, 1968). Questions have also been raised whether the 'claimed effects' are altogether constructive to participants (Yalom and Lieberman, 1971), to the organizations in which they function or to society at large (Cooper, 1976). Highly diverse views have been expressed. Almost lyrical descriptions of positive consequences have appeared alongside reports of extreme adverse effects in connection with experiential groups (Cooper, 1975).

The group methods in question have been assigned a multitude of different names such as laboratory methods, T-groups, sensitivity training, encounter groups, leadership training, consciousness-raising, human relations workshops, experiential methods, group development techniques, team-building, personal growth seminars, group dynamics training, etc. These names sometimes correspond to a real difference in method, but two different labels may also indicate highly similar pedagogical and psychological phenomena. Conversely, any of these designations may be used to describe a wide variation of group leader behaviour and influence strategies. One of the most striking results of the Lieberman, Yalom, and Miles (1973) research is that differences in actual leader behaviour may well be greater between two trainers who adhere to the same theory (and therefore are likely to describe their activities in the same terminology) than between trainers from different schools of thought. This fact has been noted with increasing frequency and intensity (Bunker, 1974), and some attempts towards classification and conceptual clarification have been offered (Lomranz, Lakin, and Schiffman, 1972; Singer et al., 1975). This paper is intended as a further contribution to that tradition.

With the proliferation of experiential group techniques not only differentiation but also definition of the similarities between methods has become a problem. We unfortunately lack a comprehensive label which would encompass this multitude of group activities. The term 'experiential social processes', created by the editors of this volume, could probably be viewed as a response to this problem, being a more meaningful phrase than the 'group event' used by Singer et al. (1975). In this chapter a wide coverage of 'experiential social processes' will be used (for stylistic reasons, the term 'experiential groups' will be used synonymously).

In order to provide an impression of the field, experiential social processes are suggested to contain each of the following features:

(1) The relationships between the group's task and the psychological phenomena which arise in a group at work are of primary concern ('task-sentience emphasis').

(2) Direct experiencing of these relationships is a core process.

(3) 'Change' or 'choice' are central concepts.

(4) The experiential process is a deliberate, designed event.

(5) 'Feelings' are essential.

(6) The group develops with the assistance of a group leader ('trainer', 'facilitator', 'consultant').

With these communalities as a background, we now proceed to explore the differences which are important to experiential learning 'outcome'. We shall do so under four headings: variations in intention, variations in focus, variations in knowledge-constitutive interests, and variations in change strategies.

Variations in intention

It may seem almost unneccessary to point out that the reasons for planning and arranging an experiential group event may differ. However, earlier theories have seldom stressed the importance of such differences in 'intention'. The emphasis on the 'task system' is, for example, one of the important contributions of Singer et al. (1975). It does make a difference whether a group is devised to provide 'learning' or 'psychological change'. However, since there must also be a reason for wanting to provide 'learning' or 'change', I prefer to speak of 'intentions' rather than 'task systems'. A list of such intentions would include:

(1) A work group is trained in order to function better.

(2) People holding certain positions or roles involving relations with other people (foremen, teachers, managers, administrators) are trained to become better equipped to fulfil these roles.

(3) People participate in an experiential group with no specific intention but to broaden their minds or psyches. (Thus we recognize that education/ training can be regarded as a cultural activity and enjoyed as such. Groups aiming at 'personal growth' should probably be subsumed under this heading.)

(4) An experiential social setting is arranged to provide a source of personal support. Groups within institutions, with emotionally difficult tasks (e.g. therapeutic institutions), may be set up to function towards this end.

(5) The group situation can be used to provide a setting to work on personal

problems and psychopathological symptoms. Many of these therapy groups capitalize on immediate personal and interpersonal experiences, and are thus 'experiential'.

(6) Programmes for planned social change or organization development often include experiential social processes as part of a broader strategy.

(7) Future 'professional helpers' (clinical psychologists, psychiatrists, social workers, counsellors, etc.) are frequently invited to learn and develop in experiential social settings.

These intentions regarding clients are blended with the group leaders' more or less 'private' ends, making money, getting away from routine, development of one's competence, working with new colleagues, interest in group dynamics, etc. are but a few possible motives. Admittedly, professional codes demand that trainers are aware of such 'private' goals and avoid exploiting participants in their pursuit. However, besides the fact that 'professionals' are human, we must also consider the possibility of the existence of less scrupulous practitioners.

Both these lists could be expanded but are detailed enough to illustrate that reasons for utilizing experiential groups may be very different. It is only logical to assume that when experiential social processes are arranged towards such diverse ends, a corresponding variation in content and method is likely to be found.

Variations in focus

Again it seems almost superfluous to mention that it is impossible to concentrate on everything that occurs in a group. A seminar, for example, usually focuses on only a few phenomena at a time, 'authority and leadership', 'sex roles', 'creative problem-solving', 'autonomy, initiative and risk-taking', 'power and influence' etc. There is also a risk involved here. One of the outstanding qualities of experiential social processes is that they possess and demonstrate the richness and interdependency of personal, interpersonal, and group phenomena. It is one of a group leader's skills to help participants focus without losing too much of the interrelationship and complexity of human conduct.

Singer et al. (1975) also recognize differences in focus, which they label 'psychological levels'. We share the standpoint that the choice of focus must be deliberate, conscious and mutually agreed upon, and that it must be in consonance with the basic intent of the group. The last requirement is frequently violated, and we then have a 'ready-made solution' in search of a problem to solve—a means in search of its' end, so to speak.

Variations in knowledge-constitutive interests

Having noticed the importance of differences in intention and focus, we now turn to the pedagogical process. It is no easy task to describe relevant differences between methods since there exists no general theory is this area; yet an attempt must be made. I have, in previous writings (Lennung, 1974), advocated the idea that participants not only learn from 'content' but also from the way content is produced and examined. Therefore, the way group leaders arrange and conduct a workshop may be of critical importance for participant change.

Our third descriptive category differentiates between three types of knowledge-constitutive interests labelled 'emancipatory', 'hermeneutic' and 'technical'. The technical interest derives its frame of reference from the empirical-analytical sciences and contains a view of knowledge as predictable knowledge. Applied to our area of interest, experiential processes are regarded as a means to discover existing law-like regularities in social processes—the 'fact' that a group solution to certain types of problems may be superior to that of any single participant, and that there exists a relationship between group size and the quality of decision-making are examples of such law-like observables. These 'facts' assume importance since they can be used to predict and control social situations. With this view of knowledge, the group leader becomes a conveyor of facts and techniques. If his behaviour is truly congruent, the workshop will be structured accordingly, and that view of knowledge will be reinforced in participants.

A hermeneutic interest is displayed when people want to gain new or deeper insights into a situation or process—not to control but to understand it better. As Habermas (1966, p. 293) suggests:

'... in revealing reality, interpretational research is guided by a concern for the maintenance and extension of possible intersubjective understanding which is necessary for the orientation of any symbolic interaction. Meaning is understood according to its structure with a view to a possible consensus of interacting individuals within the frame of a traditional or culturally patterned self-understanding.'

Going one step further we can engage in activities

'... to discover which (if any) theoretical statements express unchangeable laws of social action and which, though they express relations of dependence, because they are ideologically fixed, are in principle subject to change' (ibid., p. 294).

Such an emancipatory interest, espoused by many consultants, may be materialized in a training design (where appropriate in relation to 'intention'). This view of knowledge becomes apparent in a powerful way when group leaders themselves engage in collaborative exploration and experimentation in the here-and-now. The hermeneutic–emancipatory interests seem to have been in the core of the original 'laboratory training' idea, and that tradition is still alive as in the 'mini-society' approach developed by Hjelholt (1972).

Research has not established whether the view of knowledge held by group leaders (as expressed in the content and process of an experiential group) does have a differential impact on participants. 'Effect studies' have simply not been directly aimed at this question, but isolated findings may be interpreted in support of this hypothesis. Cleland (1973), for instance, reports that growth-scores for participants in T-groups correlate with those of trainers but not with trainers' initial scores.

If a workshop design includes both technical and hermeneutic–emancipatory approaches, it is probably wise to be very specific about 'when' staff members are teaching and 'when' they are exploring, even to the point of reserving specific time and space for the limited study of 'the covariance of observable events' (that is, technical knowledge). The failure to identify and communicate which knowledge-constitutive interest prevails, could probably explain some unnecessary, non-constructive confusion resulting in little or no learning in participants. This is the main thesis of a Swedish report analysing and making concrete the reasons for the relative failure of a mini-society design to study and solve some of the problems of an educational institution (Grenthe, 1975).

Again, the choice of trainers and training style should be deliberate and in accord with the reasons for arranging the group. The intention could suggest encouragement of 'the hypothetical spirit, the feeling for tentativeness and caution, the respect for probable error ...' plus '... experimentalism, the willingness to expose ideas to empirical testing' (Bennis, 1964, p. 694). In such a case it would be appropriate that the group leaders introduce a design which facilitates exploration and that they actively engage in such inquiry.

Variations in change strategies

The last aspect assumed to be crucial for the understanding of experiential social processes also applies to how change/learning is produced. The starting point for analysis consists of the mechanisms or conditions which must exist for change to occur in participants. The approach is inspired by Yalom's (1975) research into group psychotherapy, in which he identifies categories of 'curative factors'. When we apply a notion of 'change mechanisms'—some of which are closely related to curative factors—similar reservations as those made by Yalom apply. Thus different factors assume differential importance depending on the goals, focus, and composition of a specific group; participants in the same group may benefit from widely different clusters of mechanisms; the factors neither occur nor function separately—yet some are definitely antagonistic. With these reservations in mind we now turn to a tentative list of potential change mechanisms.

(1) *The participant learns/changes from receiving feedback about his behaviour through the impression he makes on other participants.* Group members are thus exposed to new areas of relevant information, which were previously not accessible. The added information, which may well contradict previous assumptions, incites change. Horwitz (1964, p. 209) expresses this idea, as follows:

'The feedback process is designed primarily to enable the participant to become more aware of some of his characteristic modes or interacting, which become apparent to others in a close relationship but which are hidden from the participant himself.'

(2) *The participant learns/changes because his mental equilibrium is upset or confused.* Such a state of mind can be produced through various means. To some participants, the 'seeming' lack of structure and the loss of habitual sources for security characteristic of some experiential designs may cause such reactions. Also, the nature of the feedback received by some group members may produce this state. Marrow (1964, p. 33) gives one example from a T-group:

'The day I was dropped by my team as the least valuable member, I cried. It was the old bugaboo again—I didn't stand for anything. I hated those guys at first, but I've got to admit they had me down pat.

I'm going back home now. I know what I've got to work on—and work on it I will.'

Sometimes a group leader deliberately 'attempts to drive the patient to a climax of emotionalism, and then when he thinks he has gotten to the farthest point, suddenly stops the action ...' (Corsini, 1970, p. 30).

It may be appropriate to point out that I make no reference to whether the strategy described functions in the hypothesized manner or whether potential effects are altogether desirable. The approach of this chapter is to identify approaches to change induction in groups as they are described. It becomes a matter for subsequent analysis and research to determine what intentional and unintentional effects can be expected from these strategies.

(3) *The participant learns/changes because he clarifies, recognizes and expresses feelings.* Lieberman, Yalom, and Miles (1973, p. 362) phrase this rationale as follows:

'The mutilation of this skill (to experience intense emotions) has been described by many as at the very core of what is responsible for human problems and what needs to be corrected—hence, the emphasis on increasing sensory awareness and on the simulation of physical feelings and emotion-provoking experiences.'

(4) *The participant learns/changes because subconscious personal or inter-personal processes are made available for consideration and review.* Golem-biewski and Blumberg (1970, p. 134) express this idea as follows:

'Thus the trainer ... must seek to identify the *processes* that lie beneath the obvious. If the content of the group dwells on how difficult it is to get started, for example, adequate diagnosis must isolate the processes underlying the lackluster performance. Numerous processes could be operating. Consider only two.

Group members accept the trainer but
have low trust in one another,
because they fear rejection by peers
but trust authority figures.

The members have a problem with
authority figures and cannot express
their feelings about the "incompetence"
of the trainer who has not inspired
them out of their lethargy.'

(5) *The participant learns/changes because he is subjected to a 'corrective emotional experience'.* The precise nature of these corrective experiences may differ, but the 'peak experience' as described by Freundlich (1972, p. 45) may be used as a case in point. Freundlich's article is a detailed rationale for the curative effects of a 'peak experience'.

'Encounter groups provide such enormous support that the ego may regress and re-experience intense infantile feelings of acceptance, warmth, security, and love. In a sense, during this regression the individual relinquishes part of his ego to the group, which then functions as the mother during infancy. The individual once again feels, 'I am loved and cared for because I am I'. In this atmosphere he is ready for a personality "breakthrough" or "peak experience".'

'The Encounter' is sometimes conceived in a similar manner and is attributed growth-inducing qualities. Burton (1970, pp. 131–32) suggests:

'I have described the encountering experience as essentially passionate, phasic and flowing, gratifying and enjoyable, essentially involuntary, novel, neither highly culturally programmed nor anti-cultural, but essentially personal, and more natural then neurotic. Since I consider growth natural, and deadlocked growth as neurosis and therefore un-natural, it follows that human experience that is natural facilitates growth. In this sense, the encountering experience looms as critical in psychotherapy.'

If we disregard the logic of this statement, it is still obvious that a trainer who regards an 'encounter' as the paramount change-inducing factor will structure a programme, and conduct himself in a manner, considerably different from that of a consultant who considers exposure of subconscious mechanisms to be crucial. As a consequence, possibilities to change/learn will differ.

(6) *The participant learns/changes because he can rid himself of unnecessary constraints and inhibitions.* The unshackling may be achieved in various ways. Checking self-perceptions with others' perception may produce such a result, but more forcefully directive means are sometimes employed. Trainers may purposefully ask, direct or in other ways influence participants to act in a manner they would not have done in other settings. Bodily contact with one's own sex (or with the opposite); the expression of disapproval (or approval) in a face-to-face encounter with one's fellow man; the expression of anger or joy may all be examples of previously restricted areas opened to use. In all instances the aim is '... to move the individual (away) from constriction, tightness, defensiveness, the wearing of masks, and the use of facades ...' (Lakin, 1972, p. 22). Some procedures recommended by Ellis (1970, p. 114–15), to be included in 'rational encounter' could serve such a function.

'The group leader says: "Think of something risky you can do at this moment. Do it."...
The leader directs: "What member of this group would you like to tell off? Why?
Tell him or her off, right now."...
The leader says: "With what member of this group would you like to have a love experience? Ask this person if he or she will cooperate with you in having this kind of experience"...'

(7) *The participant learns/changes because some needed important skills have been infused.* Increased 'interactional awareness' (Lakin, 1972, pp. 20–25), 'how to make contact with others', 'how to listen', 'how to give feedback', 'how to be assertive' are examples of skills which may be deemed strategic by group leaders. Workshops based on structured exercises *à la* Pfeiffer and Jones (1969) are exponents of this idea (but could also be based on other change strategies).

(8) *The participant learns/changes because he feels more secure and/or sure of himself.* This state can be reached in various ways: favourable feedback, '... the simple act of fully participating in a group discussion...' (Dickoff and Lakin, 1964); the realization that others have problems similar to his. The increased security facilitates further learning and growth.

'A person learns to grow through his increasing acceptance of himself and others. Serving as the primary block to such acceptance are the defensive feelings of fear and distrust that arise from the prevailing defensive climates in most cultures.' (Gibb, 1964, p. 279)

Gibb's strategy therefore becomes one which helps participants learn to build defensive–reductive climates, and in this way a 'constructive circle' is initiated or a vicious one broken. Note that the 'security-strategy' is completely antagonistic to the 'disequilibrium-approach', and that a good deal of trainer skill is required to integrate it with the 'feedback-change' and the 'unshackling of inhibition' models.

This list can certainly be appended. Those of Yalom's curative factors not explicitly included here may all operate in experiential social processes. As noted earlier, the aim of this analysis is not, however, to establish whether change mechanisms function as hypothesized. The emphasis is placed on the fact the purveyors of experiential groups plan, design, manage and intervene as if a given factor or a given combination of change factors are *the* change mechanism. Doing so, they provide other opportunities for learning/change than they are necessarily aware of. The exposure of a group leader's strategy for change thereby provides us with a logically backward but linguistically convenient way to suggest salient differences in the pedagogical process, including the important difference in possibilities for participants to learn about the learning/changing process itself (e.g., Lennung, 1974). (Note that this approach is based upon the assumption that group leaders plan, design, and intervene in a consistent, logical manner accessible to rational description and analysis.)

Why this backward approach? The answer is that we know far too little about design-decisions, interventions and change strategies to be able to describe them in concrete terms. Plans are now being developed at the University of Lund for a study of group managerial behaviour and leadership in relation to the purposes of a wide variety of experiential social practices (as these are applied in the field). Until such research is undertaken we shall have to make do with inferences from leaders' *assumptions* about change mechanisms.

This emphasis on change strategies is not incompatible with Lieberman's sobering view of the role of leadership (1976, pp. 232–37). He remarks that '... the behaviour, personality, and skill level of the leader has taken on mythic proportions as a basic force for successful personal change in groups' (ibid, p. 233). Although doubtless a minimum requirement in behaviour, personality and skill level of group leaders must be upheld, increased leader competence *within a given change strategy* probably does not contribute substantially to participant outcome (but almost certainly to what the trainer himself gets out of the experiential process). In fact, the Lieberman, Yalom and Miles typology of leadership behaviour (1973, pp. 226–67), which could be interpreted to represent behavioural corollaries to different change strategies, was found to correlate with significant differences in participant outcome.

Concluding comments

Any model-builder inevitably faces the problem of striking an optimal balance between generality, abstraction and conceptual scarcity on the one hand, with specificity, clarity and descriptive precision on the other. The suggested procedure to classify experiential social processes under four main headings reflects a realization that important differences exist and proposes that the most relevant of these are to be found in intention, focus, knowledge-constitutive interest, and change strategy. Due to the number of variables, we are unable to present a complete typology—this is the price paid for specificity. The inclusion of categories for highlighting the pedagogical process by determining knowledge-constitutive interest and change strategy is the corresponding gain. The proposed conceptual framework, while making no claim to provide the ultimate answer, is general enough to subsume a vast variety of the constantly expanding field of experiential approaches; but it is also specific enough to differentiate in relevant ways between these experiential processes— including the novel ones presented in this volume.

References

Bennis, W. G. (1964) 'Goals and meta-goals of laboratory training.' In W. G. Bennis, E. H. Schein, D. E., Berlew, and F. I. Steele (eds.), *Interpersonal Dynamics* pp. 692–98. Homewood, Ill.: Dorsey Press.
Bunker, D. R. (1974) 'Social process awareness training: an NTL approach.' In D. S. Milman and G. D. Goldman (eds.), *Group Process Today: Evaluation and Perspective*, pp. 51–62. Springfield, Ill.: Charles C. Thomas.

38

Burton, A. (1970) 'Encounter, existence, and psychotherapy.' In A. Burton (ed.), *Encounter*, pp. 7–26. San Francisco: Jossey-Bass.

Cleland, J. (1973) 'Changes in sensitivity training groups associated with changes in trainer characteristics.' *Dissertation Abstracts International*, **34** (2), 1271–72.

Cooper, C. L. (1976) *Developing Social Skills in Managers*. London: Macmillan.

Cooper, C. L. (1975) 'How psychologically dangerous are T-groups and encounter groups.' *Human Relations*, **28**, (3), 249–60.

Corsini, R. J. (1970) 'Immediate therapy in groups.' In G. M. Gazda (ed.), *Innovations to Group Psychotherapy*. Springfield, Ill.: Charles C. Thomas.

Dickoff, H. and Lakin, M. (1964) 'Patient's view of group psychotherapy.' *International Journal of Group Psychotherapy*, **14**, (1), 61–73.

Dunnette, M. D. and Campbell, J. D. (1968) 'Laboratory education: impact on people and organizations.' *Industrial Relations*, **8**, (1), 1–27.

Ellis, A. (1970) 'A weekend of rational encounter.' In A. Burton (ed.), *Encounter*, pp. 112–27. San Francisco: Jossey-Bass.

Freundlich, D. (1972) 'A psychoanalytic hypothesis of change mechanisms in encounter groups.' *International Journal of Group Psychotherapy*, **22** (1), 42–53.

Gibb, J. R. (1964) 'Climate for trust formation.' In L. P. Bradford, J. R. Gibb, and K. D. Benne (eds.), *T-Group Theory and Laboratory Method*, pp. 279–309. New York: Wiley.

Golembiewski, R. T. and Blumberg, A. (1970) 'Introduction.' In R. T. Golembiewski and A. Blumberg (eds.), *Sensitivity Training and the Laboratory Approach*, pp. 2–13. Itasca, Ill.: F. E. Peacock.

Grenthe, E. (1975) '*Utvecklingstendenser inom laboratoriemetoden. En studie i värderingar.*' (Developmental tendencies within the laboratory method. A study in values.) Beteendevetenskapliga Institutionsgruppen, University of Lund.

Habermas, J. (1966) 'Knowledge and interest.' *Inquiry*, 6–7, 285–300.

Hjelholt, G. (1972) 'Group training in understanding society: the mini-society.' In C. L. Cooper (ed.). *Group Training for Individual and Organizational Development*, pp. 140–51. Basel: S. Karger.

Horwitz, L. (1964) 'Transference in training groups and therapy groups.' *International Journal of Group Psychotherapy*, **14**, 202–13.

Lakin, M. (1972) *Interpersonal Encounter: Theory and Practice in Sensitivity Training*. New York: McGraw-Hill.

Lennung, S.-A. (1974) 'Implicit theories in experiential group practices—a pedagogical approach.' *Interpersonal Development*, **5**, (1), 37–49.

Lieberman, M. A. (1976) 'Change induction in small groups.' In *Annual Review of Psychology*, pp. 217–50. *Vol. 27*. Palo Alto, Calif.: Annual Reviews Inc.

Lieberman, M. A., Yalom, I. D., and Miles, M. B. (1973) *Encounter Groups: First Facts*. New York: Basic Books.

Lomranz, J., Lakin, M. and Schiffman, H. (1972) 'Variants in group sensitivity training and encounter: diversity or fragmentation?' *The Journal of Applied Behavioral Science*, **8**, 399–420.

Marrow, A. J. (1964) *Behind the Executive Mask*. New York: American Management Association.

Pfeiffer, J. W. and Jones, J. B. (1969) *A Handbook of Structured Exercises for Human Relations Training*. Iowa City, Iowa, and La Jolla, Calif.: University Associates Press.

Singer, D. L., Astrachan, B. M., Gould, L. J., and Klein, E. B. (1975) 'Boundary management in psychological work with groups.' *The Journal of Applied Behavioral Science*, **11**, (2), 137–76.

Yalom, I. D. (1975) *The Theory and Practice of Group Psychotherapy*. New York: Basic Books.

Yalom, I. D. and Lieberman, M. A. (1971) 'A study of encounter group casualties', *Archives of General Psychiatry*, **25**, 16–30.

Chapter **3**

Sequence and Consequence in the Experiential Psychotherapies

Alvin R. Mahrer

University of Ottawa, Canada

There are at least three ways of defining the experiential psychotherapies:

(1) These psychotherapies are rooted in existential, phenomenological, and humanistic philosophical foundations. Prominent here are the writings of Kierkegaard, Husserl, Sartre, Heidegger, Merleau-Ponty, Binswanger, Boss, Maslow, May, Laing, Gendlin, Frankl, Buhler, and others. *Experiential psychotherapies are those whose philosophical roots grow out of existentialism, phenomenology, and humanistic thought.*

(2) Experiential psychotherapies are also defined by the pivotal ingredient in the effecting of therapeutic change. Some therapies count on insight or understanding, e.g. grasping what one's personality is like, or how one relates to the world, or the interrelationship of one's present and past life. Some therapies count upon the development and use of a good therapist–patient relationship, whether for analysis of a transference neurosis or for support or for its impact on intrapsychic processes. Some therapies count on controlled modification of behavioural contingencies—altering the cues, stimuli, and other variables upon which the target behaviour is more or less contingent. Some therapies count upon *experiencing* to move the therapeutic process forward. Recognizing that each therapeutic approach may draw upon one or more of these effective ingredients, *the experiential psychotherapies are those which use experiencing as the pivotal ingredient in the effecting of therapeutic change.*

(3) There is a family of therapies which either rest upon an existential-phenomenological-humanistic foundation, utilize experiencing, or both. These family members include client-centred therapy, existential therapy, Daseins analysis, encounter therapy, *Gestalt* therapy, phenomenological therapy, humanistic therapy, primal therapy, experiential therapy, and others. The proponents of this therapeutic family include Rogers, Warkentin, Whitaker, Perls, May, Gendlin, Kempler, Schutz, Mahrer, Boss, Bugental, Jourard, Janov, Polster, Binswanger, Ellenberger, Holt, Van den Berg, Shorr, Enright, Serban, Laing, van Dusen, Felder, and others. *Experiential psychotherapies include those therapies as presented in the writings of the above persons.*

The therapist–patient relationship: a new departure

The history of psychotherapy is virtually the history of the patient–therapist relationship. Throughout psychoanalysis, neo-psychoanalysis, ego therapies, all of the psychoanalytic derivatives, and client-centred therapies, the patient–therapist relationship was a paramount defining feature. So important was this relationship that schools of therapy were differentiated from one another by the nature, depth, intensity, and function of the relationship. Indeed, the patient–therapist relationship nearly served as the definition of psychotherapy itself. With the advent of behaviour therapies, the centrality of the patient–therapist relationship receded in favour of the controlled modification of behavioural contingencies. Although some writers (see Patterson, 1968, 1974) insist on identifying a regnant role for the patient–therapist relationship in the behaviour therapies, the predominance of behaviour therapists see this relationship as a relatively minor ingredient. In the last two decades, however, experiential psychotherapies preserved the centrality of the patient–therapist relationship in a form first introduced by the client-centred school: the exceedingly open and available humanness of the therapist. In this relationship, the therapist was to be full there, fully open to the patient, fully willing to 'encounter' the patient. This kind of relationship emerged as the hallmark of the experiential therapies, and remains a distinguishing characteristic in many of the contemporary experiential therapies. I submit, however, that such a patient–therapist relationship runs counter to what the experiential therapies would and will look like following a systematic deduction from their existential-phenomenological-humanistic foundations. I predict that the proper study of these foundations suggests a radical departure wherein the therapist assumes a new role. Accordingly, in this chapter I shall bypass the experiential psychotherapist as the one who relates to the patient as a human being, disclosing and sharing, encountering and relating intimately. I shall describe the roles of patients and therapists as more faithfully consistent, in my opinion, with existential-humanistic-phenomenological philosophy and theory. Interestingly enough, the roles of therapist and patient and their relationship will be closer to those defined in the behaviour therapies, but for altogether different theoretical reasons, addressed to altogether different purposes, and using altogether different therapeutic methods.

In this departure, it is appropriate that the therapist openly share the goals of psychotherapy with the patient. Accordingly, the balance of this chapter is addressed to the person who elects to enter the role of patient and to carry out the work of experiential psychotherapy. It is a summary condensation of what the patient learns over the course of many sessions. Because I will be addressing the *patient*, the reader who is a psychotherapist, personality theorist, or psychological researcher, but not a patient, will find much that has been omitted. Largely, what is omitted is a discussion of those goals which the psychotherapist maintains *about* the patient, more or less privately, as a theoretician, a personality theorist, therapeutic strategist, historian, teacher, social philosopher, social scientist or researcher—*about* psychotherapy and *about* the patient. For the person who enters into experiential psychotherapy, it is not germane to discuss the social implications or the goals I hold for the person, nor is it germane to discuss goals in terms which are meaningful only to the therapist, theorist, or researcher. In eschewing a discussion *about* goals and *about* the patient, I elect to describe our goals *to* and *for* the person who undertakes the therapeutic journey.

If you seek to undergo experiential psychotherapy, you are the one who does the work. You are the one who sets out on the journey and you are the one who moves us along. How rapidly we proceed is up to you. I will be asking you repeatedly whether you wish to take the next step, and I will honour your decision. At times you will be ready, and at other times you will not be ready, but always the decision is yours. You are the leader, the boss, the one with the responsibility. Whenever you wish to pause or stop for a while, I shall honour your decision. Whenever you wish to end our work or to take it up again, I accept a commitment to honour your decision.

Therapist as instructor. I am your instructor. I will teach you what to do, what it accomplishes, and how to do it, at each step in your work. My commitment and responsibility is to be your teacher and your guide in your work. In large measure, the goals of experiential psychotherapy consist of the learning of a method for undergoing personal change. The learning of this method involves the acquisition of skills. These skills can be learned, but they are not easy to learn. They will not be learned by wanting alone. They require hard work to master them. It is my responsibility to teach you these skills. To some extent, how much you learn depends upon the kind of person you now are, whether you really want to learn, and whether you are ready to learn (Maslow, 1970; Maupic, 1965). How much you learn also depends upon how much knowledge there is available, and upon my knowledge and skills as a teacher. We know some, but not much, of the science and art of how to undertake this journey. What there is to know, and what I know of what there is to know, I will try to teach you.

Therapist as integral part of patient. In addition to being your instructor, there will be times when I will become a part of you, feeling and experiencing what you are feeling and experiencing. I will join in with you, fuse with you, conjoin with you in undergoing what you are undergoing. As you look out upon and grasp your encompassing world, I will become a part of the you who looks out upon and grasps your encompassing world. As you relate to that which is within you, I will join together with you in relating to that which is within you. I will also become a part of that which is within you, feeling and experiencing what that deeper part feels and experiences, fusing and conjoining with it, undergoing what it undergoes, looking upon its encompassing world as it looks out upon its encompassing world. I will share and become fused with you and what is within you, being what each part of you is being.

I will accompany you on your own experiential journey, risking what you risk, experiencing what you experience.

Patient as worker versus patient as relater to therapist. Your focal centre is your work—your own self, your own feelings and experiencings, your own encompassing world, the special world in which you exist. When the focused centre of your attention is your work, you enable me to be your instructor, and you enable me to be an integral part of you who is carrying out your work. When your focused centre of attention turns to me, everything stops. I cannot do what I must do if your relationship is with me rather than with your work. To the extent that you turn from your work to me as a person, to a relationship with me, our work ends. If you are to move forward in your work, you must relate to your own insides, your inner feelings and experiencings, your own meaningful world in which you exist. You must not make me into your best friend or your worst enemy, your lover or your tormentor. I am not your source of strength or your wailing wall. I am neither your parent nor your child. I am not your opposition, the one against whom you struggle, rebel, fight, or contest. I am not your confederate against the world, your ally in self-pity, your protector against others. I am not your priest, confessor, judge or jury. I am not here to provide you with love, sympathy, understanding, acceptance, positive regard, belongingness. I am not here to be your model or your saint, your ideal or your god. I am not here to clasp you, have it out with you, have emotional outpourings with you. I am not here to do anything to or for you, to help you, cure you, adjust you, make you feel better. I am not here to anchor you to reality, get you to understand the world, explain what life is all about, scold you, criticize you, inspire or exhort you. You must not woo me, seduce me, please me, give me gifts. Once you turn your focused attention upon me, and it is enormously easy to do that (Bugental, 1964; Lawton, 1958; Mahrer, 1970a; Perls, 1969), out work stops.

We now turn to a summary condensation of what we can accomplish in our work, i.e., our goals. This will be described in the order in which we take up each of these steps. What is omitted is how, the method by which each step is taken and accomplished so that we may move on to the next.

1. Discovering the deeper potentials for experiencing

Our first aim is to discover what is within you. We will understand, see clearly, study, come to know what is just inside you. This something is just beyond that of which you are aware. It is dimly sensed but never clearly felt or experienced. It is that which is just on the other side of momentary feelings such as watchfulness, anxiety, discomfort, distress, inner alienness. In existential theory we refer to this as a deeper mode of existence, modes of being in the world, potentials for being or existing or experiencing. I shall refer to them as *potentials for experiencing.* Our aim is to open up your insides and to look within, to engage in an insight, an inner vision (Wilhelm, 1962) of that which you have avoided, pushed away, closed off, sensed, not clearly known. Sometimes that deeper potential appears in a form which is grotesque and monstrous, but is always indicates the larger, deeper, somehow more real and authentic you. It may, when we first discover it, appear as a potential for experiencing emptiness, nothingness, pervasive meaninglessness. It may appear as a dogged failure, blocking your every effort, dooming every fruitless venture, foreclosing every possibility. It may appear as an erosive hate, seeping into every warm relationship, eating away in bitterness and acrimony.

You will be learning a method to remove the veils from the deeper potentials for experiencing. You will learn how to identify and illuminate what you have partially sensed but have never known. As you gain proficiency in this method, you will be able to grasp the nature of what is momentarily within you, imminent and about which you are uncomfortable, turning away, wanting to not know, closing your self off to. You will be able to illuminate what is just beyond the outer periphery of your self, your sense of 'I-ness', your vague and cloudy inner discomfort.

2. Ending the existence of the person whom you are

You exist as an 'I-ness', a sense of self, a personhood, a self which is conscious and aware of itself and of its existence. You exist as the centre of the existence which is you, as the self which has consciousness, which plans, judges, watches—the person behind the person, the self behind the self. It is the Dasein. This fundamental person whom you are will be faced with a choice. It is the ultimate choice of preserving the person whom you are or ending its existence. It is the choice of ending everything that you are. It is a complete giving up of the very heart of what you are, the core of your existence as a self (May, 1967). It is the ending of your self, your I-ness, your centre of consciousness and awareness, the very core of your being (Suzuki, 1956). It is a complete ending of the person whom you are (Byles, 1962), every last shred of the you who has consciousness of what is occurring. This closing off, ending, sacrificing, no longer being, death of the person whom you are—this has all the certainty and absolute finality of suicide, of the void, emptiness, death of your existence (Ellenberger, 1958; May, 1958b; Schachtel, 1959).

This step is in flat contrast with that of virtually all other psychotherapies, and you should know the differences. Whereas experiential psychotherapies invite you to bring to a final close the whole of the person whom you are, another direction, and one offered by other psychotherapies, is to preserve and strengthen the person whom you are (see for example Fenichel, 1954; Knight, 1941, 1952), to lend it support, to help it adjust or cope with what is within, what is without, and its way of behaving in relationship to what is within and what is without. In contrast, to end the very existence of the person whom you are is beyond changing of your behaviour, your character, or way of looking at your self and your world. It is beyond changes in the way you relate to your insides or to your external world. It is beyond a straightening

44

out of your problems or your psychopathology. It is, instead, the final ending of the existence of the you who has the behaviour, who adjusts or has difficulties adjusting, who relates well or poorly to what is within and to your external world, who has the problems and the psychopathology. Our invitation is the radical metamorphosis of the you who has all of these behaviours, hopes, problems, pains, hurts, anguishes, and struggles.

The person whom you are known what it is like to be caught in problems and decisions, to be in dilemmas. You know what it is like to be stuck, to be struggling against 'it', to live in a world of impossibilities, impasses, confinements. These are not solved; you end the existence of the person who exists in this kind of world. The person whom you are has pain and anguish, anxiety and depression, worry and fear, symptoms and imminent bad possibilities. All of these are left behind as you close off the existence of the person who has all of these.

The person whom you are has hopes and ambitions, wishes and wants. It has immediate goals and lifelong directions. It has loves and pleasures, that which it cherishes and that which it guards as precious. It has an existence which it maintains at all costs. The invitation is to give up all of that, to end the existence of the personhood, self, I-ness which zealously protects all of that. It is an ending of all that you are and all that you hope to become, all that you are moving toward and all that you have accomplished. It is an ending of everything wonderful and promising, exciting and maintaining of the person whom you now are.

The culmination of this step is a resolve, an eager readiness to give up one's existence. It is a complete willingness to enter into a whole new existence which requires the absolute ending of your present total existence. If you are ready, the next step is the doing of it. If you are not, we cannot and will not proceed. The decision is yours, wholly.

3. Being the deeper-potential

In the first step, you discovered the nature of potentials which are within. In the second step you became ready to close out the person whom you are. The third step is being that deeper potential. It is a being of that which you struggled not to know, which you have avoided, fought against, sought to deny and disprove, defended against. It is being the deeper potential which threatened you, menaced you, loomed out against you, hurt and terrorized you, victimized and cackled at you.

Fully being that deeper potential can be described in two ways. One consists of a hurling of your self into it, falling completely into it, actively being its very core, its personhood, its self. It is a headlong rush over the abyss and into the chasm of its central being. This is the final leap of faith. The certainty and the criterion of being the deeper potential is that there is no longer any you who gauges and assesses and knows what you are doing. It is not you who are being the deeper potential. Having sacrificed your self, the person who emerges is the person of the deeper potential—an entirely new person, distinct and intact in and of its self. A second way of describing the being of a deeper potential consists of a passive posture. Let it fill you, invade you, saturate your very being until you die. You give in to it until that point where you are no more and what emerges is the deeper potential which occupies your body and thinks with your head and exists with the body which had been you. Here is the trust of going under, of falling asleep, knowing that you will exist no more, and knowing that the person who wakes will be the person of the deeper potential.

Whether you actively hurl your self into the core of the deeper potential or passively allow the deeper potential to invade your whole being, the critical step, the point of *kairos* (Ellenberger, 1958) is the ending of your existence and the appearance of the other self, I-ness, being which is the deeper potential. The new self cannot occur until *you* have passed out of existence, and this metamorphosis is an experientially cataclysmic uprooting (Janov, 1970; Levitsky and Perls, 1970; Mahrer, 1975a; Maupin, 1965; Ouspensky, 1957). To accomplish this is neither cerebral nor experientially mild. It may occur suddenly, but to get to that point requires the pinnacle of experiencing. Even when the shift occurs in an instant, the experiencing which brings it about has several components. One is volume. The sheer volume of experiencing is beyond the ordinary peaks. A second is repetition, an overagainness until the new self is present. A third component is primitiveness, a being of archaic feelings and doings. A fourth component is complete bodily being of it in full physical saturation. A fifth component is the intense being of the deeper potential for experiencing, a being of its precise nature and content. The sixth component is the doing of its behavioural action in the appropriate situational contexts in which it occurs. In this, the emerging person lives in another world, another existence in which the situation is present and occurring.

The person whom you are will have learned the skills to enable all of this to happen. You will know how to pass through this metamorphosizing journey. *All* of the person whom you are will undergo this journey. A *part* of the person I am will go with you on our journey. I risk what you risk, but you risk more. I have been on such journeys, and the part of me which is the instructor stays near, ready to guide us through the right next steps. But before we discuss the next step, we must consider the consequences which follow from the successful achievement of the first three steps.

4. The consequences

There will occur a set of consequences as a result of your successful achievement of the first three steps. The more you undergo the first three steps, the more these consequences will occur, so that there is a kind of cumulative effect to the magnitude of the consequences. It is important to understand that these are consequences, products of your work. They are evidence of your having successfully accomplished the first three steps. Each of these consequences may also be seen as a goal of experiential psychotherapy. But they are goals which can never be sought directly. The more you seek to accomplish these directly, the more elusive they become, for they are expressions of a radical metamorphosis in the person whom you are becoming (Hora, 1961).

Transformation of the nature and content of the deeper potential

The nature and content of the deeper potentials rely upon your being the person whom you are and relating to them in the way you do. When you discover these deeper potentials, they are in a form which, almost inevitably, is frightening. It is that form of their nature and content which you have avoided and defended against, which you have struggled with and from which you have recoiled. Once you have ended the existence of the person whom you are, and once you have surrendered fully into being these deeper potentials, there is a radical transformation in their nature and content, a radical mutation of their very nature and content (Gendlin, 1962, 1964). They undergo change by your undergoing change. This notion of the openness of deeper potentials of fundamental change in their nature and content is in stark contrast to the psychoanalytic conviction of the absolute unalterability of basic personality processes (Allport, 1937).

What you had recoiled from as an awful homosexuality is transformed into a potential for the experiencing of intimacy and closeness, or softness and dependency, or forthrightness and toughness. Your isolation and withdrawal may give way to a lush sexuality with men or women or both. What had menaced you as a monstrous sucking parasitism may be transmuted into a potential for the experiencing of simple, straightforward trust. What you had avoided as a consuming depression is transformed into a potential for being with oneself or for extricating yourself from intolerable situations. What you had defended against as homicidal rage is transformed into a sense of control or loving closeness or a direct straightforwardness. The deadness and petrification emerges into a potential for strength or toughness or iron firmness. The catastrophic competitiveness, dominance, and superiority may transmute into leadership or belongingness or respect for others. The painful exposure and vulnerability may become a refreshing emotionality or feelingness or open expressiveness. Death may become a rebirth, a freedom from the confining, a sense of mastery.

Although you could never have known it as the person whom you were, the form in which the deeper potentials occur varies with the person whom you are. As a person who is alien to them, who fears and hates them, who recoils from and struggles with them, they occur in their monster form, grotesque and twisted, alien, fearful, hateful. When *you* undergo the changes outlined in the first three steps, no longer do these deeper potentials loom as their former images and icons, forms and shapes spurts of behavioural possibilities, The whole sweep of ways in which the deeper potentials might occur is now washed away as you are within their centre. Now these potentials are free to occur in more cordial, more integrative, more assimilated forms and shapes. This transformations is a transformation of how the potentials are manifest, are seen and related to. They may become more or less socially acceptable to those around you, but within you their nature and content are transformed.

Extinguishing of the person with the problem behaviour

Extinguishing of the problem behaviour. You are no longer the person who behaved in problem ways. The person whom you become will be free of problem behaviours which themselves are painful, anguishing, hurtful. These problem behaviours will simply extinguish. Whole sets of problem behaviours will extinguish because they served, without you ever knowing, to preserve the person you were, to insure that there is no change in the core which is you. When you no longer must be preserved as the person whom you were, all of these self-protective behaviours fade away. There will be an extinguishing of all the problem behaviours which culminated in bad feelings of anxiety, fear, feeling in pieces, torn apart, meaningless. So many of your problem behaviours were designed to prove that you are not the kind of person you fearfully sensed you really were, to proving that you were not wicked, not crazy, not cruel, not nothing, not dead, not grotesque. Once the person is no more, these behaviours have no further reason for being, and they extinguish. With that extinguishing occurs the washing away of being stuck, being at an impasse, being caught—together with the problem behaviours which brought about such manacling situations. All of these problem behaviours will slide away when the person you were is no more, and their extinguishing occurs without concentrated effort or attempts to get rid of them directly.

Some of these problem behaviours may remain, but they will be carried out by a new person—and therefore, in a paradoxical way, they are radically different. The husk of the old problem behaviours will be filled out and used by the new personhood, the new sense of I-ness, and that changes the behaviours fundamentally. Before you undergo the ending of the person whom you are and the being of the deeper potential, you may hesitantly inquire about both problem behaviour and more preciously cherished behaviour. Will I no longer impose a barrier between myself and my wife? Will I be rid of my excessive drinking, my making others ridicule me, my antagonizing of my children, my having to be the clown, my terrible compulsiveness? Will I still smile the way I do, love riding my bicycle, enjoy lovemaking, still be a parent, cellist, good neighbour? Where the person whom you were hopes to get rid of problem *behaviour* and to retain cherished *behaviour*, the risk is of far greater proportions, namely that the *person* whom you become may carry out all of them, none of them, or some of them. The *person you are* will change, and the old problem behaviours may or may not change. If the new person drinks a lot or plays the cello, it will be a new person who carries out these behaviours. All of these behaviours will somehow be different, their whole meaning altered, their manifest form changed because the behaver is a new person (Holt, 1968). In flat contrast to Skinner (1967), the behaviour itself is drastically altered when the behaving person alters.

Extinguishing of cognitions. Included in the slab of extinguished problem behaviours is the whole realm of cognitions, basic premises, ways of thinking, conceptual structures, modes of grasping the world, fundamental cognitive assumptions, expectations and attitudes, beliefs and values, ideational systems. This whole array is coupled to the person whom you were, and when you are no longer that person, they extinguish. They are attached to the person you were, a part of its way of being, and they are left behind when you no longer are the old personhood. Experiential therapies free you of these cognitive structures by your disengaging from being the person who has them. In this regard, the experiential psychotherapies differ markedly from those therapies which attack your fundamental cognitive structures while leaving you the same person you were (e.g. Adler, 1927, 1969; Dreikurs, 1956, 1967; Ellis, 1962, 1967; Kelly, 1955, 1967).

Extinguishing of physical bodily problems. Problem behaviour includes the domain of the physical body, for there is an extinguishing of those physical bodily manifestations which constitute problem behaviour. The body, in this perspective, is described as far more than the site of feelings. It is also a domain in which is manifested phenomena isomorphic with external problem behaviour, and phenomena which occur within the body but are unexpressed in actual external behaviour. As the person undergoes change, there will occur actual, physical, tangible changes in the structure and function of the body. These changes include the washing away of tumours, muscular constrictions, valve leakages, inflammations, obesity, malignancies, ulcers, internal bleedings, toxaemias, skeletal abnormalities, endocrine imbalances, asthmatic conditions, brain tissue impairment, and hundreds of other localized, generalized, internal and external bodily phenomena.

Awakening of dilated consciousness

The awakening. Although it seems paradoxical, the closing out of one's self, I-ness, and consciousness leads to a radically expanded and dilated sense of consciousness. This consequence of therapeutic experiencing is frequently expressed as a surprising sense of awe, an opening of a third eye, a sudden awakening from a hypnotic sleep in which one only now knows he had been in (Maupin, 1965; Watts, 1961). Only after awakening in this state of dilated consciousness can the former state be recognized as one in which the consciousness was numbed, truncated, narrowed, delimited. Each state of consciousness carries with it a sense of being complete, a state which is only recognized as incomplete and self-illusory when you pass into a state of even more expanded consciousness. Each outward dilation of consciousness is experienced as an awakening, and with this awakening comes other changes.

Freedom, choice, self-consistency. One of these changes is a sense of freedom. It is a freedom of being the former person, of having to be that person, of not knowing that one has the freedom to be or not to be that person. There is a sense of choice, a freedom to choose to enter into the world of the former personhood, and the freedom to choose not to enter into that world, the freedom to choose to exist within the personhood you are now or perhaps to exit from this person also. This is a freedom from a kind of imprisonment in which you had existed without knowing that you had existed in it (Frankl, 1959). It is clear now that you had existed in a former state which imprisoned you with the illusion of being free, the deception of being in charge, the false reality of having choice (Ouspensky, 1957). Indeed, this new found sense of freedom is laced with a giddy, silly playful liberation in which you experience the utter nonsense of it all (Watts, 1960). More than mere freedom, you now have the skills to acquire even greater freedom, the skills to free one's self from whatever one now is. It is the freedom of being-able-to-be (Binswanger, 1958).

In addition to the sense of freedom, there is the sudden new world of choice. It is as if one now lives in a world filled with opportunities, and one is the chooser—able to accept or to decline hundreds upon hundreds of presented invitations. Sometimes these invitations require active moving into. At other times the invitations allow you passively to surrender and let happen, or to disengage from and stop from happening that which is starting to fill you, to saturate you from within, to constitute your experiencing. Whether choosing in the active or passive mode, there will be that quality of being centred, organized, all of a piece. It is a sense of self, of consistency and stability, of being able to be in charge of one's driftings, of control and governance, of self-confidence, mastery, self-reliance, independence, intactness and self-direction (Loevinger, 1966; Ouspensky, 1957; Rogers, 1970; Szasz, 1956; Van Dusen, 1957).

Receptivity to inner sensings. This dilated consciousness means that you will be receptive to the realm of inner feelings, sensations, messages. You are now in a position of welcomed receptivity to what is happening within. It will seem that you are more at one with these inner physical sensations which, for example, tell you that something is wrong or amiss. Listen to us, we are trying to tell you that something is not right. These are the tiny inside warnings, inner voices warning you that you are on the wrong track, or that you are about to launch onto some action which your insides are telling you is wrong. Watch out, this is not the right thing to do. Instead of closing off these inner messages, you will be responsive to them (Rogers, 1970). Each slight increase in inner experiencing will be received into your consciousness, present and available to you. This is the skill of consigning a part of your awareness to attentive hovering, watchful and receptive, to what is happening within. You will be knowing what these inner messages are, attuned to where they are in your body, to what they signify (see Gendlin, 1969; Wilhelm 1962), used by you as guideposts, signals, warnings, danger signals (Rogers, 1963). On the basis of these inner signs, you will be able to stop an ongoing behaviour, to not do something you are doing. When they say that something is wrong, that you are proceeding along the wrong path, you will have the capacity to call a halt to your behaviour. These inner guidelines will be trusted and used to monitor the way you are, both in the tiniest of mundane life decisions and as trustworthy guides in the major decisions of your life (Mahrer, 1967; Maslow, 1963; Reik, 1948).

Centring one's self. With dilated consciousness, with an expansion of the sense of self, you will be able to learn the skills of aligning the person whom you are with the nature of the internal bodily sensations or feelings. This has been termed 'centring' (May, 1967), and consists of letting your self be properly coupled with the actual ongoing internal bodily feelings. When the feelings are those of buoyancy and excitement, you are able to 'have' these feelings, and to integrate your self with those feelings. When there is a separation between your self and internal bodily feelings of being jangled, tight, torn apart, when you are headed in one direction and the internal bodily feelings are headed in another direction, you have the skills of centring and realigning your self with those feelings. There is the acquired skill of stopping the beginning disconnection, of letting the person whom you are settle into a centred reconnection with those internal bodily feelings—and thereby reintegrated the whole personhood right now.

By being able to centre your self, by being able to maintain the connectedness with your own internal feelings, you keep your self immediately right here. To accomplish this centring means that you prevent your self from falling asleep, from being on automatic pilot, from being and acting mechanically. You maintain a presence of being, a sense of organized immediacy. You prevent the possibility of falling into a state of becoming a robot, being activated and governed by external stimuli and cues, external forces and influences.

Greater freedom of movement. Because the domain of your self is expanded, it now includes sets of potentials with easy freedom of movement into and out of them. Each of these potentials is now open and available to you, able to be stepped into and out of. More than merely being able to be these potentials, you will also have friendlier relationships with them. That is, you will be able to joke with them, to poke fun at them, to enjoy and be proud of them (Watts, 1961). Whatever potential you have just been can be kidded about or a source of pride because you are so very free to slide out of what you were just experiencing and establish a relationship with it. You can, in other words, respond to your self as being pompous or dumb, thick-headed or irresponsible, clever or jealous, narcissistic or defensive. All the reactions which others have, or are invited to have, about you, yourself can have and enjoy having about yourself (*cf.* Bullard, 1959). With such an expanded domain of your person, you can assert that what you just did was above your usual standards, or so appalling that you sometimes wonder how you manage to do such things.

In addition to having reactions to what you are, there is a wider range of potentials which you are now able to be. Now you are able to experience affection, and to slide into experiencing competition, and to move into a kind of hilarity, on into a soft sensuosity, and on into the experiencing of intellectual achievement. There are more potentials for experiencing which are open to you, where before they existed only deeper and unavailable.

Changes in feelings

When the person who you were is no longer the imprisoning limit of your being, when that person is no more, perhaps the landmark consequence is changes in feelings. These changes in the felt bodily sensations are regular accompaniments to successful accomplishment of the first three steps of experiential psychotherapy (cf. Gendlin, 1964).

Increase in good feelings of integration. One of the most prominent consequences is the automatic increase in certain kinds of good feelings. Increases in these good feelings refer to actual felt physical bodily sensations. Where before you may have mild good feelings, now they are of heightened magnitude. Where before you may have had such good feelings a few minutes every day or so, now they occupy a much larger proportion of your life. Where before they may have been localized in a part of your body, such as your upper chest or your head, now they occupy most or even all of your body—in body regions which practically never had experienced such good feelings. The presence of such good feelings often constitutes a qualitative new dimension of feelings whose absence can be diagnostically discernible (cf. Rado, 1956; Rado and Daniel, 1956). Such good feelings fall into the following kinds:
(a) There will occur a felt bodily sense of a wholeness, unity, oneness, togetherness, good organization, *Gestalt* (Bergman, 1949; Buytendijk, 1950; Byles, 1962).
(b) There will occur a felt bodily sense of internal peace, harmony, tranquillity.
(c) There will occur a felt bodily sense of welcoming, taking in assimilating, fusing, becoming, growing, opening up, expanding, receiving.

These good feelings are quiet and benign, soft and unobtrusive. They constitute the bulk of that which is described as a state of *satori* (Maupin, 1965) or a state of integration.

Decrease in bad feelings of disintegration. When you successfully undergo the first three steps of experiential psychotherpay, there will occur decreases in certain kinds of bad feelings:
(a) There will occur a reduction in a state of unfeeling, of deadness, of numb-

ness, of nothingness. You will begin to feel, to have felt bodily physical sensations. Your body will no longer be a thing of deadness and unfeelingness.

(b) There will be a reduction of felt bodily sensations of being in pieces, torn apart, fractionated, disjointed, broken up and broken apart, of parts being walled off or sealed off from other parts.

(c) There will be a reduction of felt bodily sensations of one's parts being at war with one another, in turmoil, set against each other, menacing and hating one another, struggling against each other.

(d) There will be a reduction of felt bodily sensations referred to by such words as anxiety, fear, threat, tension, tightness; of a restless urgency of having-to-be or must-be; of helplessness, smallness, pawnness; of shame, guilt, self-punishment; of separation, aloneness, alienation; of meaninglessness, hollowness, emptiness; of depression and heaviness; of hostility and anger, rage and hatred; of bodily aches, pains, distresses, hurts.

These classes of bad feelings will decrease along two dimensions. First, there will be a reduction in their presence, their intensity and magnitude, their strength and consistency. Indeed, it is conceivable that such bad feelings will be virtually eliminated (cf. Buber, 1957). Second, the bad feelings will take place within an integrated person. You may have a feeling of anxiety, but you will be a person who receives that anxiety well, who has the anxiety without exacerbating it, a person to whom the anxiety has possibly a constructive meaning. The bad feelings will no longer have their former catastrophic impacts because you are less vulnerable to their dirtier effects. Instead of being engulfed or torn apart by the bad feelings, you will be a person who can be whole and unified, all of a piece, and still have tension or guilt or emptiness.

Integration with your own external world

As the person whom you are undergoes change, so too will there be change in the world in which you live, and in your way of being in and relating with that world. Your own personal external world will itself change. It will undergo substantive change in its very fabric, its physical nature, as well as the relationships among and between its parts. By successfully undergoing the first three steps of experiential psychotherapy, your own relationships with the deeper potentials will alter in ways which are expressed in similar altered relationships with an altered external world:

Integrative openness. There will occur an increasing openness between you and your external world. This openness will show itself in your providing others with more space, more room to be, more letting-be. You will be less inclined to push others out of their natural contours, to make them into what you were inclined to make them into. You will be marked by less of a tendency to try to change others, to get them to be different, to pressure them to be a way that you want them to be, to be distressed by their being inconsistent or contradictory (Enright, 1970; Jourard, 1968). Their own ways of being are given more freedom to be, more welcomed reception. In the same way, your world will relate to you with greater openness. Other persons will grant you more space and freedom to be, less crowding and pushing you out of your own natural contours. Both in you and in your world, and in the relationships between you and your world, there will be less restless pushing, forcing, having to be, frenetic urgency to do something to the other. There will be less pressure to conform or be conformed, to rebel or be rebelled, to must do or to be done to.

Integrative openness means that your relationships with others will become more on an equal stature, more person-to-person, more I–thou. This kind of open relationship has feeling characteristics of wholeness and unity, oneness and peacefulness, tranquillity and harmony. It includes a mutual welcoming, expanding, becoming. In short, it is a relationship of love, a dual mode of existence in love (Binswanger, 1958; Enright, 1970). In such a relationship, your own feelings will be increasingly transparent, and you will behave with fewer avoidances and defences. You will become more trusting in being passive and more openly available. The world in which you exist will likewise take on a similar transparency and diminution of defences and avoidances, increasing trust and ease of being passive. In both you and your world, and in the relationship between you and your world, there will occur a greater sense of genuineness, realness, authenticity (Shostrom, 1967; Szasz, 1956; Rogers, 1967).

With this openness in you and in your world, you will be more able to sense, listen to, receive, know, resonate to what is occurring in others, to what they are saying, feeling, thinking, sending, doing. Here is increased contact between you and the external realities, a decreased distancing which you most likely did not know had been a distance at all, until you enter into more real contact. Patients have frequently mentioned how new it is to be in direct contact with an external world free of veils, moats, gaps, and distances which had always been there without their ever knowing. You will be able to lose yourself in the external world, to entrust yourself actively or passively to it, and thereby to know your world in ways you had never known. In this state of heightened contact with aspects with which you had never been in contact, you will have far more knowledge; you will know your world—and be known by it—more deeply, more realistically, more intimately, more systematically, more veridically.

Integrative being-one-with. In addition to your personhood becoming more open to the external world, there will also occur an extension of your self into parts of the external world. It is as if the outer periphery of your self will dilate to encompass something which is out there (Fromm, Suzuki, and de Martino, 1960). In being-one-with a friend or a lake or a painting, you have gone beyond being a separate, intact person in close or open relationship with what is out there (Suzuki, 1949). It is as if the centre of the person you are is able to close down and move out of your physical self with the result that you are able to throw yourself into being-one-with the external thing, you will be able to lose your self in it. You will have the skills to be invaded by the other thing, to be filled and saturated with it. You will, thereby, be able to be within its skin, and to exist within its world. You will be able to fuse with it, to assimilate with it, to integrate with it.

This quality, like that of being open to your world, enables you to know the world in which you exist. You have now acquired a way of knowing what occurs within the other person or object. In this way you can become magnificently intimate with the real phenomena which comprise your world (Rogers, 1959), for now you know what it is like from the inside of those phenomena. Once you allow your self to be-one-with the other person or object, you have acquired a very special domain of knowledge about it. Quite often, patients are surprised by the seeing of it as if for the first time. Your son will be sturdy for the first time; suddenly you will see a backbone in your daughter; you will see a symmetry to the house, a rootedness in the tree, a very ugly nose on your husband. In this new seeing of the person or object, there is often reported a kind of rightness, a luminosity (Watts, 1960).

Extinguishing of your painful external world

To the extent that you are successful in undergoing the first three steps in experiential psychotherapy, there will occur an extinguishing of the world which you had co-participated in constructing, and in which you have existed painfully, hurtfully, constrictively. Its very nature and content will alter to such a significant extent that it can be said the world in which you will exist will be qualitatively new (Needleman, 1967).

Extinguishing of disintegrative relationships. You will no longer participate in constructing a painful world wherein relationships are characterized by disintegrative feelings; that is, by feelings of deadness and unfeeling, of being torn apart and in pieces, of being in turmoil and internal struggle, of being anxious or depressed. Your world will be freed of relationships of fighting, struggling, antinomic tension, hatred, and unending opposition which you have, without knowing, co-participated in constructing. These kinds of painful relationships will wash away because you will no longer be a person who engages in the construction of conflict situations in which you are stuck, unable to move, impasses with no way out. No longer will you work toward the building of worlds designed to disprove and deny that which you sense is an inner truth—such as your sensed deeper instability or worthlessness or rigidity or incompetence. No longer will you construct worlds in which you are consigned to fruitless, impossible, lifelong groupings after illusory love, respect, oneness, intimacy, belongingness. No longer will you engage in the construction of external worlds which relate to you in the same disintegrative manner in which you relate to what is within—by clamping down on you, rejecting you, assaulting and confining you, disliking and fearing you, pushing you down and away. As you become your own person, as you behave in ways which indeed may be unique and singular, different, and even deviate, your relationships with others will nonetheless be free of invitations for others to fight you, hurt you, resist and crucify you (Rogers, 1963). So too, your relationships with social norms, standards, and values will become more friendly and congruent. You will neither slavishly follow nor defy them, neither attack nor have to defend them, neither be impelled to adjust to them nor worship them (see Bandura, 1961; Fromm-Reichmann, 1958; Jung, 1933).

The world in which you exist will be freer of disintegrative relationships because it no longer must be twisted painfully out of its own natural contours nor must you accept its invitations to twist you painfully out of your natural contours. These disintegrative relationships extinguish when you no longer must modify the external world, push upon it, change it, turn it into what you had worked hard at turning it into (Jung, 1962). By the same token, the world in which you exist will no longer be one which issues invitations for you to participate in painful relationships. That world will no longer be one which ensnares you, entraps you, sucks you into painful relationships. In these senses, you will leave the world alone, and it will be allowed to leave you alone. You will decline invitations of entrapment, and exist with far fewer of such painful relationships.

Extinguishing of an external world constructed of your own potentials. The external world in which you live will be different because it no longer will include your own externalized or extended ('projected') potentials. Only when you live in such a revealed world can you see that your former world included so much of your own projected potentials. There is virtually nothing you can do directly to deprive the external world of your present projections. You have no way of knowing they are present in your world. But after you take back what you had projected, after you 'own' what you had externalized, then that world is significantly changed. If you house deeper potentials for being moribund, then your present world will include elements of death and dying, erosion and crumbling. As the person whom you are changes, then those elements will wash out of your external world.

5. Actualization

In your work, the first step consisted of discovering your own deeper potentials for experiencing. The second step involved the ending of the existence of the person whom you are and, in the third step, the being of the discovered deeper potentials. Successful accomplishment of these three steps led to the consequences discussed above. Going further, taking the next step, means actually *being* the person you have now become, experiencing the potentials which constitute the new personhood, actualizing the newly dilated person whom you now are (Boss, 1963; Bullard, 1959; Fromm-Reichmann, 1958; Mahrer, 1972; Maslow, 1970; May, 1958b; Rogers, 1963; Van Dusen, 1957). Arriving at the point where you are ready to take this step requires successful accomplishment of the first three steps. It means acquiring a good measure of internal integration. The step we are about to discuss is thus one from which more or less integrated persons, and often this includes older persons, are by no means excluded. Indeed, this step is quite cordial to older persons (Jung, 1933). However, whether or not to proceed further is your decision, each time you arrive at this point. Indeed, it *requires* your decision and commitment. The person whom you are now may well find the next step, for whatever reasons, unimportant. It is your choice whether or not to move onto the next step.

Identifying the Right Behaviour

The right behaviour is a way of being which provides for actualization. Being the dilated, integrated new person means engaging in behaviour, in the right behaviour. Experiencing the potentials which are you means behaving, and the right behaviour provides for these experiencings. In order to experience, behaviour is required; inversely, the right behaviour unlocks the experiencing. It is as if the new person is a heightened readiness for experiencing, and that readiness for experiencing itself requires its own new behaviour. The state is that of a vacuum to be filled with the right behaviour, a vacuum of experiencing which is a context wherein the right behaviour is the necessary element. This hunger is a strong ally in the search for the right way of being, for the behaviour which enables the experiencing to occur. Thus the search for the right behaviour is a providing of what is sought, and not a tacking on of a distal behaviour to a neutral person (Mahrer, 1975b).

The right behaviour is a *positive* defined behaviour. It is never a *not* doing of something. It is never a matter of some sort of resolve to stop drinking or nail biting or masturbating or lending money or being with that kind of person. It is not an attacking or eliminating or reducing or any kind of blockade against some behaviour. It is not a vague effort to be amiable or understanding or assertive—but is, rather, a behaviour with specificity, definition, concreteness.

The nature of the right behaviour is seldom, if ever, that which constituted the bad form of the formerly deeper potential for experiencing. When you feared and struggled against it, the images were those of throat-slitting, crumbling into dust, sexual exposure, eating insatiably, devilishly torturing, smashing, suiciding, falling apart, eroding—behavioural images from which you had recoiled. As the potential becomes integrated, as its nature and content change, as you dilate to assimilate the potential for experiencing, the new person-whom-you-are will identify an appropriate behaviour whose nature ordinarily has nothing in common with the old, feared, behavioural images. You know this now, as the new person whom you are, whereas the former person knew only the frightening behaviouralized images of the feared and hated deeper potential.

The right behaviour is that which is acknowledged by the physical body. Experiencing is a bodily process; feeling is a bodily process. The right behaviour is found by consulting the body. Identifying the right behaviour is not a cerebral enterprise, not one which calls for reasoning or intellectual analysis. The key criteria are bodily processes, and you must learn how to listen to what is occurring in the body in order to identify that as the right behaviour.

The criterion: increased bodily experiencing. The right behaviour is that one which fills you with a full measure of that particular potential for experiencing. If the potential is love and affection, the right behaviour is that which provides a full measure of *depth* and *breadth* of bodily experienced love and affection. Having tried it out, wait, listen to what is happening in the body. If the body radiates depth and breadth of love and affection, that particular experiencing, the behaviour is the right behaviour. If there is minimal or no such bodily experiencing, the behaviour is not the right one, no matter what you think or reason or believe. The body will let you know that you are on the right track when the *intensity* of experiencing is increased. The right behaviour will release a full measure of intense experiencing of love and affection, and it is the scope of bodily phenomena which will attest that loving and caring is occurring. More than likely, the degree of intensity will be beyond that which you have ever experienced before, and when that occurs, the body will let you know—when you stop and wait and listen carefully.

The criterion: bodily feelings of actualization. You know that the behaviour is right when the body has the good *feelings* of actualization. The body is not only the site in which the potential itself is experienced; there also are bodily feelings which accompany the experiencing of that potential. These good feelings of actualization are described by words such as the following: aliveness, vitality; lightness, buoyancy, 'high'; vibrating, tingling, excitement; happiness, satisfaction, pleasure; joy, giddiness, exhilaration, ecstasy; power, force, energy. These words refer to bodily phenomena, sensations, physical feelings. It is interesting that similar words to describe such a state of feelings are employed, not only by experiential psychotherapists, not only in the Nietzschean meaning of power (May, 1958a), but also in the description of the state attained by following the precepts of Zen meditation and contemplation (Chang, 1959; Herrigel, 1956; Kondo, 1952, 1958; Wilhelm, 1962).

When you listen and attend carefully to your body, you can guage whether the behaviour is right by consulting the magnitude of the bodily experiencing and feeling throughout your body. For at least a moment, large portions of the body, or even the body as a whole, can have these kinds of good feelings. If they are localized in and confined to the hands or head or chest or genital area, the behaviour is less 'right' than if the total body is involved in the experiencing and the feeling. Wait, listen, attend. The bodily feelings will serve as a systematic critierion, for they are real, palpable, tangible. They will have a locus, a nature, and a magnitude which you will know reliably and validly.

Because you are now more integrated, these good feelings occur without residuals of the bad bodily feelings of *dis*integration. There is, for example, an excited aliveness without a tightly bound urgency, a fearful constrictedness, an explosive super-stimulation, a pressured anxiety, a menace. The behaviour is right when the feelings of actualization occur in this good way, with a purity of nothing but good feelings.

The criterion: selflessness. The third criterion is the degree to which 'you' (the I-ness, sense of self) fuse into the experiencing. The behaviour is more the right behaviour when the experiencing engulfs I-ness and fills it with experiencing. Under these conditions, the whole person experiences with a kind of selflessness, an extinguishing of the sense of self, an assimilating fusion of the personhood into the experiencing (Ouspensky, 1957). This state may be contrasted with a splitting wherein only a part of you is experiencing while a separated self thinks, knows, assesses, is aware of the experiencing other part. In the search for the right behaviour, you will know that it is right only *after* experiencing occurs. Looking into the loved person's eyes and grinning may be the right behaviour to fill you with the experiencing of love and affection, but in that moment you will be experiencing—and not assessing the degree to which your self was thrown into the experiencing. Only *after* the right behaviour is tried out can you gauge the degree to which the self was thrown into experiencing (indicating the behaviour was right), or the self was removed, standing by, not participating (indicating the behaviour was not right).

By using these criteria, you will be posturing yourself toward being a different way in your actual, daily life outside therapy. You will have identified a particular behaviour which, occurring in a specific situation, will provide you with a full measure of experiencing. The experiencing which is to occur will take place in the immediate world waiting outside therapy; the behaviour will take place in the actual world in which you exist; the situational context in which the behaviour is to occur is available in the imminent future. In effect, you are poised on the brink of your actual, real world, ready to behave in a situational context which provides a full measure of experiencing.

Being-in-the-world

Once you have identified the right behaviour, the next step is being the person who actually is (does, carries out) that behaviour. This is the point where psychotherapy makes a significant intrusion into one's actual life, for behaviour means being the person in one's real life. It is now a matter of doing, of movement, activity, of carrying it out in the world in which you exist (Byles, 1962). This is the momentous step from the sanctuary of the therapeutic office to the real world of one's daily life. The person whom you now are has the choice of the actual experiencing of the potential through actual behaviour in the actual world. This choice leads toward highest plateaus of experiencing, but that requires a doing, a being, a behaving for real in the real world.

If you choose to take this step, the commitment to carry out the behaviour is yours. The new behaviour cannot occur in the actual world unless you undertake to do it, and that decision is a commitment you make in the therapeutic context before it can be carried out in the actual world. In the actual world you may withdraw the commitment and decide not to do it, but the behaviour will not be carried out in the real world unless you commit your self in the therapeutic context to do it, *really* to do it. Only you can undertake such a commitment.

What you are committing your self to is a behavioural change with consequences. Sometimes the consequences are those of heightened depth, breadth, and intensity of experiencing as you carry out a way of being which itself may be subtle—such as a way of touching, or saying the right words, or grinning, or posturing your body. These may be subtle behaviours coming from a new person, providing for new experiencings through simple new actualizing behaviours. Sometimes, however, the new behaviours consist of gross decisions— having the baby, leaving the job, entering a whole new life, leaving or entering a marriage, buying or selling it all, beginning a whole new life. Regardless whether the behaviour itself is subtle or gross, it is always consequential. There will be new feelings and experiencings, changes in whom you are, how you behave, and the world in which you exist. These consequences always bear a component of exciting risk.

Sometimes the new behaviour will be *in* already intact situations, and sometimes the new behaviour will itself *build* situations. Experiencing requires the right situational contexts in which the experiencing can occur. By means of your own behaviour, you will become the one who constructs those situations so that the experiencing can occur. This in itself is a defined class of behaviours of their own. To experience closeness and intimacy may call for a whole new set of behaviours in which you go and get another person, say that you want to talk with the other. To do this is not, in itself, providing directly for the experiencing of closeness and intimacy, but it is building the appropriate situational context in which it can occur. Again, building these situations calls for moving out, starting, doing.

Whether the situation is already there, or whether you construct the situation, carrying out the new behaviour means that you are the one who initiates the doing of it. You get is started. You are the activator, the one who thrusts the new behaving into the world in which you exist. There is always a critical moment when you either do it or you do not do it—regardless whether the behaviour is simple, easy, and subtle, or conspicuous, substantial, and gross. There is a critical moment in which you either throw your self into being it, doing it, or you stop your self. This quality of active initiation of the new behaviour is present even when the behaviour is one of being passive, soft, dependent, taking in, receiving. It is an active initiating effort to behave in a passive manner.

Being the new behaving person calls for effort, guts, courage, will. It is lonely, for whether or not you initiate and actually carry through the new behaviour is a matter of you, and only you. Being the new person, experiencing in the real world, these occur or fail to occur because of you—there is no alien, separate force to carry you along. There is no intrinsic natural actualization process to assist you or to do it for you, in contrast to the thinking of some humanistic writers (cf. Maslow, 1968; Rogers, 1970; Tauber, 1960).

6. Consequences

Following the first three steps, consequences occur (step 4). In the same way, consequences of a different order will result from the fifth step. Again, these consequences require that actualization first take place, and the more that actualization occurs, these consequences will follow. The consequences are regularly coupled with actualization, and cannot be obtained directly.

There are at least two reasons why it is virtually impossible to provide a precise description of what you will be like following progressively increasing actualization. One is that the kind of person you will be is a function of your particular array of *potentials* for experiencing, and your particular array of *behaviours* which provide for that experiencing. Since these differ in significant ways from person to person, approximating guesses can only be made after a careful study of you. Second, you can only really know what it is like fully to *be* your potentials for experiencing when you actually *are* them. Until you actually experience them, you can only see them from the side, as it were, and that is qualitatively different from the actual being and experiencing of these potentials.

Heightened experiencing and feeling. Your body will be characterized by heightened experiencing and feeling. This refers to the heightening of both the potentials for experiencing and the feelings of actualization. Instead of being more or less in a state of bodily deadness, unfeeling, nothingness, or a state of bad feelings, the body now is engaged in physical experiencing and feeling of that which characterizes actualization. Moreover, the greater part of the body is filled with experiencing and the feelings. So pivotal is this dimension from actualized experiencing and feeling, and away from a state of un-actualization, unfeeling, narrowed and truncated experiencing, death, frozenness, numbness, an absence of experiencing and feeling, that Perls (Shostrom, 1967) champions such a dimension over the psychiatric dimension from sickness to health.

You will have increased depth, breadth, and intensity of experiencing your own potentials for experiencing. That is, of all the potentials for experiencing which you now are, you will experience each to greater depth and intensity, and you will experience more of them. Potentials which had been out of sight, beyond consciousness, deeper, are now here to be experienced. So too are potentials which had been inconsistent or polar to one another. There is more to you, more to be experienced, and all of this is experienced more fully, deeply, intensely. So too, there will occur a greater magnitude of the good feelings of actualization. Not only does the occurrence of these feelings serve as a major criterion of the right behaviour, they also define the way you become. More of the time will be characterized by more of these good feelings—e.g., aliveness, lightness, excitement, joyful pleasure and energy. Furthermore, the presence of these good feelings brings an added dimension to the experiencing itself. Not only is there greater experiencing of belonging, but it is a belonging with aliveness. Not only is there an experiencing of thrusting or trust or wonderfulness or mastery or soft passivity, but it is a thrusting joyfully, a trusting pleasurably, an exhilarating wonderfulness, an energetic mastery, a soft passivity experienced with feelings of buoyancy and tingling.

The actualization of potentials means being fully in the moment. This quality has a sense of immediacy to it (Watts, 1960), a here-and-nowness (Perls, 1969). Experiencing with intensity and depth and breadth means a kind of full being of what one is in the immediate moment, a full being and experiencing from moment to moment, so that the proportion of heightened experiencing and feeling in one's life increases. Instead of a minute or so every few hours or days, you will experience and feel much more of the time.

Expansion of behaviours. Behaviours which formerly served as a means of providing for the experiencing of one or few potentials will now carry out a greater range of services. They will serve for the experiencing of a greater compass of potentials. New behaviours will be added which construct the appropriate situational contexts in which potentials can be experienced. Other behaviours will be added which provide for the experiencing of new potentials. Potentials which had been experienced through a small number of painful and distressing behaviours will, if they are still around, be experienced by means of a larger number of non-painful, non-distressing new behaviours. You will behave in ways which formerly were inconsistent or incompatible or contradictory or even opposite to one another. This too leads to an expanded array of behaviours. You can be both outgoing, social, gregarious, and also solitary, by yourself, withdrawn. You can be both passive, a follower, a drone, and also a leader, dominant, commanding. Each of these pairs of potentials includes additional sets of behaviours to expand the repertoire of the ways in which you are. The net result is the expansion of the spectrum of behaviours. Not only will you behave differently, but you will have more behaviours in your repertoire.

Without trying, without conscious effort, you will be existing in a world of situations appropriately outfitted for good experiencing. By the same token, and again without effort and with a kind of easy grace, you will become a person who avoids inappropriate situations, does not get entrapped in situations which are inappropriate, and you will be able to extricate your self from situations which constrict or narrow the possibility of a good measure of experiencing (Byles, 1962; Mahrer, 1970b; Mailloux, 1953). Thus the repertoire of behaviours will be increased to include ways of constructing situations cordial to experiencing, and ways of declining invitations to participate in inappropriate or non-actualizing situations.

Two interrelated processes of change. The net result of experiential psychotherapy is two processes running along in parallel. One is the work of experien-

62

tial psychotherapy. It includes the sequence of steps 1, 2, 3, and 5. In these steps you will be engaged continuously in discovering deeper potentials, ending the existence of the person whom you are, being the deeper potentials, and actualizing. This process occupies a few hours a week or a month or so. It leads to a continuous unfolding change in the person whom you are and in the worlds in which you live. The second process is living your life, being the person whom you are in the worlds in which you live. This second process includes the consequences described under 4 and 6; it occupies all the other hours in the week or month or so. Although these two processes are parallel, there are intimate interconnections between them. In your daily life you are being the person whom you are, e.g., married, obstinate, a little overweight, a responsible worker with a good sense of humour. When you engage in the work of experiential psychotherapy, you are exposing that person to the likelihood of change so that, as you emerge from experiential psychotherapy into your daily life, you may or may not be the person whom you were. Yet in your daily life, you are the person whom you are, even if that person and your change over time. Experiential psychotherapy is a continuous destructive force, revamping and basically altering the person whom you are, sending a constantly changing person into a constantly changing world of daily living.

References

Adler, A. (1927) *Practice and Theory of Individual Psychology*. New York: Harcourt, Brace.
Adler, A. (1969) *The Science of Living*. New York: Anchor-Doubleday.
Allport, O. W. (1937) *Personality: A Psychological Interpretation*. New York: Holt.
Bandura, A. (1961) 'Psychotherapy as a learning process.' *Psychological Bulletin*, **58**, 143–59.
Bergman, P. (1949) 'The germinal cell of Freud's psychoanalytic psychology and therapy.' *Psychiatry*, **12**, 265–78.
Binswanger, L. (1958) 'The case of Ellen West: An anthropological–clinical study.' In R. May, E. Angel, H. F. Ellenberger (eds.), *Existence: A New Dimension in Psychiatry and Psychology*, pp. 237–364. New York: Basic Books.
Boss, M. (1963) *Psychoanalysis and Daseins Analysis*. New York. London: Basic Books.
Buber, M. (1957) 'Guilt and guilt feelings.' *Psychiatry*, **20**, 114–29.
Bugental, J. F. T. (1964) 'The person who is the psychotherapist.' *Journal of Consulting Psychology*, **28**, 272–77.
Bullard, D. M. (ed.) (1959) *Psychoanalysis and psychiatry. Selected Papers of Frieda Fromm-Reichmann*. Chicago: University of Chicago Press.
Buytendijk, F. J. (1950) 'The phenomenological approach to the problem of feelings and emotions.' In M. L. Reymert (ed.), *Feelings and Emotions*, pp. 127–41. New York: McGraw-Hill.
Byles, M. B. (1962) *Journey into Burmese Silence*. London: George Allen and Unwin.
Chang, Chen-Chi (1959) *The Practice of Zen*. New York: Harper and Row, 1959.
Dreikurs, R. (1956) 'Adlerian psychotherapy.' In Frieda Fromm-Reichmann and J. L. Moreno (eds.) *Progress in Psychotherapy*, pp. 111–18. New York: Grune and Stratton.
Dreikurs, R. (1967) 'Goals of psychotherapy.' In A. R. Mahrer (ed.), *The Goals of Psychotherapy*, pp. 221–37. New York: Appleton-Century-Crofts.

Ellenberger, H. F. (1958) 'A clinical introduction to psychiatric phenomenology and existential analysis.' In R. May, E. Angel and H. F. Ellenberger (eds.), *Existence: A New Dimension in Psychiatry and Psychology*, pp. 92–124. New York: Basic Books.

Ellis, A. (1962) *Reason and Emotion in Psychotherapy.* New York: Lyle Stuart.

Ellis, A. (1967) 'Goals of psychotherapy.' In A. R. Mahrer (ed.), *The Goals of Psychotherapy*, pp. 206–20. New York: Appleton-Century-Crofts.

Enright, J. (1970) 'An introduction to Gestalt techniques.' In J. Fagan and I. L. Shepherd (eds.), *Gastalt Therapy Now*, pp. 107–14. New York: Harper and Row.

Fenichel, O. (1954) 'Symposium on the theory of the therapeutic results of psychoanalysis.' In H. Fenichel and D. Rapaport (eds.), *The Collected Papers of Otto Fenichel: Second Series*, pp. 19–24. New York: Norton.

Frankl, V. E. (1959) *From Death Camp to Existentialism.* Boston: Beacon Press.

Fromm, E., Suzuki, D. T., and de Martino, R. (1960) *Zen Buddhism and Psychoanalysis.* New York: Harper and Row.

Fromm-Reichmann, F. (1958) *Principles of Intensive Psychotherapy.* Chicago: University of Chicago Press.

Gendlin, E. T. (1962) *Experiencing and the Creation of Meaning.* New York: The Free Press of Glencoe.

Gendlin, E. T. (1964) 'A theory of personality change.' In B. Worchel and D. Byrne (eds.), *Personality change*, pp. 100–148. New York: Wiley.

Gendlin, E. T. (1969) 'Focusing.' *Psychotherapy: Theory, Research and Practice*, 6, 4–15.

Herrigel, E. (1956) *Zen in the Art of Archery.* New York: Pantheon.

Holt, H. (1968) 'The problem of interpretation from the point of view of existential psychoanalysis.' In E. F. Hammer (ed.), *Use of Interpretation in Treatment*, pp. 240–52. New York, London: Grune and Stratton.

Hora, T. (1961) Existential psychiatry and group psychotherapy.' *The American Journal of Psychoanalysis*, 21.

Janov, A. (1970) *The Primal Scream.* New York: Putnam.

Jourard, S. M. (1968) *Disclosing Man to Himself.* New York: Van Nostrand-Reinhold.

Jung, C. G. (1933) *Modern Man in Search of a Soul.* New York: Harcourt, Brace.

Jung, C. G. (1962) 'The detachment of consciousness from the object.' In R. Wilhelm, *The Secret of the Golden Flower: A Chinese Book of Life*, pp. 122–27. London: Routledge and Kegan Paul.

Kelly, G. A. (1955) *The Psychology of Personal Constructs. Vols. I, II.* New York: Norton.

Kelly, G. W. (1967) 'A psychology of the optimal man.' In A. R. Mahrer (ed.), *The Goals of Psychotherapy*, pp. 238–58, New York: Appleton-Century-Crofts.

Knight, R. P. (1941) 'Evaluation of the results of psychoanalytic therapy.' *American Journal of Psychiatry*, 98, 434–46.

Knight, R. P. (1952) 'An evaluation of psychotherapeutic techniques.' *Bulletin of the Menninger Clinic*, 16, 113–24.

Kondo, A. (1952) 'Intuition in Zen Buddhism.' *American Journal of Psychoanalysis*, 12, 10–14.

Kondo, A. (1958) 'Zen in psychotherapy: The virtue of sitting.' *Chicago Review*, 12, 57–64.

Lawton, G. (1958) 'Neurotic interaction between counsellor and counsellee.' *Journal of Consulting Psychology*, 5, 28–33.

Levitsky, A. and Perls, F. (1970) 'The rules and games of Gestalt therapy.' In J. Fagan I. L. Shepherd (eds.), *Gestalt Therapy Now.* New York: Harper and Row.

Loevinger, J. (1966) 'Three principles for psychoanalytic psychology.' *Journal of Abnormal Psychology*, 5, 432–43.

Mahrer, A. R. (1967) 'The goals of intensive psychotherapy.' In A. R. Mahrer (ed.), *The Goals of Psychotherapy*, pp. 162–79. New York: Appleton-Century-Crofts.

Mahrer, A. R. (1970a) 'Some known effects of psychotherapy and a reinterpretation.' *Psychotherapy: Theory, Research and Practice*, 7, 186–91.

Mahrer, A. R. (1970b) 'Interpretation of patient behavior through goals, feelings, and context.' *Journal of Individual Psychology*, **26**, 186–95.

Mahrer, A. R. (1972) 'Theory and treatment of anxiety: the perspective of motivational psychology.' *Journal of Pastoral Counseling*, **7**, 4–16.

Mahrer, A. R. (1975a) 'Metamorphosis through suicide: the changing of one's self by oneself.' *Journal of Pastoral Counseling*, **10**, 10–26.

Mahrer, A. R. (1975b) 'Therapeutic outcome as a function of goodness of fit on an internal–external dimension of interaction.' *Psychotherapy: Theory, Research and Practice*, **12**, 22–27.

Mailloux, N. (1953) 'Psychic determinism, freedom, and personality development.' *Canadian Journal of Psychology*, **7**, 1–11.

Maslow, A. H. (1963) 'Fusions of facts and values.' *American Journal of Psychoanalysis*, **23**, 117–31.

Maslow, A. H. (1968) *Toward a Psychology of Being* (2nd edition) New York: Van Nostrand-Reinhold.

Maslow, A. H. (1970) *Motivation and Personality.* (2nd edition) New York: Harper and Row.

Maupin, E. W. (1965) 'Zen Buddhism: A psychological review.' *Journal of Consulting Psychology*, **29**, 139–45.

May, R. (1958a) 'The origins and significance of the existential movement in psychology.' In R. May, E. Angel and H. F. Ellenberger (eds.), *Existence: A New Dimension in Psychiatry and Psychology*, pp. 3–36. New York: Basic Books.

May, R. (1958b) 'Contributions of existential psychotherapy.' In R. May, E. Angel and H. F. Ellenberger (eds.), *Existence: A New dimension in Psychiatry and Psychology*, pp. 37–91. New York: Basic Books.

May, R. (1967) *Psychology and the Human Dilemma.* Princeton, N. J.: Van Nostrand.

Needleman, J. (1967) 'Preface.' In L. Binswanger, *Being-in-the-World*, pp. viii–xvii. New York: Harper Torchbooks.

Ouspensky, P. D. (1957) *The Fourth Way.* London: Routledge and Kegan Paul.

Patterson, C. H. (1968) 'Relationship therapy and/or behavior therapy?' *Psychotherapy: Theory, Research, and Practice*, **5**, 226–33.

Patterson, C. H. (1974) *Relationship Counseling and Psychotherapy.* New York: Harper and Row.

Perls, F. S. (1969) *Gestalt Therapy Verbatim.* Moab, Utah: Real People Press.

Rado, S. (1956) *Psychoanalysis of Behavior.* New York: Grune and Stratton.

Rado, S. and Daniel, G. (1956) *Changing Concepts of Psychoanalytic Medicine.* New York: Grune and Stratton.

Reik, W. (1948) *Listening with the Third Ear.* New York: Grove Press.

Rogers, C. R. (1959) 'A theory of therapy, personality, and interpersonal relationships, as developed in the client-centered framework.' In S. Koch (ed.), *Psychology: A Study of a Science, Vol. 3*, pp. 221–31. New York: McGraw-Hill.

Rogers, C. R. (1963) 'The concept of the fully functioning person.' *Psychotherapy: Theory, Research and Practice*, **1**, 17–26.

Rogers, C. R. (1967) 'The process of the basic encounter group.' In J. F. T. Bugental (ed.), *Challenges of Humanistic Psychology*, pp. 261–76. New York: McGraw-Hill.

Rogers, C. R. (1970) *On Becoming a Person.* Boston: Houghton-Mifflin.

Schachtel, E. G. (1959) *Metamorphosis.* New York: Basic Books.

Shostrom, E. L. (1967) *Man, the Manipulator.* Nashville: Abingdon Press.

Skinner, B. F. (1967) 'What is psychotic behavior?' In T. Millon (ed.), *Theories of Psychopathology*, pp. 324–37. Philadelphia: Saunders.

Suzuki, D. T. (1949) *Living by Zen.* Tokyo: Sanseido Press.

Suzuki, D. T. (1956) *Zen Buddhism.* Garden City: Doubleday.

Szasz, T. S. (1956) *The Myth of Mental Illness.* New York: Hoeber-Harper.

Tauber, E. S. (1960) 'Sullivan's conception of cure.' *American Journal of Psychotherapy*, **14**, 666–76.

Van Dusen, W. (1957) 'The theory and practice of existential analysis.' *American Journal of Psychotherapy*, **11**, 310–22.

Watts, A. W. (1960) *This is It and Other Essays on Zen*. New York: Random House and John Murray.

Watts, A. W. (1961) *Psychotherapy East and West*. New York: Pantheon.

Wilhelm, R. (1962) *The Secret of the Golden Flower: A Chinese Book of Life*. London: Routledge and Kegan Paul.

Chapter 4
Experiencing Video Tape

Gordon A. Walter

University of British Columbia, Canada

Appreciation of the pervasiveness and power of television is growing and it is now acknowledged, by some experts, that television can be thought of as a third parent to Western children. The development of inexpensive portable videtape recording equipment has led to widespread utilization of this influential technology by experiential leaders. A decade of research and practice in therapeutic and training contexts now provides proof of and explanation for the effects of video tape presentations in change processes. Similarly, communications research documents the powerful force video presentations constitute throughout society.

The objective of this chapter is to develop, in the reader, a comprehensive understanding of the utilization of video tape in facilitating individual change. It first describes a feedback and modelling paradigm for learning with video tape. Second, salient research and anecdotal evidence provides an in-depth and detailed description of the way in which these mechanisms effect change in the domains of therapy, training and society. The societal level of analysis provides a rich appreciation for modelling in the absence of feedback while the therapeutic level of analysis emphasizes feedback more than modelling. Finally, the three levels of analysis provide clear conclusions regarding experiencing video inputs that transcend the limitations of method and discipline boundedness and give guidance for the utilization of the 'feedback–modelling' paradigm. Development of the feedback–modelling paradigm is the first step toward understanding the video experience.

The Dynamics of video tape feedback and modelling

Modern video tape equipment can provide individuals with vivid instantaneous personal feedback about their behavioural effects on others and can, almost simultaneously, also provide presentations of models, which have been developed and stored over a long period of time. Given the technical simplicity of video tape feedback and a natural desire of most individuals to see themselves on television, it would be easy to overemphasize feedback in a learning situation. However, this would be a serious mistake leading to gross underutilization of this important technology. Feedback and modelling have quite distinct effects on individuals. A short description of the *role* of feedback and modelling *in change* is presented here to describe the general mechanisms by which these processes bring about change. The combined feedback and modelling paradigm is then finalized and its most central implications for experiencing video tape are discussed.

Feedback

Feedback can confirm or negate an individual's behaviour or merely provide information in a domain where neither negation or confirmation are involved. Schein and Bennis (1965) argued for the basic Lewinian premise that lasting behavioural and attitudinal change occurs via a three-stage process: unfreezing, changing, and refreezing. Discrepant feedback, feedback which shows the individual that his self-perceptions are not precisely shared by others, has the effect of unfreezing people in the T-group context. Once unfrozen, the individual searches 'within *the self* and the environment' for clues about alternative behaviour and for new goals—change then begins. Refreezing of newly acquired behaviours into the individual's repertoire depends upon (1) congruence between these behaviours and the individual's self-perception, (2) positive reinforcements, and (3) non-discrepant feedback within the group and elsewhere. Many T-group and encounter group trainer orientations emphasize discrepant feedback (Lieberman, Yalom, and Miles, 1972). The rationale here is that changing and refreezing subprocesses involve individual freedom which should not be compromised. Often the only acceptable refreezing to occur within training is an increased willingness and ability to give and receive feedback.

A second function of feedback is to provide cues and guidance to the individual to facilitate behavioural adjustment during efforts to increase congruence between the desired and actual presentation of self (Harrison, 1970). Thirdly, non-discrepant feedback lets the individual know that attempts to change are effective. Near the end of many personal growth and therapy groups, moreover, a relatively high proportion of non-discrepant feedback is emphasized (Stoller, 1968). This serves primarily as support for continued change following termination of the group and secondarily to refreeze a few new behaviours. The more subtle reinforcement contingencies of 'life back home' bring about refreezing.

Modelling

The behavioural and attitudinal *modelling* process central to 'social learning' does not emphasize the unfreezing aspect of change. Instead, for example, Bandura and Walters (1963) emphasized the importance of the *acquisition* of imitative responses (changing) and *performance* of the imitatively learned responses (refreezing). A willingness and readiness to change is virtually assumed. Imitation of a model is the consequence of identification (Bandura, 1969, Allen and Liebert, 1967). Identification occurs when (1) the model has a

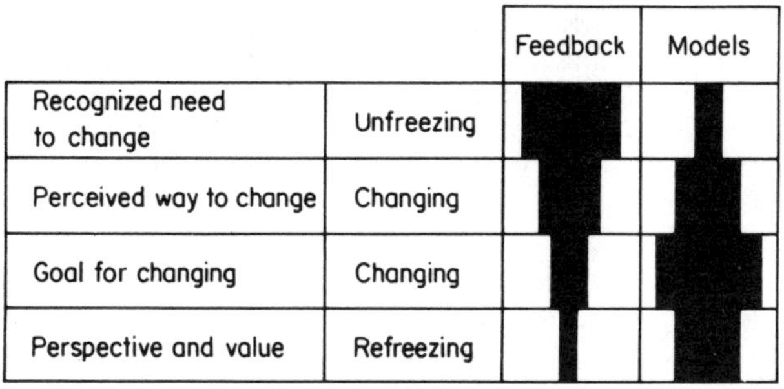

		Feedback	Models
Recognized need to change	Unfreezing		
Perceived way to change	Changing		
Goal for changing	Changing		
Perspective and value	Refreezing		

Figure 1 Feedback and modelling in change

special relationship to the individual, such as a parent to a child; (2) when the model is attractive, such as a highly competent specialist; and (3 when the model provides 'vicarious positive reinforcement', such as O. J. Simpson's financial arrangements for his performance as an athlete. Quite simply, vicarious reinforcement refers to the propensity of people to imitate someone they see being rewarded. In a more complex way, Bandura (1969) argued that both acquisition and performance are affected by vicarious reinforcement contingencies, knowledge about the controlling environmental factors and incentives with activating properties. Thus models provide goals for change and demonstrate mechanisms for change as shown in Figure 1. Refreezing of acquired behaviours is facilitated by reinforcement which results from matching one's own behaviour with the behaviour of the valued, attractive, or rewarded model. Thus, closure on growth is attained and this sense of completion increases refreezing.

Interactive effects of feedback and modelling

Feedback and modelling when used separately to promote change can each be highly effective but each has limits and can be supplemented by the other. In the case of modelling, one limit is the large number of competing models which exist in normal circumstances. Further, it is impossible to select systematically an arrangement which maximizes identification for a wide variety of individuals. The unfreezing aspect of discrepant feedback, however, involves an inherent focusing of the individual's concern on a specific area and increases the probability that a chosen modelling presentation will have predictable effects. Efforts to match behaviours with models is normally in terms of self-perception, and feedback can provide better information for adjustment and closure than the individual might be able to develop alone. Finally when matching does occur, positive reinforcement can be formalized and more deeply received with the aid of feedback.

Feedback alone, by contrast, makes change essentially a trial and error process, within which experimentation is demanded instead of allowed or encouraged. Harrison and others emphasized that individuals need to know where they are going as well as from where they are coming.

'The individual may be ready for growth but fail to find in the behavior of other members patterns which provide alternatives which are meaningful at the cognitive level at which he can respond. For example, a dependent person may be able to comprehend the opposite, counter-dependency, as a meaningful alternative. True collaboration in which authority is irrelevant, neither sought out or defied, may be beyond this current range of understanding.' (Harrison, 1965, p. 412.)

Modelling can clearly supplement the dynamics of feedback. Models provide cues, goals, and mechanisms which facilitate rather than demand change. Finally, the goal structure inherent in the modelling process provides a clear conclusion to the learning process in contrast to non-discrepant feedback which may mean different things to different individuals.

The impact of feedback and modelling for each element in the change process is portrayed by the thickness of the bar in Figure 1. Feedback is shown to be highly effective in unfreezing but has a diminishing impact as one moves beyond to refreezing. Models, on the other hand, show little effect in the unfreezing domain and maximum effect in the goal-related aspects of change. Modelling is shown to be much more effective in the refreezing aspect of the process than feedback. The complementarity between the two techniques is emphasized by the additive possibilities of the respective bars and the importance of this complementarity may be the greatest in the very early and very late stages of training. The following discussion of video in therapy, training and society explores the practical application of these general change principles, and serves as empirical evaluation of the effects of video feedback and modelling inputs on individuals.

Research findings on video presentations

Feedback and modelling processes and their study have yielded a high appreciation of the effectiveness of video presentations in individual change. It would be impossible to review all relevant contributions from the three domains in the space available. Instead a broad sampling of perspectives and results is offered from empirical researchers as well as conscientious and thoughtful participant observers which illuminate the general pattern of findings. Methodological in adequacies exist in all areas and to some degree results should be considered tentative.

Not surprisingly, different aspects of the feedback–modelling paradigm are emphasized in each domain with feedback techniques more widely used in therapeutic interventions, modelling intricacies the key to most societal applications, and training somewhere between the other two. In spite of these differences, results are quite mutually consistent. Further, differences as well as similarities aid in appreciating the effective utilization to video tape in change. The following discussion considers first, the therapeutic applications, second, training and third, society-related issues.

Video tape in therapy

Therapeutic utilization of video tape originally emphasized feedback and has more recently added facets of modelling. Similarly, the following discussion treats first the feedback and then modelling aspects of video tape utilization.

Feedback. Psychotherapy considers feedback in two distinct ways. The first and most simplistic of these is consistent with the ideas of Schein presented above. Feedback unfreezes the individual and provides data for adjusting behaviour. The second and more fundamental consideration of video feedback involves a confrontation of one's fundamental self-image. Self-image is to a great degree a function of the physical realities of early experiences and George Herbert Mead argued that self-consciousness is what separates man from animals. He stated:

'Self-consciousness, rather than affective experience with its motor accompaniments, provides the core and primary structure of the self, which is thus essentially a cognitive rather than an emotional phenomenon. The thinking of intellectual process—the internationalization and inner dramatization by the individual, of the external conversation of significant gestures which constitutes his chief mode of interaction with other individuals belonging to the same society is the earliest experiential phase in the genesis and development of the self.' (Strauss, 1956, p. 228.)

Thus feedback in a self-confrontation mode actually updates self-image. Further, feedback is seen to expand *awareness* so as to increase self-control and self-direction since

'That which is outside self-awareness is also beyond control. Self-control is important because it involves forming images of oneself in relation to an anticipated audience and redirecting behavior in the light of this. The more communication there is with oneself about the behavior that is being undertaken, the more control can be exercised.' (Stoller, 1968, pp. 216–17.)

Self-confrontation implies a more fundamental unfreezing than Schein considered. Further Bailey and Sowder (1970) argued that the chief contribution of video tape feedback was its motivational effect on the individual. The following discussion simultaneously considers both levels of 'feedback-induced' unfreezing, assumes a motivational component, and looks at the issues of timing, purposes, and limits of video tape feedback in therapy.

The timing of video tape feedback is the most pragmatic and concrete of all issues and is divisible into the facets of contiguity, length of sessions and storage of feedback. Stoller (1968) and Hogan and Alger (1969) emphasized the desirability of temporal contiguity for feedback, arguing that the immediacy of the feedback forces patients to confront themselves and to be more reflective about and more aware of their impact on others. A dynamic can be established in the therapy group in which members 'react to themselves on the television monitor, and others react to this reaction' (Stoller, 1968, p. 32). Feedback virtually becomes the second half of a therapy session. Similarly Boyd and Sisney (1967) presented feedback of the completed interview with neuropsychiatric patients and clearly documented reduction in pathology level. In another approach, emphasizing contiguity, Kagan, Krathwohl, and Miller (1963) recommended instantaneous feedback as an ongoing subprocess within the group. In the opposite direction, Geertsman and Reivich (1965) showed feedback of the previous week's group meeting at the beginning of each therapy session and Goldstein et al. (1966) did not show video tapes in family therapy until the fifth session, lest the feedback be too confrontive too early in the process. It appears that more instantaneous feedback is more confrontive and in some circumstances this may be desired while in others it may not.

Various lengths of feedback have also been utilized. Kagan, Krathwohl, and Miller (1963) used very brief segments and Stoller (1968) suggested that each segment should terminate when a comprehensible bundle of data had been given to the individual. In both approaches the group was allowed to react to the feedback and the recipients response to the feedback. In contrast again, Geertsman and Reivich (1965) showed full 45-minute playbacks of previous therapy sessions. Danet (1968) warned against overloading individuals with information or overwhelming them by the confrontation, but these risks seemed to be mitigated somewhat by the waiting period between the taping and viewing sessions of the Geertsman and Reivich approach. Some balance between fragmentation and information overload clearly must be sought during feedback sessions. Further, stored feedback seems to require longer sessions with fewer objectives. Resnik et al. (1973) stored tapes of the hospitalization procedures for individuals who had attempted suicide. Patients often reach a point in therapy where they deny their self-destructive acts or attempt to remove themselves from the therapeutic experience before making progress. A video tape self-confrontation which shows 'intraveneous puncture, gastric lavage, and (entry) psychiatric interview' leads to expressions of repressed feelings, awareness of projections and denials, and acknowledgement and acceptance of responsibility for the actual suicidal act. Therapy can resume and progress. Stored tapes of early behaviours can also be used to demonstrate an individual's progress near the end of therapy (Stoller, 1968).

Video feedback appears to have a number of different purposes. Confrontation implies that a fundamental aspect of self-image is reconsidered, and that unfreezing is dramatic. Self-confrontation can be applied to specific acts such as suicide or to a particular process such as ego-functioning or thinking (Berman, 1972). A second purpose is that of behavioural adjustment and a third is that of augmenting group processes. For example, Kagan's instant feedback 'interpersonal process recall' (IPR) technique enables participants to 're-experience' feelings and thoughts on the tape and then share the 'recall' with others in the group. The important confrontation is often interpersonal rather than directly with the video tape feedback.

Each approach has both value and also limitations and requires supplements. Stoller's approach acknowledges this in a number of ways. First, each tape sequence is directed as a particular individual and requires a team of two therapists to record, make decisions and provide feedback. Alterations in feedback include presentations without sound which increase the focus on a particular behaviour and reduce the potential for information overload. Berman (1972) showed that without therapist intervention, schizophrenics did not benefit significantly from video tape confrontation. It is thus not surprising that no single video feedback procedure stands out as superior to all others.

Modelling. Enthusiasm for the use of video-taped models is therapy is more recent than feedback—and research is even less extensive. Discussion of models in therapy considers three applications; social modelling, affect simulation and systematic desensitization.

Social modelling, in therapy is used in two quite distinct ways. First, video tapes of smoothly functioning therapy groups can be presented to disturbed patients to prepare them for psychotherapy. These presentations reduce patient anxiety and demonstrate 'in a low threat way' how to behave to get value from the therapeutic process (Hansen, Niland, and Zani, 1969; Krumboltz and Thoresen, 1964). The second use of social modelling is in providing the patient with behavioural objectives or change targets. The models of desired behaviours differ only slightly from patients. Over the period of therapy the modelled behaviour more and more closely approaches the ideal envisaged by the therapist. This hierarchy of models thus provides patients with cues and goals for change, and a sense that change is attainable (Woody, 1971a). Eisler (1973) clearly showed the effectiveness of modelling in therapy.

The second approach, *affective simulation*, utilizes models but in a more specific and limited way than true social modelling. Woody (1971b), pp. 34–35 describes affect simulation as follows:

'Professional actors are filmed or recorded presenting scenes designed to stimulate intense degrees of feelings, such as hostility, affection, fear of hostility, and fear of affection. The objective is to give the patient a confrontation with the kinds of affect which he has trouble dealing with and which might not arise appropriately or adequately in conventional psychotherapy. In essence, the psychotherapist diagnoses what affects should be worked on in the course of psychotherapy with a particular patient, and then uses the films or recordings to stimulate those feelings. The patient is asked to assume that the actor is talking directly to him, to experience the feelings (i.e., his internal reactions), and to then introspect about the psychodynamic implications.'

Models here are stimulus sources rather than identification sources. Kagan and Schauble (1969) indicated that this may be a more powerful source of change than IPR due to the clarity, intensity and simplicity of the emotions and awarenesses evoked. A second level of model inputs can be provided which demonstrate coping with the stimulus object. Here the approach is more typical of social modelling, with the important exception that the individual is identifying with the situation in addition to the model. No empirical analysis of this two-staged, evoked reaction and modelled response approach was found in the therapy literature.

The third technique, *systematic desensitization*, differs somewhat more subtly from the true social-modelling approach. Here video tape stimuli usage is based on:

'The reciprocal inhibition principle that asserts that an anxiety-provoking stimulus will have a decrease in provocation power, if it is counteracted by an anxiety-free stimulus; and a progressive series of pairings of these two types of stimuli will eventuate in elimination or at least significant alleviation of undue in anxiety.' (Woody, 1971b, p. 35.)

It thus utilizes the central principles of all systematic desensitization. No modelling in the social learning sense occurs, yet critical vicarious processes can and do proceed. The stimulus is vicarious but the reinforcement is not (Woody and Schauble, 1969a, 1969b), and the process is most accurately termed vicarious classical conditioning. One clear principle in modelling is that for identification purposes—same-sex models seem to be best in most cases although this is not necessary for affective stimulation. Further in affect stimulation, the stimulation is only the beginning of the therapeutic event, and therapist and group factors are critical. Systematic desensitization depends most significantly on the ability to generate and maintain a relaxed state in participants in the face of vivid stimulation. Therefore, it may require hypnosis or relaxation training prior to this utilization (Woody, 1971b).

Therapy implies internal change for the individual yet social modelling emphasizes changing response patterns and is thus quite behaviouristic. Many therapists argue the sufficiency of behaviourism in a wide variety of cases (Bandura, 1969; Krumboltz and Thoresen, 1969) but Keys and Vane (1975, personal communication) found no effect to result from vicarious reinforcement of modelling presentations to hospitalized schizophrenics. Their interpretation was that schizophrenics were unable to focus adequately on the modelling, so the process was short-circuited. This explanation seems to apply equally to video tape self-confrontation of schizophrenics (Berman 1972).

Modelling requires capacity, willingness and opportunity for the viewer to truly experience the model. Time, circumstance and model characteristics can significantly increase the chances of identificatory learning for most individuals, and it must be emphasized that the general conclusion from the therapy literature is that modelling does have effects. More dramatic is the evidence for the pervasive use of video tape feedback in therapy. Combinations of modelling and feedback by Kagan, Schaubel, and others points to a large number of additional creative uses of modelling. There is no doubt that video tape is a powerful source of change especially when adequately supplemented.

Video tape in training

Training differs from therapy in many obvious ways, but issues and examples in training at times overlap those of therapy, as is seen in the following discussion. This overlap shows the high degree of applicability of insights from therapy to training. As with previous sections, the following discussion will treat feedback first and then modelling.

Feedback. Video tape feedback has been popular in training over the last decade but there has been little systematic study of its effects. The power of interpersonal feedback in training combined with the popularity of video feedback in therapy, have yielded assumptions as to the inevitable value of video tape feedback in training. The simplistic faith that if people see themselves they will perform better, ignores the complexity of video stimuli and the multitude of changes possible as a result of viewing feedback. To aid in an initial clarification of change directions, the following discussion is divided into two parts: (a) skill acquisition with a specific clear focus and (b) general process awareness.

Training directed at specific skills occurs in individualized as well as group modes and generally includes a supplemental device which aids the individual in focusing on some particular aspect of the feedback. Dehon (1967) and Payne (1967) argued from a practitioner base that instructions from a consultant were the key to constructive utilization of video tape feedback. In an experiment, Walter (1975a) gave verbal cues to members of problem-solving groups prior to their receiving video tape feedback. Participants were encouraged to note suboptimal problem-solving acts when viewing feedback. For one change objective this procedure brought about behavioural change, for another it did not. Weber (1971) found no support for the value of written structuring of video tape feedback viewing. Further, Walter (1975b) found no group problem-solving performance improvement occurred even when feedback resulted in behavioural change. However, Ellett and Smith (1975) developed a questionnaire with 60 Likert-scaled items to be used with video tape feedback. Teachers were video-taped once a month and then allowed to (individually) view feedback while performing a self-evaluation. Significant change resulted in the direction of improvement on the questionnaire items. Thus the viewing conditions, the specific form of cueing or focusing, and the participants themselves can significantly alter the effectiveness of video tape feedback. Individual feedback eliminates distractions and for specific behavioural change this is probably more significant than whatever is lost by the absence of group support. One qualification is offered from Kennedy (1970) who described what amounted to spontaneous structuring due to group feedback following role-playing in a sales training course. Some focusing aid is valuable and it needs to be concrete and involving.

Training with more general objectives such as awareness of self and group processes implies a different approach of video tape feedback. These more general objectives in training lead to a greater degree of self-confrontation. In fact, Kagan's stimulated recall technique (IPR), discussed above, is widely used in counsellor training where personal awareness is central to the training objectives. Walter and Miles (1974) studied the effects of weekly video tape feedback on participants engaged in an eight-week task group exercise and found that participant self-acceptance scores increased comparably to those of an intensive two-week sensitivity training session. Weber (1971) found that video feedback to task group members increased general group process awareness. In both the Walter and Miles and the Weber studies, immediate feedback of about ten minutes was all that was provided and in both cases efforts to structure participants' viewing interfered with this more general change. Kennedy (1970) saw obvious improvements in coping and general awareness during the course of a video tape feedback training programme. In all cases participants received feedback in groups.

The Walter and Miles (1974), Weber (1971), and Walter (1975a, 1975b) results indicate that specific changes and general changes require different video tape feedback formats and are to some degree mutually inconsistent. The inhibitor effects of mechanistic structuring techniques are especially a factor for short viewing times or when only one specific topic is pursued. If, however, a more complex strategy is utilized, this limitation may be avoided. An example of such a strategy is offered by Furman and Feighner (1973), who successfully trained parents of hyperkinetic children to cope more productively with their children. Immediate video feedback of the children, in both the presence and absence of the parents, was viewed by the parents and a therapist. Parents acted as therapists, pinpointing problems and choosing what to do about them. Segments were limited to 15 or 20 minutes and shorter segments of good child behaviour were sometimes emphasized by multiple replay. Parents were keyed into one behaviour at a time and assigned behavioural homework. The therapist played an active but complex role. Behavioural changes in both parents and children were 'dramatic and retained'. Perhaps more importantly, parents had come to see their children as individuals with positive qualities. In summary, parents were provided with focused feedback on one specific issue but allowed to cope with the feedback in an only partially structured manner. Structuring commenced after feedback and was directed at future behaviour rather than the feedback itself. The major limitation in this approach was the time, energy and expertise required to make it effective.

The discussion of feedback and training point out the importance of structuring supplements, but yields no simple set of guideline comments, except that involved sequences of feedback–reflection–review planning can be helpful. The value of check lists and questionnaires is less clear but it seems likely that inhibition of learning will result from such structuring aids, unless significantly more time is allocated to viewing. Private viewing of feedback with structuring techniques is clearly an alternative to group viewing of feedback with discussion serving as sort of a spontaneous structuring force. In general, trade-offs of key importance and between focusing efforts, overload possibilities, and change objectives. Video presentations of models are an alternative supplement to feedback in addition to providing change impetus on their own.

Modelling. The discussion of modelling inputs in training builds upon the discussion of modelling in therapy. Three important issues in the modelling process, identification, cueing, and matching, are utilized to explore the way in which video-taped modelling can be applied to training. Bandura and

Walters (1963) argued the importance of model reinforcement for the performance of the behaviours acquired from model observation. Identification and the implied simultaneous reinforcement thus serve as a starting point for this discussion. To a certain degree, identification occurs when models are seen in some sense as 'attractive'. Interpersonal attraction is too complex a subject (Berscheid and Walster, 1969) to pursue fully here; still, a few studies can be noted that describe facets of identification. Baron (1970) demonstrated that the competence of models was an important source of identification in adults. Harvey and Rutherford (1960) established the key role of status in the development of identification. Kelman (1958) emphasized obvious similarities plus success of the model for the identification condition of his now famous social change experiment on internalization, identification, and compliance. Specifically for video tape applications in training, Walter (1975c) explored modelling effects for improved problem-solving in an experiment which determined that 'acted' models were more effective than 'natural' models. This result was partially attributed to the vicarious reinforcement in the relaxed (yet excited) way in which the models behaved. Noble (1973) found a 'realistic' model to have greater effects on behaviour of subjects and a 'stylistic' one, although Noble's stylistic models were probably much less realistic than Walter's acted models. The apparent contradiction between the findings of these two studies points out the subtleties and complexities in creating powerful identificatory video tape presentations for training. It also emphasizes the value of a societal level of analysis where video presentations rely heavily upon identificatory processes. Kacher (1973) used high status models on video tape for lecture input to increase attitude change in a management development course. This was a straightforward application of insights from society to be discussed more fully below.

Turner and Berkowitz (1970) in a more fundamental exploration demonstrated a mechanism by which identification could be encouraged and supplemented. Subjects in this study of aggression were encouraged verbally to imagine themselves as movie protagonists who win a fight. Another condition required them to act in an aggressive way each time the protagonist hit the opponent. Both this verbal encouragement component and the classical conditioning component resulted in increased willingness to inflict electrical shocks on confederates afterward. The effect of both supplements was to increase vicarious reinforcement, since the first put the subject into more emotionally intimate contact with the reinforcement, while the demand characteristics of second increased frustration and irritation and thus the salience and satisfaction inherent in the filmed events. The implication is that trainers attempting to utilize modelling input can intervene directly in the identification process, in addition to developing highly identificatory models.

The importance of *cueing* in the modelling process is comparable to the importance of focusing in the feedback process and many alternative cueing contributions are of value. Bandura and Walters (1963) argued that cueing was the key to acquisition of new responces and showed that cartoons were nearly as effective as were live models in bringing about change in children even though identification was much less. Noble (1973) found that model presentations produced at close range had greater effect than those produced at a distant range. Walter (1975c) concluded that the prime reason for superior change attributable to acted models was the overtness and clarity of the behaviour modelled. The typical training practitioner preference for colour film over either colour or black-and-white video tape is probably due to perceived increases in participant attention and satisfaction (Philips, 1971). However, there is some evidence that colour and black and white are equally effective (Booth and Miller, 1974). On the other hand, Menne and Menne (1972) showed the addition of audio cues to video model presentations to increase modelling effectiveness, and the Turner and Berkowitz (1970) study of aggression showed that verbal cues in modelling promoted change. Singer and Singer (1976) found that an adult could cue children into spontaneous and imaginative play of a television model, and Paulson (1974) emphasized the need for cues in modelling attempts within an educational television programme. Hart (1968) assigned evaluative roles to participants which aided them in focussing on relevant aspects of film presentations. Spangenberg (1973) showed that the detail available in moving models compared to fixed, photographed models increased the number of cues available to individuals and was thus more effective.

Both positive and negative implications about the need for cueing can be drawn from these studies. On the negative side, the need for clear cueing indicates the limited effectiveness of a social change strategy based on recording and presenting sequences of realistic ongoing events, no matter how productive the models in them might be. On the positive side, research results indicate clear guidelines for model development, presentation, and cueing devices and interventions. Encouragement, verbal directions, and elicitation of conditional responses are important and they inherently limit the feasible number target behaviours. Finally, clarity and believability of models are both of high importance and sacrificing one to increase the other reduces the potential effectiveness of the modelling presentation. Again, the societal presentation of video is necessary to appreciate fully the subtitles of effective modelling.

The notion of *matching* refers to a number of separate phenomena. First is the individual's comparisons of newly acquired behaviour to those of the model to ensure 'match'. The second is the degree to which real-world reinforcements match the vicarious reinforcement for the model. The third involves connections between the model's action and the individual's experiencing of the model. In the first facit, the successful matching of newly acquired behaviours with those of a model gives the individual a sense of closure on an attempted change and this end state has motivational consequences. Attempts to match are supplemented by video feedback, since otherwise matching would only be in terms of self-perception. Video feedback also seems to increase motivation to attempt matching. The inherent positive reinforcement of repetitive modelling and feedback sequences probably also increase the significance of this subprocess as evidenced by the effectiveness of multiple presentations in therapy. There the concentration was on discrepant feedback at the beginning of a change experience and relatively non-discrepant feedback near the end (Stoller, 1968). The unique strength of video tape is its equal applicability to modelling and feedback.

The matching of real-world reinforcements to the expectations generated by the model follow directly from the more specific feedback considerations. Venn and Short (1973) emphasized and documented the significance of this principle in an experiment. They showed that the effects of vicarious reinforcement on children were relatively shortlived and were easily overridden by contradictory direct experience. A more subtle level at which this real-world experience is important is internal to the individual. The Turner and Berkowitz (1970) study showed that classical conditioning occurred when individuals were encouraged to act while experiencing the models. Reinforcements had more effect on active than passive individuals because matching increased linkage between the model and the individual. Further, matching efforts seem to increase sensitivity to the awareness of behavioural cues. A key value in combining feedback and modelling derives from this aspect of matching, which increases the potency of the modelling itself.

The research discussed in this section documents the individual effectiveness of video presentations of feedback and modelling in promoting change. Further, modelling provides important goals for change and focusing cues, which supplement feedback.

Similarly, video feedback supplements the modelling process by transcending some self-perceptual distortions in the matching of behaviour to the models. While the general processes of modelling (with video tape) are well documented, research emphasizes that subtleties of model behaviour greatly affect identificatory processes. Overtness of action, perceived benefits and attractiveness all seem important and the following discussion of video presentations in society supplies further elucidation as to the character of powerful models and the manner in which the identifactory process is keyed to human needs.

Video presentations in society

Enormous energy has been directed for decades toward understanding media in relation to society. One major concern has been the impact of violent television programmes on children and many examples from this field will be used in the following discussion. Evidence for the manner in which video presentations in society affect adults as well as children is impressive and contributes especially greatly to understanding the power of television through modelling processes. While the consideration of modelling processes is a major focus in exploration of the role of television in society, one anecdotal example of the potential value of feedback is offered before considering modelling fully.

The community was bitterly divided during the school governance disputes in the Bedford-Stuyvesant district of New York City and public meetings at times bordered on chaos. At one point, meetings were video taped and continuously played back in the lobby of the meeting place on a 30-minute to one-hour delay. Thus many active 'debater' experienced a dramatic *self-confrontation* upon retiring from the meeting room for refreshments. Often their behaviour changed dramatically upon returning. Their fear, frustration and anger was channelled into more socially acceptable behavioural responses because of this very 'therapeutic' arrangement (Roberts, 1977).

The real story of video in society, however, lies in modelling processes and the remainder of this discussion considers these processes and their implications in three subsections. First, modelling and the complexities of television presentations are re-examined. The second subsection considers the subtle role of television in reflecting and transmitting the assumptions of the culture. Finally, a conclusion is offered which looks at the potentialities and risks envisaged in the industry. Much of the discussion is directly applicable to training and the remainder adds depth of appreciation concerning the power of video technology to affect human functioning.

Modelling. Does violence on television increase aggression in children? Can television programming teach complex social skills or develop cognitive ability? Is change for all viewers? Is change lasting? The answers to the first two questions are yes, the others require a fuller response, and the following discussion leads to an increased sense of the direct role television plays and can play in behavioural change throughout the society. A number of the following studies could easily have been presented in the previous section yet the specific target behaviours of change efforts (e.g., aggressive) made their presentation here more convenient.

Liebert, Neale and Davidson (1973) capture the essence of a decade of research on the impact of violence in television on children. First, children learn initially that violence gets things done and, second, they tend to perceive less of actual violence, that is, their sensitivity is blunted. Further (p. 87):

'There is, then, a remarkable degree of convergence among all of the types of evidence that have been sought to relate violence viewing and aggressive behavior in the young: laboratory studies, correlational field studies, and naturalistic experiments all show that exposure to television can, and often does, make viewers significantly more aggressive as assessed by a great variety of indices, measures, and meanings of aggression'.

It is no wonder when 'the average child between 5 and 15 watches the violent destruction of more than 13 400 persons on television' (Sabin, 1972).

Motivational studies of adults indicate that the likelihood of aggressive behaviour following viewing violent televised models can be altered. Berkowitz (1965), Hoyt (1970), and others showed that provoking subjects or building justifications for the modelled violence (such as having a hero instead of a villain as model) alter the effects. However, in Leifer and Roberts's (1972) study of children then found that;

'Whatever analysis was performed, the amount of violence in the program affected the amount of agression subsequently chosen. Nothing else about the program—the context within which violence was presented—seemed to influence subsequent aggression' (p. 89).

Liebert, Neale, and Davidson (1973) conclude an analysis of the literature with the assertion, 'Aggression in children is increased by watching violent T.V., more so for children predisposed to watching violence'.

Can television teach complex social skills? Singer and Singer (1976) showed that viewing *Misterrogers Neighborhood* increased spontaneous play and found that parental co-watching and support increased this effect. Exercises plus a live model, however, had greater effects. Parental support was the key to the total effect. Paulson (1974) concluded that teaching cooperation via *Sesame Street* required clear goals in programming and verbal cueing, (e.g., 'some for you—some for me—that's sharing!') Liebert, Neale, and Davidson (1973) documented reading skills, alphabet mastery, and other cognitive development to result from exposure to *Sesame Street* and like programming. *Again, increased exposure results in increased effects.* There is even evidence that withdrawn children can be bought out and become more social (Liebert, Neale, and Davidson, 1973). The obvious dramatizations of television appear to increase the individual's attention and identification with the model and thus lead to increased change.

Some appreciation of the complexities and limitations on modelling is provided by Evon et al. (1974). In a ten-year longitudinal study they found that the relationship between viewing television violence in third-grade boys was positive and significant. They also found that physical punishment of the child (live modelling) and rejection of the child were equally correlated with 19-year old aggression. Parental nurturance of the child, child identification with parents, child IQ and child freedom to confess to parents were the key correlates of low aggression. It is striking that viewing televised violence could have *impact comparable to these pivotal parenting practices.* Worting and Greenberg (1973) examined the relationship between verbal and physical aggression in interaction with televised violence. They hypothesized that verbal and physical aggression would rise and fall together, but found the opposite. For example, a physically violent model increased physical but decreased verbal violence They also found that lower socioeconomic class children were more affected by the violence than middle socioeconomic class children and concluded that 'we need to know more about thresholds and ceilings', that is, more about specific modelling acts and contingencies.

In spite of such complexities, Klapper (1965) provided a reminder that a number of principles of mass media persuasion are still highly applicable. Most important is to attain a monopoly position in the lives of viewers. If this is not possible the following key techniques aid in overcoming resistance or the lack of monopoly (Klapper, 1965):

(1) Utilize the principle of 'canalization', i.e., offer the individual a new way

to satisfy an old need instead of trying to create a new need.

(2) Offer rewards such as membership in the majority or an in-group.

(3) Use the status of the media or model persons themselves.

(4) Repeat themes with minor variations to exploit different vulnerabilities.

(5) For the most part shown only one side of an argument.

(6) Supplement media with face-to-face contact via, say, discussion groups. Mutual confirmation tends to have a 'clinching' effect and is a key to national movements.

(7) Combine with an action alternative.

These simple principles are remarkably consistent with the discussion above. One can easily envisage frustrated kids joining a fantasy 'team' called 'SWAT' with high status officers in repetitious programmes, and then joining their friends while playing with 'SWAT' toys. Television plays a modelling role comparable to a parent. In the more subtle process to be discussed next it has comparable effects.

Assumption reflecting and transmitting. Television programming reflects the internal needs, desires, fantasies, and assumptions of the 'average' viewing public. It reflects the viewer's inner world and at the same time increases its concreteness. Marshall McLuhan (1951) saw similar effect of advertisements and noted that 'ads can be seen as a kind of social ritual or magic that flatter and enhance us in our own eyes. What Kipling was to the aggressive British imperialists, these ads are to our domestic economy.—Don't run but look again, Reader. Find the 'Mechanical Bride' [sic], p. 113. The implication is that assumptions or biases in programming are for commercial reasons. Further, the overall programming pattern in television is a virtual *monopoly* source of influence. None of the training or therapy literature addresses either of these interdependent issues of assumption reflecting and monopoly. Clearly some assumptions in a training input must be reflected. But which ones are appropriate, necessary, or moral? Most training programmes, moreover, are of relatively short duration. With some complex use of the technology, could more of a 'monopoly' be developed? Is this an acceptable scale of training input? The Surgeon General's Advisory Committee on Television and Social Behaviour stated that 'television can be considered to be a window on the world, a school if you will, through which the child first perceives his society and then learns from repeated example to cope with vicissitudes of living' (Liebert, Neale, and Davidson, 1973).

The view from this window with regard to occupation, sex, age and violence is worth brief glance at this point to further elucidate the subtle ties of modelling. Liebert, Neale, and Davidson (1973) noted that only ten per cent of the people on television are working class. Professionals, managers and so forth comprise 51 per cent of the people on television. What do most working-class children think of their parents' place in society? What do the parents think of themselves? Telesco (1974) states, further, that the women who people prime-time television drama programmes are best described as 'powerless'. They are also less smart, rational and stable, more likely to be married than men, and seldom are seen in adventure situations. Identification and fantasy are also important to advertising and here 'women, for the most part, continue to clean house, launder, cook, severe meals while the men give orders and advice and eat the meals' (Courtney and Whipple, 1974, p. 106). Since identification with models of the same sex predominates, boys and girls learn different things from both programmes and advertisements. Arnoff (1974) shows *elderly* prime-time characters to compromise the highest percentage of 'bad guys' and the lowest percentage of 'good guys' of any age group. Further, 40 per cent of elderly characters are portrayed of all other age groups. Other television stereotypes of the old are not supported by the data according to Hess (1974) who concludes the reason to be that the old are 'poor consumers' offering little commercial incentive as a group and 'poor copy' in that they remind us of role loss, deprivation and ultimate demise, 'none of which is a helpful product association'. Again, the implications for training are profound.

Finally Liebert, Neale, and Davidson (1973) note the speculation that since violence on television also reflects the inner world of viewers it might provide sufficient catharsis to offset its training effects. Here, however, no support is forthcoming. In fact, Gerbner and Gross (1976) explored the effects of televised violence on the viewers' perception of the world, and found a high proportion of the population exhibited a heightened sense of risk, insecurity, and acquiescence to authority. Others were incited to aggression. They concluded (p. 194):

'Risky for their perpetrators and costly for their victims, media-incited criminal violence be the price inductrial cultures exact from some citizens for the general pacification of most others—T.V. appears to cultivate the assumption that fit its socially functional myths. *Our chief instrument of enculturation and social control*, television may function as the established religion of the industrial order, relating to governance as the church did to the state in earlier times' (emphasis added).

Implications. It is not surprising that media experts are increasingly concerned with the future of the technology and its policy implications. Programmers face a dilemma. On the one hand, without conscious control of offerings (e.g., violence), the societal drift could be quite undesirable. However, once manipulation of television programming is accepted, mechanisms of participation and control are demanded. Further, it is inevitable that various parties such as political governing groups could aggressively try to gain control of the television to further their aims. Some censorship is inevitable for some people. A large percentage of schizophrenic hospital patients, for example, incorporate television images into their psychoses! (Wadeson and Carpenter, 1976). But where does one draw the line on censorship?

By contrast to these gloomy considerations futurologists envisage that 200 channel broadcasting and communications satellites can lead to greater individual freedom and worldwide audiences. Clark (1971) calculated the possibility of world education for one billion children costing $1 per pupil per year. He argued the possibility of a new social order resulting from mass education in which worldwide common languages could play an important part: 'The children of the future are going to learn several languages from the third parent in the corner of the living room' (p. 959).

The Canadian federal government committed vast training and manpower resources to the bilingual capacities of government employees many years ago but did not use this modern technological approach and have only recently made the obvious societal application of Clark's vision.

In general, the potential for video tape in training is more modest than Clark's vision but so also are the ethical problems. Lessons regarding televison in society apply well to training, and policy concerns may be close behind. Moreover, the discussion of these aspects of television in society provide benchmarks against which judgements about the worth and power of the technique can be measured and appreciated.

Conclusion

Feedback and modelling offer substantially different approaches to change. The chief power in feedback is the self-confrontation which has dramatic unfreezing effects and thus is best used in training which involves reappraisal of the old ways of doing things. This effect is heightened when feedback is in contiguous short sequences of ten minutes or less. Deferred sequences have the single advantage that they are somewhat less threatening. However, deferred sequences are necessarily longer than instantaneous sequences and thus the risk of information overload is increased. Trainer focusing of feedback on a moment-to-moment basis or at critical points is valuable. Written structuring techniques must be involving and specific since broad guidelines are of marginal value. Further, trainer contribution includes aiding individuals move beyond the feedback to action. Individual feedback limits distractions but group support and mutual focusing is also valuable and thus some variety here is called for Feedback for specific skills development has some incompatibilities with feedback for general personal reappraisal and complex arrangements of feedback and trainer contributions are needed to accomplish both change goals, if pursued simultaneously. Feedback on a continuous basis in a variety of actual work situations could have interesting results as evidenced by the school dispute anecdote.

The first and most fundamental use of modelling is that of social learning. Other uses create feelings around situations where the individual can gain competence and confidence. Identification with the social model is affected by a variety of factors including: model competence, status, success, excitement, comfort, general 'attractiveness', believability, and of course, demonstrated vicarious reinforcement. However, it is important to keep in mind that, when sponsoring change, an attainable model is preferable to a perfect model. Verbal and co-action supplements increase the impact of the identificatory process. Cueing is increased by clarity, action, assigned focal activities and verbal direction. Matching increases cueing, identification, and motivation increased involvement and provides the individual with closure to change efforts. Video tape feedback has unique value in the matching process.

Analysis of the impact of television in society demonstrates the value of multiple presentations of highly personally satisfying models, and that change is a function of total viewing time. Trainers might do well to look to commercial groups such as Walt Disney Studios and Madison Avenue advertising firms as their models for the advancement of this approach in training. Behaviour models must also fit a wide set of cultural values to ensure that change is seen as acceptable to adults. Discussion before and after both feedback and modelling presentations can serve as a structuring aid and provide support and confirmation. Finally, creative combinations of feedback and modelling have high potential value. However, this value is as yet not fully explored. Combinations of feedback and modelling in both therapeutic measures and training do indicate that a blending of the inputs is desirable and further study or utilization attempts should consider the needs for repetition, cueing, focusing, matching, goals and the time necessary for reflection and integration of the messages from video presentations.

References

Allen, M. K. and Liebert, R. M. (1967) 'Effects of live and symbolic deviant modeling clues on adoption of a previously learned standard.' *Journal of Personality and Social Psychology*, **11**, (83), 253–60.

Arnoff, C. (1974) 'Old age in prime time.' *Journal of Communication*, **24**, 4, 86–87.

Bailey, K. G. and Sowder, W. J. (1970) 'Audio tape and video tape self-confrontation in psychotherapy.' *Psychology Bulletin*, **74**, 127–37.

Bandura, A. (1969) *Principles of Behavior Modification*. Toronto: Holt, Rinehart and Winston.

Bandura, A. and Walters, R. H. (1963) *Social Learning and Personality Development*. New York: Holt, Rinehart and Winston.

Baron, R. A. (1970) 'Attraction toward the model and model's competence as determinants of adult imitative behavior.' *Journal of Personality and Social Psychology*, **14**, 345–51.

Berkowitz, L. (1965) 'Some aspects of observed aggression.' *Journal of Personality and Social Psychology*, **2**, 359–69.

Berman, A. (1972) 'Videotape self-confrontation of schizophrenic ego and thought processes.' *Journal of Consulting and Clinical Psychology*, **39**, 78–85.

Berscheid, E. and Walster, E. H. (1969) *Interpersonal Attraction*, Menlo Park, Calif.: Addison-Wesley.

Booth, G. D. and Miller, H. R. (1974) 'Effectiveness of monochrome and color presentations in facilitating affective learning.' *A. V. Communications Review*, **22**, 4, 409–22.

Boyd, H. S. and Sisney, W. (1967) 'Immediate self-image confrontation and changes in self-concept.' *Journal of Consulting Psychology*, **31**, 291–97.

Clark, A. C. (1971) 'Beyond Babel: the century of the communications satellite.' In Schramm, W. and Roberts, D. (eds.) *The Process and Effects of Mass, Communications, Revised Edition*, pp. 952–65. Chicago: University of Illinois Press.

Courtney, A. E. and Whipple, T. W. (1974) 'Women in commercials.' *Journal of Communication*, **24**, 2, 110–18.

Danet, B. N., (1968). 'Self-confrontation in psychotherapy reviewed.' *American Journal of Psychotherapy*, **22**, 245–47.

Dehon, W. N. (1967). 'Self-confrontation via T.V.: videotaped feedback for training at Scardia Laboratory.' *Training and Development Journal*, **17**, 42–46.

Eisler, P. M. (1973) 'Effects of modeling on components of assertive behavior.' *Journal of Behavioral Therapy and Experimental Psychiatry*, **4**, 1–6.

Ellett, L. E. and Smith, E. P. (1975) 'Improving performance of classroom teachers through videotaping and self-evaluation.' *A. V. Communications Review*, **23**, 3, 277–88.

Evon, L. P., Husemann, L. R., Monroe, M., Lefkowitz, M. M., and Walder, L. O. (1974) 'How learning conditions in early childhood—including mass media—relate to aggression in late adolescence.' *American Journal of Orthopsychiatry*, **44**, 3, 412–23.

Furman, S. and Feighner, A. (1973) 'Video feedback in treating hyperkinetic children: a preliminary report.' *American Journal Psychiatry*, **130**, 7, 792–96.

Geertsman, R. H. and Reivich, R. S. (1965) 'Repetitive self-observation by videotape playback.' *Journal of Nervous and Mental Diseases*, **141**, 29–41.

Gerbner, G. and Gross, L. (1976) 'Living with T.V.: the violence profile.' *Journal of Communication*, **26**, 2, 173–99.

Goldstein, A. P. (1966) *Psychotherapy and the Psychology of Behavior Change*. New York: Wiley.

Griffiths, R. D. P. (1974) 'Videotape feedback as a therapeutic technique: retrospect and prospect.' *Behavioral Research and Therapy*, **12**, pp. 1–8.

Griffiths, R. D. and Hinkson, J. (1963) 'The effects of videotape feedback on the self-assessments of psychiatric patients.' *British Journal of Psychiatry*, **123**, 223–24.

Hansen, J. C., Niland, T. M., and Zani, L. P. (1969) 'Model reinforcement in group counseling with elementary school children.' *Personnel and Guidance Journal*, **47**, pp. 741–44.

Harrison, (1970). 'Defenses and the need to know.' In Golembiewski, R. T. and Blumberg, A., *Sensitivity Training and the Laboratory Approach*, pp. 80–86. Itasca, Ill. Peacock Press.

Harrison, R. (1965) 'Group composition models for laboratory design.' *Journal of Applied Behavioral Science*, **1**, (4), 409–32.

Hart, H. A. (1968) 'Using films for attitude change: an "Evaluative role play technique".' *Training and Development Journal*, **15** or **18**, 32–34.

Harvey, O. J. and Rutherford, J. (1960) 'Status in the informal group: influence and influencibility at differing age levels.' *Child Development*, **31**, 377–85.

Hess, B. B. (1974) 'Stereotypes of the aged.' *Journal of Communication*, **24**, 2, 76–87.

Hogan, P. and Alger, I. (1969) 'The impact of videotape recording on insight in group psychotherapy.' *International Journal of Group Psychotherapy*, **19**, 158–64.

Hoyt, J. K. (1970) 'Effect of media violence "Justification" or Aggression.' *Journal of Broadcasting*, **14**, 455–65.

Kacher, J. D. (1973) 'Development of a training program at R.C.A.' *Training and Development Journal*, **27**, 5, 3–9.

Kagan, N. Krathwohl, D. R. and Miller, R. (1963) 'Stimulated recall in therapy using videotape: a case study.' *Journal of Consulting Psychology*, **10**, (3), 237–43.

Kagan, N. and Schauble, P. G. (1969) 'Affective simulation in interpersonal process recall.' *Journal of Counseling Psychology*, **16**, 309–13.

Kelman, H. C. (1958) 'Compliance, identification, and internationalization: three processes of attitude change.' *Journal of Conflict Resolution*, **2**, 51–60.

Kennedy, J. B. (1970) 'Using A. V. techniques in training the hard-core.' *Training and Development Journal*, **2**, 30–32.

Keys, G. and Vane, P. (1975) 'Informal communications.'

Klapper, J. T. (1965) 'Mass media and persuasion.' In Schramm, W. (ed.) *The Process and Effects of Mass Communication*, Urbana: University of Illinois Press.

Krumboltz, J. D. and Thoresen, C. E. (1969) *Behavioural Counseling: Cases and Techniques.* Toronto: Holt Rinehart.

Krumboltz, J. D. and Thoreson, C. E. (1964) 'The effects of behavioral counseling in group and individual settings on information seeking behavior.' *Journal of Counseling Psychology,* **11,** 324–33.

Leifer, A. and Roberts, D. (1972) 'Children's responses to television violence.' In J. P. Murray, E. A. Rubinstein, and G. A. Constock (eds.) *Television and Social Behavior Vol. II,* pp. 43–180. Washington D.C.: Televisionland Social Learning, Government Printing Office:

Lieberman, M. A., Yalom, I. D., and Miles, M. B. (1972) 'The impact of encounter groups on participants: some preliminary findings.' *Journal of Applied Behavioral Science,* **8,** 1, 29–50.

Liebert, R. M., Neale, J. M., and Davidson, E. S. (1973) *The Early Window: Effects of Television on Children and Youth.* Toronto: Pergamon.

McLuhan, M. (1951) *The Mechanical Bride,* Boston: Beacon Press.

Menne, J. M. and Menne, J. W. (1972) 'The relative efficiency of bimodal presentation as an aid to learning.' *A.V. Communications Review,* **20,** 2, 170–80.

Noble, G. (1973) 'Effects of different forms of filmed aggression on children's constructive or destructive play.' *Journal of Personality and Social Psychology,* **26,** 1, 54–59.

Paulson, F. L. (1974) 'Teaching cooperation on television: an evaluation of *Sesame Street* social goals.' *A.V. Communications Review,* Programs, **22,** 3, 229–46.

Payne, J. G. (1967) 'Video tape recording for management training.' *Training and Development Journal,* **17,** or **14,** 18–25.

Philips, G. E. (1971) 'Films vs. video tapes in educational programs.' *Training and Development Journal,* **25,** 4, 39–42.

Resnik, H., Davidson, W., Schuyler, P., and Christopher, P. (1973) 'Video tape confrontation after attempted suicide.' *American Journal of Psychiatry,* **130,** 460–63.

Roberts, D. (1977) Informal Communications.

Robinson, J. A. (1968) 'Videotape in training: some limitations and criteria to help select its best applications.' *Training and Development Journal,* 14–17.

Sabin, L. (1972) 'Why I threw out my T.V. set.' *Todays Health* (February). Quoted in Liebert, Neale, and Davidson (1973).

Schein, E. H. and Bennis, W. G. (1965) *Personal and Organizational Change Through Group Methods: The Laboratory Approach,* New York: Wiley.

Singer, D. G. and Singer, D. L. (1976) 'Family television viewing habits and the spontaneous play of preschool children.' *American Journal of Orthopsychiatry,* **46,** 3, 496–502.

Spangenberg, R. W., (1973) 'The motion variable in procedural learning.' *A.V. Communications Review,* **21,** 4, 419–36.

Stoller, F. H. (1968) 'Focused feedback with videotape: extending the groups' functions.' In G. M. Gazda (ed.) *Innovations in Group Psychotherapy,* pp. 207–55. Springfield, Ill. Charles C. Thomas.

Strauss, A. (ed.) (1956) *George Herbert Mead on Social Psychology,* Chicago: University of Chicago.

Telesco, N. S. (1974) 'Patterns in prime time.' *Journal of Communication,* **24,** 2, 119–24.

Turner, C. W. and Berkowitz, L. (1970) 'Identification with film aggressor (covent role taking) and reactions to film violence.' *Journal of Personality and Social Psychology,* 21–2, 256–64.

Venn, J. R. and Short, J. G. (1973) 'Vicarious classical conditioning of emotional responses in nursery school children.' *Journal of Personality and Social Psychology,* **28,** 2, 249–55.

Wadeson, H. and Carpenter, W. T. (1976) 'T.V. in the hospital: programming patients' delusions.' *American Journal of Orthopsychiatry,* **46,** 3, 434–38.

Walter, G. A. (1975a) 'Effects of videotape feedback and modeling on the behaviors

88

of task group members.' *Human Relations*, **28**, 121–38.

Walter, G. A. (1975b) 'Effects of video tape training inputs on group performance.' *Journal of Applied Psychology*, **60**, 3, 308–12.

Walter, G. A. (1975c) 'Acted versus natural models for performance oriented behavior change in task groups.' *Journal of Applied Psychology*, **60**, 3, 303–307.

Walter, G. A. and Miles, R. E. (1974) 'Changing self acceptance: task groups and video tape or sensitivity training?' *Small Group Behavior*, **5**, 3, 356–64.

Weber, R. J. (1971) 'Effects of video tape feedback on task group behavior.' *Proceedings of the 79th Annual Convention of the American Psychological Association*, 499–500.

Woody, R. H. (1971a) *Psychobehavioral Counseling and Therapy: Integrating Behavioral and Insight Techniques*. New York: Appleton-Century-Crofts.

Woody, R. H. (1971b) 'Clinical suggestion in video taped psychotherapy: a research progress report.' *American Journal of Clinical Hypnosis*, **14**, 1, 32–37.

Woody, R. H. and Schauble, P. G. (1969a) 'Desensitization of fear by video tapes.' *Journal of Clinical Psychology*, **25**, 102–103.

Woody, R. H. and Schauble, P. G. (1969b) 'Videotaped vicarious desensitization.' *Journal of Nervous and Mental Disease*, **148**, 281–86.

Worting, C. E. and Greenberg, B. S. (1973) 'Experiments in televised violence and verbal aggression: two exploratory studies.' *Journal of Communication*, **23**, 446–60.

Chapter 5

Open Interaction:
Form, Function, and Feasibility

Robert E. Kaplan

Case Western Reserve University, U.S.A.

The experiential social process under consideration in this chapter is open interaction or that special form of social encounter in which conversants talk about their own behaviour and feelings. To qualify as openness, a conversation must be an explicit and extended exchange—more than a passing comment, an oblique reference, or attributions embedded in action or injunctions. The object of the talk may be interpersonal in that the participants examine together their experience of the relationship. The object may also be personal in that attention centres on one or more of the individuals present. Person-based openness can take either of two complementary forms, depending on whether one's remarks apply to oneself or one's partner. To refer to oneself is to engage in self-disclosure, confession, self-criticism. Reference to the other it termed feedback, criticism, admonishment. It is understood that to characterize another person is often, in effect, to reveal oneself.

Openness turns out to be a rarity in our society. For one thing, the inherently repressive nature of civilization (Freud, 1930) not only generally prohibits infantile, narcissistic, and labile expressions of sexuality and aggression but also greatly restricts the *verbal* expression of feeling. Secondly, openness tends to be regarded as an invasion of privacy, whether one talks personally about oneself or is commented on by someone else (Altman, 1975). And thirdly, as Goffman (1967) contends, the infrequency of open interaction is due to the hazards it poses for the social order: if people reveal their true opinions of one another, their mutual 'working acceptance' might be jeopardized.

In a society in which openness is the exception rather than the rule, the appearance of the T-group 25 years ago caused something of a stir. It was, of course, as much the precipitate of an age of self-consciousness as the precipitant of it. And it appeared at a time when similar developments such as Bion's process-oriented group therapy were occurring independently. From the original focus on group and interpersonal dynamics, the T-group has given rise to new forms such as the encounter group whose concentration on the development of the individual borders on group therapy, and to organizational applications for surmounting interpersonal obstacles to work effectiveness.

The T-group and its derivations constitute a sort of prototype of openness, at least in the scientific and professional subcultures in which this experiential social process originated and continues to be practised. In this setting, there has developed a certain cultural insularity, a kind of intellectual myopia which blurs apprehension of other analogous forms of openness. And a variety of other forms, albeit often remote and exotic, do exist. Examples include: personal reclamation programmes for overcoming addictions to drugs, cigarette smoking, overeating, etc.; utopian communes, in which a commitment to 'telling the truth' prevails; religious conversion and religious confession; and brainwashing as a social means for accomplishing political indoctrination. These and other instances of openness that might be enumerated have in common the purposes of instituting personal or social change or of maintaining the change.

Thus, while the type of openness introduced by the T-group is quite properly regarded as an advance, it is important not to take the T-group as the embodiment of the universal properties of openness. This paper is intended to point up the cultural relativity of T-group openness and to transcend ethnocentric traces in applied behavioural science concerning openness. In the process of widening vistas on openness, this chapter will hopefully deepen understanding of the behavioural science version of it. Particular attention will be given to identifying the variety of *forms* openness can take and to relating these to the several *functions* it can perform. Emphasis will also be placed on setting out the moral function, which is either neglected or rejected in the T-group world. Finally, the paper will concern itself with the applicability of openness to everyday interaction. By examining the conditions under which openness is able to gain a foothold, a determination will be made as to the *feasibility* of introducing openness, as a special, exceptional social form, into ordinary settings.

Form

Just as there is a tendency to overlook or underplay structurally related instances of openness, there has been a tendency among T-group partisans (including the author) to regard openness as *sui generis*—as a thing unto itself and disjunctive from conventional interaction. In fact, a dispassionate view of social interaction will detect a continuity between direct verbal expression about things interpersonal and personal and the myriad ways in which people continuously signal each other indirectly, non verbally, implicitly about their emotional states, the state of the relationship, and their views of self and others. Metacommunication, which may take place explicitly but usually is expressed through non-verbal behaviour, is a process by which an individual indicates how he and his verbal message ought to be taken. Injunctions, which consist of the perpetual stream of things people ask or tell each other to do, constitute another important medium through which a person's sense of himself and of his partners in interaction is conveyed (Laing, 1961). Thus, openness is a dramatic and conspicuous, but not at all the sole, channel for communicating personal and interpersonal content.

A related polarity worth avoiding is the one which pits the freedom from restraint of open interaction against the oppression and control of everyday social life. Openness as it usually occurs is very much 'bounded'. Like any other kind of socially acceptable behaviour, it is defined by expectations and constraints and moderated by consideration of its impact on other people. One early writer on this subject showed an appreciation for this need for emotional self-restraint in remarking that 'the successful introduction of this institution . . . require[s] a certain amount of . . . civilization of the passions' (Noyes, 1876).

Openness of any variety is shaped by a particular set of boundaries, which themselves derive from the purpose for which people have come together as well as by the values regarding proper treatment of human beings. Informed by the social systems theory of the Tavistock Institute, Singer et al. (1975) took the view that authenticity is a role which leader or member assumes and which is defined by the task of the group. Therefore, to be open in a particular setting, is to abide by a particular set of role expectations? In a T-group, for example, constraints apply especially to criticism of, or feedback to, others. Feedback is to be based on concrete behaviour presented descriptively and non-evaluatively, stated in terms of one's perceptions, framed in terms of the relationship rather than the person, and concerned with the 'here-and-now' rather than the biographical history of the participants. These prescriptions are responsive to the task of the T-group—to educate people about themselves as persons-in-relation, without administering therapy and without applying undue pressure to the individual. T-group openness no doubt also owes its make-up to its scientific origins in the fields of social psychology and group dynamics. From this source presumably has come the stress placed, for example, on valid data and on non-evaluative, value-free observation.

That openness as a social phenomenon is not equated with T-group openness, and that openness is structurally variable rather than fixed is seen in the following discussion of the several dimensions of openness. The four dimensions discussed at some length are: considerate vs. abusive, subjective-affective and objective-normative, symmetrical vs. asymmetrical, and contemporaneous vs. historical. (It is understood that openness be characterized on other dimensions as well—for example, it can take place either by formal arrangement or informally.)

Considerate vs. abusive

One of the cardinal rules of openness, as those of us in applied behavioural science know it, is that criticism be constructive. It is meant to be an *offering* to the person on the receiving end. Naturally, reactions are given with feeling, often with angry and frustrated feeling, but there is absolutely no license to abuse, disparage, or humiliate.

In other settings, however, this sacred standard of consideration is observed less stringently or abandoned altogether. An example of nearly complete abandon is Chinese Communist thought reform, or 'brainwashing', as practised at the time of the Korean War. It was the fate of Western civilians in prison for example, to be abused psychologically and grossly mistreated physically. Prisoners were subjected to 'humiliation, revilement, and brutalization':

> 'Most prisoners were put into a cell containing several Chinese prisoners who were further along in reforming themselves and who saw it as their primary duty to "help" their most backward member to see the truth about himself . . . Each cell had a leader who was in close touch with the authorities . . . In this setting the cell mates found ways of putting *extreme pressure* on their unreformed member, particularly since he was often completely dependent upon them for help in feeding himself, eliminating, etc.' (Schein, 1964; emphasis added.)

This is an instance of openness so extreme, heavyhanded, and inhumane that it is relevant to socially acceptable uses of openness only as a near-diametrical opposite.

A more problematic case comes from the world of drug addiction and rehabilitation. Both Synanon and its descendant, the Delancey Street Foundation, attempt to reach hard-core drug addicts through a high-powered, emotionally violent type of encounter known as the Game. Delancey Street is a residential community, which holds its groups for all residents in various combinations every weekday evening after work as well as for longer periods on the weekends. In his account of Delancey Street, Hampden-Turner (1976) reports the following instance of a Game, which involved an individual named Bryant.

> 'Bryant, a tall, middle-class, black youth with large sad eyes . . . says softly, "I'd like to put the Game on myself."
> "Did you hear an unpleasant noise?"
> "Something crawled out from beneath a stone. It's rattling."
> "At least let me speak!" Bryant blazes. "How can you hope to do justice if you won't hear me?"
> "Justice, ha! If you'd got what you deserved, you'd be f—' *dead.*" '

When he is allowed to speak, Bryant makes a contrite statement about himself and cites some minor instances of wayward behaviour during the last year. Someone in charge impatiently points out a gross omission: 'About a year ago his two room-mates accused him of being loaded. That's not an easy thing to do. They said he was scratchin', he was nodding off, and he watered his TV set instead of the azaleas'. At the time Bryant had denied the charge, managed to make himself believed, and later was found to have lied. The next person "in the ring" tells Bryant:

> ' "I resent the hell out of you college educated middle-class f—... We uneducated slobs keep repeating to ourselves, "gotta educate our children and ourselves and prepare for the day." Then we look at you . . . , and we think "wait a minute! I could graduate from college and *still* be a slave. I could end up like Bryant—the most erudite liar that ever tied himself up in supersophisticated knots and used his brains against his own life.' Ain't *no one* believes you but yourself!" ' (Hampden-Turner, pp. 39–41).

In addition to the rather entertaining display of sarcastic wit, the hard-hitting style is manifestly obvious. The abusive type of confrontation is assumed to be necessary in order to get through to the thick-skinned, exceptionally well-defended clientèle and to make contact with the negative images they have of themselves (Hampden-Turner, 1976). To help a person become aware of the unconfessed image he has of himself as a punk, one must call him a punk. The abusive style can be seen as an adaptation of T-group openness for use with the lower class: the polite middle-class approach simply would not work (Maliver, 1973). Furthermore, it is important to recognize that the insults and gross exaggeration are part of the Game and come to be expected. The participants are not affected by name-calling and curses in the way that an individual in an otherwise well-mannered group would be. Thus, the definition of authentic and concerned role behaviour is different; the Game is a setting where one can count on, in a sense, raucous music with the volume turned up. But no one is fooled. Despite the noise, real concern for the individual comes through clearly.

Under what conditions considerate and abusive forms are regularly found will not be addressed here. But the example of Delancey Street should not lead to the erroneous conclusion that stridency in openness is necessarily and exclusively a lower-class phenomenon. Groups populated by the middle-class are fully capable of rampant intolerance and invective, and advanced groups at Delancey Street reach the point of decorous and reflective exploration.

Subjective-affective vs. objective-normative

Openness as it has grown out of applied behavioural science is tentative and and relativistic. Feedback is framed in terms of the perceptions of the deliverer, and in this way allowance is made for the possible distorting influence of a critic's perceptions. Subjective feedback is based on the phenomenological assumption that an individual confronting another can present only his experience, and can never presume to set out the objective reality, of the other.

Despite the sometimes righteous conviction that feedback is inherently subjective, and therefore must be cloaked in qualified language, cases abound of objectivity given feedback. An example comes from a utopian commune known as the Farm, which is a spiritual community of more than 1000 people with locations in several states in the United States. The Farm dispenses, for the most part, with phenomenological qualifiers and purports to characterize a person's behaviour objectively. In the words of Stephen, the spiritual leader of the Farm: 'Your friends will hassle if you ain't groovy. They'll say, "Hey, man, where's it at, how come you're being a pain in the ass? Shape up!"' (Stephen, undated). Implicit in Stephen's example is the readiness with which residents of the Farm will speak of *you* and what *you* are doing, without acknowledging the humble perceptual origins of their statements.

Whereas subjective feedback is assumed to describe the giver as well as the receiver, objective feedback presumes simply to characterize the receiver. Subjective feedback is taken to be a product of the interaction between giver and receiver, while objective feedback centres unabashedly on the receiving individual. At the Farm the spotlight often plays upon the individual, especially in so far as his behaviour fails to meet collective expectations. The Farm subscribes to a largely explicit code of moral conduct which calls, in essence, for selflessness and a spirit of cooperation. As Farm residents say, 'If a person's ego sticks out, we'll pare it down for him'. Thus, much of the criticism given at the Farm is levelled squarely at individuals, who are held responsible for acting in accordance with community values.

The difference between subjective and objective feedback is associated with a difference in level of analysis. The Farm is concerned with the tie between the individual member and the community. Consequently, the critics in a given open exchange are presumably acting not so much on their behalf as agents of the minisociety. This is *normative* feedback, by means of which the individual is stood up alone against the yardstick of community values. In contrast, in the T-group there is no organizational or societal level of analysis, no overarching moral framework against which to judge the individual *qua* individual. Participants do, of course, have available the general social mores regarding desirable social behaviour, about which, however, there will undoubtedly be no sharp consensus. What the T-group deals in primarily is *affective* feedback, which arises from the thicket of interpersonal relationships. Critics speak on the authority of their personal values, preferences, and sentiments as well as make due allowance for the causal influence of interaction on the actions of the individual.

Furthermore, T-groups place a premium on merely describing another person's behaviour, as concretely as possible, and steering clear of judgements. The value on minimizing evaluation makes sense in light of the largely affective nature of feedback in a T-group; for the moral consensus required to make judgements readily is largely absent. (Norms regarding authenticity *are* present, and form the basis of unambiguous assessments as to the extent to which individuals are assuming the role of authentic group member.) Moral judgements are avoided for the further reason of easing the pressure on the individual.

By the same token, one could expect normative feedback and judgemental tendencies to go hand in hand. This, in fact, is the case. Clear and agreed-upon standards of conduct lend themselves to evaluation. The Delancey Street Foundation, with its moral code for residents, exhibits no shyness about judging people. Similarly, the confessional is a place where neither clergyman or penitent hesitates to take the latter's measure against the canons of Christian morality.

Symmetrical vs. asymetrical

The T-group specializes in symmetrical interaction, operating on the assumption that everyone in the group, including the leader, is a potential player in open interaction. All are obliged to allow comment on their behaviour, and all are empowered to comment on everyone else's behaviour. This reciprocity is, in part, necessitated by the interpersonal focus of the activity: a productive discussion of a relationship is impossible without the participation of the parties to the relationship.

The T-group is not alone in providing for mutuality between leader and members. Some recent variants of psychotherapy and group psychotherapy make similar provisions for the therapist to partake of open interaction on more or less equal terms with patients (Durkin, 1964). But openness by no means requires a symmetry in the relation between leader and members. There are numerous instances in our society in which the behaviour and inner life of a person are discussed with an authority of some stripe or other without the favour being returned. Such instances include dealings between parent and child, teacher and pupil, coach and player, organizational superior and subordinate, confessor and sinner, social worker and client, and many therapists and their patients. These are, of course, all hierarchical relationships, which are all inherently asymmetrical to some degree. This is part of a general phenomenon noted by Goffman (1967, p. 14) in which:

'the superordinate [has] the right to exercise certain familiarities which the subordinate is not allowed to reciprocate ... Perhaps the clearest form of this is found in the psychiatrist–patient relation, where the psychiatrist has the right to touch on aspects of the patient's life that the patient might not even allow himself to touch upon, while of course this privilige is not reciprocated.'

In pure form, asymmetry in open interaction consists of a conversation in which both parties talk about the inferior member and neither broach the subject of the superior. Psychoanalysis may seem to provide a counterexample, since the analysand legitimately discusses his reactions to the analyst. But in the psychoanalytic framework these characterizations of the analyst are classed as transference, and therefore taken to be the projections of the patient and fundamentally descriptive of him rather than the therapist. And countertransference, or the (projective) reaction of therapist to patient, is regarded as something the professional should minimize and certainly not introduce into the therapeutic conversation.

At the root of the differential parts taken in open interactions such as these is a differentiation in roles. The lack of equal treatment is justified by the position of the superior as an authority representing a larger system and its values and by the position of the inferior as someone who is learning or potentially deviating from these values.

Contemporaneous vs. historical

The classic T-group limits its attention to the present interaction among members—to the 'here-and-now'. Technically, of course, the here-and-now is a misnomer, since one cannot reflect on events precisely as they occur but only just after they have occurred (Schutz, 1932). The sense of the term, then, is that T-group participants address issues arising during their current social encounter or current meeting, or during previous meetings of the group. Among other things, the contemporaneous focus serves to restrict the portion of personal space open to public inquiry.

For a group to grapple with nothing but its shared contemporaneous existence is unique, and other types of open interaction do not restrict themselves so severely. For example, therapy is traditionally an approach with primary attention to personal history. Beyond opening up private areas for scrutiny, the historical perspective is part of a process of reinterpreting past events in terms of the framework offered by the change agency. If one is to change—and, for example, become better adjusted to society, converted to a new religion, or indoctrinated into a new political philosophy, then the person one becomes must be reconciled with the person one has been (Berger and Luckman, 1967). Hence a systematic revaluation of one's past, with special attention to deviations from the newly adopted code, is in order. The person striving for mental health comes to understand his pathogenic origins, the individual seeking religious purity confesses and atones for past transgressions, and the person in quest of political enlightenment renounces the violations committed in his former life. This inquiry into personal history involves a bringing to awareness of past inconsistencies with present values and an accompanying arousal of guilt (aggression towards self) or aggression towards others for one's failure to be *then* what one wishes to become *now* (Frank, 1963).

While an historical orientation tends to intrude more deeply into the self, a contemporaneous approach is not necessarily associated with lack of depth. *Gestalt* therapy, for example, breaks ranks with childhood-probing tendencies of psychoanalysis but nevertheless achieves considerable depth by having the participant face his internal conflicts as they manifest themselves in the present. Despite being contemporaneous, *Gestalt* therapy remains substantially intrapsychic and thus differs from the essentially interpersonal and outward orientation of the T-group.

The distinction between contemporaneous and historical blurs when, for example, people with prior relationships such as the members of a work group assemble for a T-group. If their history prior to the T-group is, as it realistically should be, admissible, then the scope of the group scrutiny is appreciably widened. While such an expanded scope includes shared relational history, it still excludes the independent past of the individual.

Summary

In addition to demonstrating that the characteristics of a T-group are not universal givens in the practice of openness, this treatment of form has hopefully begun to bring out the ends served by the T-group's particular constellation of properties. One apparent end is to moderate the pressure applied to the individual participant. This, patently, is the effect of requiring consideration in the way people are handled, showing appreciation for the origins in the self of expressed views of the other, exposing the giver of feedback—including the leader—to feedback himself, and minimizing evaluation in the characterizations of people. The second apparent underlying function of the characteristics of T-group openness is to limit the scope and depth of intrusions into the private reaches of the person. This, patently, is the effect of restricting the agenda to present shared events, assigning cause not just to persons but also to situation and relation, and refraining from global assessments of character. These twin brakes on power exercised and privacy invaded support the T-group's expressly educational and non-therapeutic mission. When, as we have seen, the uses to which openness is put become avowedly change-oriented, the form taken by openness also changes.

Function

In his tract on 'mutual criticism', as practised in the Oneida Community a century ago, John Noyes (1876) spoke of two primary functions—education and regulation. Education is the personal development of the individual, and regulation is the social control of the members of a collectivity. In addition, openness can perform a third function, integration, or the enhancement of social unity. We in applied behavioural science are well familiar with the educational potential of openness: the opportunity for individuals and aggregates of individuals to learn about themselves is the chief advertisement made for openness. By comparison, the other two functions are poorly recognized. This section is devoted, therefore, towards demonstrating the importance of these two functions.

Regulation

It is not difficult to uncover the regulatory function at work in the T-group, despite rhetoric to the contrary. An obvious example is the social pressure to conform to the norm that openness is worth engaging in. The contradiction between the ideology of freedom and self-determination and the reality of social pressure is a point driven home forcibly by such critics of the 'human potential movement' as Koch (1971). But let us assume that, while the regulatory element of openness is no doubt more strongly in evidence than proponents of T-groups may recognize, the T-group does in fact represent a relatively benign, non-coercive type. And let us look to other settings for clear-cut, unabashed instances of openness for social control. [Social control can be defined as 'the influence exercised by authorities, or any person for that matter who acts as an agent of the social system and whose targets are those people whose actions can potentially disrupt the orderly functioning of the system' (Gamson, 1968, p. 18).]

The regulatory function of openness is perhaps best seen in small utopian societies, on the order of 1000 members, where the system of values is comparatively explicit and the social mechanisms for enforcing the values are in plain view. Writing about Oneida, Noyes (1876), for example, referred to mutual criticism as a 'regulator of morals' (p. 70). Nordhoff (1875), writing on the same subject, observed that mutual criticism was 'in fact their main system of government'. It served as an instrument of community governance in the sense that it was the means by which departures from community expectations were confronted. As Nordhoff noted, the members of Oneida

'depend[ed.] upon criticism to cure whatever they regard[ed.] as faults in the character of a member; for instance, idleness, disorderly habits, impoliteness, selfishness, a love of novel-reading, "selfish love", conceit, pride, stubbornness, a grumbling spirit—for every vice, petty or great, criticism [was] held to be the remedy.'

Similarly, the Bruderhof, a twentieth-century utopian society now located in the United States, possesses a moral system that specifies good attitudes such as 'joy (above all), openness, eagerness to participate in communal activities . . . , cooperation, and friendliness . . .' and 'wrong attitudes such is aloofness, grumpiness, a desire for solitude, . . . judgementalism . . . and an unwillingness to work . . .' (Zablocki, 1971, pp. 57–58). The Bruderhof's method for contending with counter-normative behaviour and attitudes is articulated in its only codified moral requirement, which holds that under no conditions whatsoever is gossiping allowed and that 'the only possible way is direct address as the spontaneous brotherly service to the one whose weaknesses cause something in us to react negatively' (Zablocki, 1971, p. 58). At the Farm, a like body of explicit 'agreements' exists, as well as a similar remarkable ability to achieve voluntary moral consistency.

Clearly, the combination of normative structure and mutual criticism in these three communes constitutes a system of deviance and control. In each case the values betoken a strong collective identification and oppose tendencies in members which threaten or weaken involvement in the collectivity. There is, of course, nothing unusually about a normative infrastructure and mechanisms for obtaining compliance with normative requirements. What is different about these communes is the extent to which monitoring is accomplished explicitly and continuously.

The utility of openness for social control becomes apparent in utopian communes because of the saliency of the normative system. By contrast, the T-group is conflicted and confused about its moral identity, even as to whether it has a moral identity. Perhaps a more balanced and differentiated statement would be that the T-group is clear about norms regarding how people ought to act in the group itself—specifically, that openness is desired—but it tends to avoid prescriptions as to what the good life or the good person is. One can speculate that the skittishness about making moral pronouncements derives, in part, form the T-group's origins in science with its aspiration to

non-moral, or value-free, observation. It is also worth noting that any dis-
inclination to moralize is born not only of ambivalence but also of the relative
inadequacy of the T-group's moral framework.

The utopian commune neither suffers from the lack of an undeveloped
value system nor hesitates to make moral prescriptions. Paraphrasing Frank
(1963, p. 219): the presence of a single all-embracing world view which is
shared by the individual, the person confronting him, and the communal
society greatly increases the pressure that can be brought to bear on the individual. The salient and encompassing nature of the commune's moral system
is reflected in the nature of the feedback given. Feedback tends to be normative,
comparing the behaviour of the individual member against collective values.
The central relation becomes that between the individual and the social institution. The centrality of this relation is seen in the following statement by
Noyes (1876, pp. 54–55): 'Neither our estimation of an individual's character
nor our affection for him should be determined by our personal relations to
him, but by his *relations to general society* . . . (emphasis added)'. In this way,
openness is the servant of social control—of the control of the individual
for the social system's purposes.

It is interesting to note that, based on my observations of the Farm and
of T-groups, normative feedback tends to be put forth more strongly and less
equivocally than affective feedback. At the Farm, the confronting individual
speaks not so much for himself but as a representative of the community,
and consequently can be more impersonal and less tentative. This explanation
is consistent with Simmel's insight into the differing natures of subjective and
objective conflict (conflict being a category of social process which subsumes
criticism). It is his view that conflict tends to be fiercest when the parties are
fighting for an external, objective purpose or cause rather than for their private
or selfish interests (Simmel, 1908).

There is perhaps no clearer instance of openness for moral purposes than
religious confession. Confession is a social institution in which a member meets
with a representative of the church hierarchy to disclose his failure to live up
to moral standards. The two join in commenting on the moral slippage and in
providing for ways to avoid similar mistakes in the future. Luther's instructions
to the individual, for example, were to 'reflect on your condition in light of
the Ten Commandments: . . . whether you have been disobedient, unfaithful,
lazy, ill-tempered, or quarrelsome, whether you have harmed anyone by word
or deed; and whether you have stolen, neglected or wasted anything, or done
other evil' (quoted in Belgum, 1969). In addition to confession, the Church
came to terms with moral inadequacy with admonition. According to Calvin
also quoted in Belgum, 1969): 'If anyone does not perform his duty willingly,
or behaves insolently, or does not live honorably, or has committed any act
deserving blame—he should allow himself to be admonished by his brother.'

Clearly, from the point of view of the Church, one function of confronting
departures from Christian morality is to reaffirm that morality. This is in
keeping with Durkheim's notion that deviance in society, although on the face

of it a threat to the social order, is an opportunity seized by society for the purposes of reasserting the ascendancy of the violated social mores (Durkheim, 1893). From the standpoint of the individual, confession serves the function of alleviating his guilt. In this connection Mowrer (1964) makes an interesting tie between the guilt-relieving capabilities of religion and psychotherapy. In his view, this function in western civilization has been for two millenia the province of religion but it has been transferred in the last century to psychoanalysis and its various derivatives. He contends that unexpiated guilt is often the source of emotional distress and mental illness. He argues further that the expiation of guilt is best accomplished socially. In its early stages Christianity conducted confession as a community event but later confined it to a private audience with the priest. In its attempt to reform the church, Protestantism removed confession entirely from the self-serving reach of the church bureaucracy and made it a private matter between the believer and God. In this way confession was reduced to a solitary experience and thus stripped of its social character and, in Mowrer's opinion, much of its salutary effect. While psychoanalysis heralds a return to at least a dyadic exchange, Mowrer favours a more public event, involving those significant others in one's life affected by the failures in question.

Integration

In addition to education (concerned with the edification of the individual) and regulation (concerned with the maintenance of social morality), there is a third purpose potentially served by openness. This is integration, a lateral function, which brings persons together as persons. Its primary instrument is *affective* feedback. Noyes (1876, pp. 31–32) apparently was prejudiced against feedback for personal reasons and advocated instead morally based criticism: 'Sometimes people criticize those around them merely or chiefly because they are personally annoyed by the faults they complain of; but the true motive is to edify Christ'. Providing a contrast is the T-group which lacking an encompassing system of values, emphasizes the person-to-person rather than the person-to-organization relation, and uses affective feedback as the coin of the realm.

Elsewhere Noyes (1876) commented that 'the system of mutual criticism ... takes the place of backbiting in ordinary society, and is regarded as one of the greatest means of fellowship'. Nordhoff (1875) in reporting a formal session of criticism which he personally witnessed at Onedia, commented that 'while [the object of criticism] might be benefitted by the "criticism", those who spoke of him would also be the better for their speech; for if there had been bitterness in any of their hearts before, this was likely to be dissipated by the free utterance' (p. 293). The notion that anger can best be dispelled by expressing it directly is consistent with the Freudian view that displaced expression of a wish (in this case, to aggress against another) never decathects the wish as effectively as does direct expression (Freud, 1950). Also relevant is Mills' theory (reported in Slater, 1966) that aggression taken in relation to an object facilitates identification with that object. (This tendency applies to objects with valued characteristics.) On the assumption that all relationships are moved simultaneously by urges to approach and avoid and to love and hate, Mills suggested that the expression of negative affect can pave the way for positive identification. And identification with the other is an essential ingredient in close personal relations.

It seems to me no accident that the Farm, the Bruderhof, and Oneida all place a taboo on gossiping. (Noyes, 1876 spoke scornfully of 'tea-party back-biting'.) The question of what one does with resentment toward others is, in sociometric terms, substantially a question of 'who talks to whom about whom'. Gossiping is a case of talking about the object of one's resentment with another party. The effect of this triangular relationship is often to bring the gossipers together in opposition to the absent individual. Confronting, on the other hand, is a case of talking about a person with that person himself. In such a conversation, one cannot talk nearly as freely or ungenerously as one can in gossiping. But if one can prove equal to the task of communicating both with candour and with consideration for the other person, then the uniting effect accrues to the two individuals.

Just as criticism is capable of healing breaches, so is confession. The theory is that interpersonal breaches are caused by covering up wrongdoing and the attendant guilt. In religious terms, 'unconfessed sin isolates the sinner' (Belgum, 1969). Arguing for private confession (outside the institutional context), Calvin is quoted as saying that 'for our neighbour's sake, we appease him and *reconcile him to us* if through fault of ours he has been in any way injured' (in Belgum, 1963, p. 80; emphasis added). In sociological terms, this process can be understood as the 'intrinsically isolating effect of immorality', this because 'the immoral hides itself' and the immoral person withdraws in some measure from his fellows (Simmel, 1950, p. 331). Again from a sociological perspective, Kanter (1972) classed both confession and criticism as 'morti-fication' (of the egoistic and antisocial tendencies in the individual), which she thought of as a 'commitment mechanism' for enhancing social unit.

The example of confession is also useful in demonstrating the utility of absolution. To disclose a misdeed and the feelings of regret prompted by it does nothing necessarily to preclude recurrences in the future. Apart from whether confession fortifies the person against future lapses, it accomplishes in the present a release from guilt evoked by past actions. In the T-group world, absolution is lost in the shadow of resolution. If, for example, a problem between a pair of individuals surfaces, energies are channelled towards *re-solving* the problem. But not a few interpersonal conflicts are immune to resolution, and much can be accomplished nevertheless by simply acknowledg-ing the problem and expressing regret. Thus, independent of resolution, ab-solution—or what in the church is known as a process of contrition, confession, and satisfaction (Belgum, 1969)—has a value in and of itself.

Summary

Openness is assumed to have three functions—education, regulation, and integration. Education is an individual-oriented function, concerned with the promotion of growth and development in the individual via throughgoing and lasting processes of internalization. The utility of openness for educational purposes is well illustrated by the T-group, where the participant's self-awareness and emotional education are the sought-after outcomes. Regulation is a moral function bearing on the relation between individual and collectivity. Openness can promote regulation by serving as a highly personalized and emotionally arousing way of monitoring the conformity of individuals to collective values. Religious confession in the church is an excellent example of the morally tinged regulatory function of openness. Integration is a social function, directed at strengthening bonds between people. Openness can be seen as furthering social connectedness both through criticism, by mitigating hostility in the offended party, and through confession, by alleviating guilt in the offending party.

Although they have been presented as distinct, these three functions are potentially very much interrelated. Education can be the handmaiden of regulation by socializing new additions into a society. This is nicely illustrated by Nordhoff's statement about the function of mutual criticism for Oneida: '[Criticism] is useful as a means of eliminating uncongenial elements, and also of *training those who remain in harmony with the general system and order*' (emphasis added). It is also apparent that the functions of regulation and integration are intricately intertwined. Social relations take place in a medium infused with a mixture of collective morality and personal feelings. The resentment and guilt that separates people, and that openness can surface and dispel, result from failures to live up to shared values as well as from more purely affective sources, and more often from an inseparable combination of the two. In addition, the moral element inherent in the regulatory use of openness has a definite integrative effect: holding the same set of beliefs, individuals find it easier to enter, and enter fully, into relation.

Feasibility

As we have considered it here, openness refers to the practice of talking in the company of relevant others about one's views, opinions, feelings, descriptions, and prescriptions regarding self, others, and the various interrelations. In this chapter we have thus far examined the variety of forms in which openness can occur and the functions which it is capable of performing. The concern of the present section is with the low incidence of this social phenomenon—with the fact that it is by far the norm for people to eschew this sort of thing rather than embrace it.

Openness is an essentially private and personal activity that can be assumed to occur in people's family lives and intimate relationships. This assumption must be tempered, however, by the knowledge that, for example, certain segments of the population (such as men) have traditionally been disinclined to engage in self-disclosure (Jourard, 1964); and that couples tend to avoid mutual confrontation or to be inept at it (Bach and Wyden, 1968; Bach and Deutsch, 1970).

In public and organizational spheres, whether in the context of enduring relationships at work or in fleeting relationships in public, openness is a rarity. It seems to occur in organizations only under highly specialized conditions. The performance-appraisal interview is one such rare occasion in work organizations, and it is characteristically a formal occasion, taking place at widely spaced intervals, at the behest of the organization, conducted in private and one's immediate superior who presumably has the authority to intrude in a manner such as this. Despite these enabling features, performance appraisal is for both superior and subordinate typically an unwelcome event and many times trivialized if not avoided completely (Hall and Lawler, 1969). Confession is another instance of openness in an institutional context, and it is also noteworthy for the special conditions under which it occurs. In effect, since it takes place in utter privacy and under strict confidentiality, it is sealed off from the rest of the congregation and the rest of the person's life.

Besides the incidence of openness in private life and under encapsulated conditions in public life, openness is also found in exotic and out-of-the-way settings such as utopian communes. The fact that it flourishes in such places is both a testament to its ability to exist at all and a statement about its rare and precious nature. The T-group can be seen as a similar exotic phenomenon. The quintessential version is a comparatively short burst of activity, completely consuming for the weekend or week that it lasts, totally removed from people's lives and society, answering to an unconventional set of social dictates—in short, like the utopian commune, a 'cultural island'. The comparison of T-group and utopian commune becomes particularly instructive when one recognizes that both can be classed as instances of 'communitarianism'. Along with revolution and reform, communitarianism is a method of social change; it attempts to effect change by creating a miniature ideal society which is intended to serve as a model and inspiration for the larger society (Zablocki, 1971). Thus, a communitarian strives for change on a macroscopic level by demonstrating the viability of his vision on a microscopic level.

Few would argue that communal experiments represent a social ideal that is not about to be widely adopted. I would maintain that the same fate is reserved for the T-group. While, at the climatic stage, it may be a paragon of candour, authenticity, and intimacy, it has little chance of becoming standard practice in society. At best it will be accepted as a special form of social interaction worth invoking on an exceptional basis for the emotional education of individuals and the repair of social relationships. It is doomed, it seems, to a relatively peripheral role because it requires conditions not ordinarily met in society.

The relative inapplicability of the T-group is demonstrated by the case of organization development (OD). One facet of OD has been what amounts to an attempt to translate the T-group to the work place. Although the first such efforts were made about 20 years ago, there are still, to my knowledge, few recorded instances of a work organization that has adopted openness of the T-group type *on a large scale*. It is interesting to note that recently the T-group approach has been modified to fit the realities of organizational life. 'Role negotiations', for example, a technique developed by Harrison (1973), has participants deal with less personal matters such as role expectations, performance, group goals, and group process, and has them do so at a greater social distance. Such efforts notwithstanding, one is led to wonder about the feasibility of open interaction and the condition under which it can be success-fully introduced.

Prerequisites for open interaction

There are a select few conditions in the absence of which open interaction will not occur. By far the most important one is a strong collective identification. The collectivity consisting of the potential partners in open interaction must possess a high degree of internal cohesion. In a T-group, solidarity—both in intermember relations and in the group's relation to the task—must materia-lize before openness will occur. In a similar vein, Noyes (1876) in his tract on mutual criticism advised that love must accompany criticism: 'Society should be *knit together in love* before the strain of criticism is put on', p. 29 (emphasis added). In other words, any social unit that would be open must possess a high degree of mutual attraction, must generate abundant commitment on the part of its member to one another and to the unit itself. Kanter (1972) spoke of commitment mechanisms—that is, social structures and processes for promot-ing social unit—and included confession and criticism in this category. In short, openness is a social mechanism which can enhance commitment but, paradoxically, can only be used in groups already enjoying high commitment (or the potential for high commitment.)

Commitment, cohesion, mutual attraction, and collective identification are essential because these properties of a group or organization support an incursion into areas of the person normally regarded as private. Privacy can be defined as the 'selective control of access to self' (Altman, 1975). For a group to engage in open behaviour is to submit the private internal states of its members to external control (Kanter, 1972). And individuals will parti-cipate voluntarily only if they identify profoundly with the controlling social identity. Openness both requires and itself betokens an investment, and some-times even a submergence, of the individual in the collectivity. Openness is associated with a dampening of individualistic tendencies and a heightening of collectivistic ones.

The condition of commitment and cohesion is associated with and depends upon two lesser conditions—minimal competition and minimal hierarchy. Minimal competition is a state in which the members of a group put collective ends over self-interest. In a work setting, for example, the members of a department would at the very least not seek to advance their personal careers so avidly that investment in common pursuits was precluded. At the Farm, the tension between self-interest and organizational ends is mitigated by the Farm's egalitarianism and an antimaterialism and by the relative absence of status advantages and material possessions to strive for.

In general, competition is negatively correlated with an 'identification of ends'. This sense of shared purpose is, in turn, closely akin to a value consensus, an agreement as to what is important in the life together. It is no coincidence that the utopian communes in which openness abounds are also places with highly developed and widely accepted moral systems. By virtue of being a 'creedal community' (Berger, Hackett, and Miller, 1972), the religious commune unifies its members. (Furthermore, the 'assumptive world' of the commune provides 'detailed guides to behavior' which facilitate the practice of openness (Frank, 1963). The monism of this type of social organization expedites the process of coming to terms with deviant or questionable behaviour. In a monistic group the parties to an analysis of the actions in question are all likely to share a common standard and can thus occupy themselves with its application to the given instance. The pluralistic group, which is the more typical, may be impeded in evaluating behaviour by conflicts over the standards to be applied.

Like minimal competition, minimal hierarchy pertains to the reduction of social barriers. If openness depends on social solidarity, then status and power distinctions will undermine solidarity and consequently also openness. In considering the 'attitude change' method of resolving conflict, of which openness is an example, Walton (1965) theorized that attitude change is feasible only when the parties to a conflict enjoy relative parity. His position supports idea that openness and hierarchy are, to some degree, incompatible. Of course, hierarchy does not necessarily rule out openness. We can all point to leaders who inspired sufficient trust for their subordinates to disagree with them, confide inspired sufficient trust for their subordinates to disagree with them, confide in them, and even confront them personally. The point is that hierarchical distinction drives a wedge, of varying dimensions, between people such that the individual with less power feels less free to be open. Hierarchy breeds asymmetry. Henry (1965) observed, for example, that in heterosexual couples, the traditional ascendancy of the male predisposes the female to sham. (Status differences can also inhibit the social superior, who may, for example, fear that an expression of anger would be magnified out of all proportion.)

It is not that vertical differentiation makes openness impossible; it simply limits the possibilities. *Asymmetrical* openness for instance, is well within the realm of possibility in a hierarchical relationship. In fact, hierarchy and asymmetrical openness are closely associated empirically. Asymmetrical openness is almost necessarily of the moral type, of which religious confession, performance appraisal, and parental socialization are instances. That is, the superordinate in his role as regulator of the subordinate's morals and instructor of the subordinate's competent social behaviour points out deviations from what is expected. By the same token, asymmetrical openness is almost necessarily not the effective, or interpersonal, type. Any meaningful work on personal relations requires that the parties to the relationship are willing to participate on equal terms in the exchange of perceptions and feelings.

The Bruderhof provides an interesting case in point. There openness among members is symmetrical, but between the membership and the top two echelons it is asymmetrical. The leaders, or Servants of the Word, hear members' confessions of wrongdoing or wrong thoughts, but members do not feel free to confront the leadership, and only give vent to their hostility towards a given leader once he steps down from his position (Zablocki, 1971.) Quite different from the ordinary superior in an organization, the position of Servant is endowed with tremendous, awesome authority. In more typical superior–subordinate pairs, openness is not necessarily inconsistent with strong leadership. Even symmetrical openness can thrive in a leader–member relationship which the leadership is democratic and the relationship is mutual.

The reader may have noted the resemblance between the social configuration needed for the introduction of openness and what in sociology has been called the 'primary group' (Cooley) '*Gemeinschaft*' (Tonnies), and 'familistic relations' (Sorokin). Sorokin's familistic relations are described, for example, as:

'... permeated by mutual love, sacrifice, and devotion. They are most frequently found among members of a devoted family and among real friends. Familistic relations represent a fusion of the ego into the "we". Both joys and sorrows are shared in common, and those involved need one another, seek one another, sacrifice for one another, and love one another. Norms of such relations require that participation be all-embracing, all-forgiving, all-bestowing and unlimited' (McKinney, 1963, p. 18).

Although stated in flowery and absolutist language, this description of the familistic relation captures the social features necessary for openness to take root. It is clear that openness has no place in social relations characterized purely by contractual ties, an instrumental and self-centred orientation, and social distance. On the other hand, while it is clear that so-called primary relation is a necessary condition, it is not a sufficient condition for openness. In addition to a strong social bond and the absence of such impediments as divisive competition and prohibitive hierarchy, it is apparent that openness must be actively introduced.

Hence, an additional precondition of openness—institutionalization. Institutionalization is in important measure a matter of legitimation, of establishing the idea that openness is an acceptable and expected mode of interaction. There is, after all, no necessary association between cohesion and openness; the world is littered with cohesive groups that shun self-revelation and mutual confrontation. Moreover, openness is something that must be believed in because it must be entered into willingly. If this invasive method of social control is to work, a person's response to it must be one of 'voluntary cooperation' (Zablocki, 1971). Relevant here is Etzioni's framework regarding the bond between individual and organization. Openness requires that the organization's authority over the individual be *normative* and that the individual's orientation be *moral* in the sense that the individual participates on the basis of his belief in the inherent rightness and worthiness of the organization's purposes. A case which violates this principle is brainwashing, in which organizational authority is coercive and the individual's orientation is one of alienation. Besides being morally reprehensible by our standards, brainwashing tends to be ineffective because it frequently draws compliance as a response. A large proportion of its targets learn to resist by doing a convincing job of going through the motions of revealing themselves, of receiving criticism, and of reinterpreting their lives in terms of the proffered framework (Schein, 1964).

Institutionalization has been defined as the control of human conduct through predefined patterns of conduct; to institutionalize a segment of human activity is to subsume it under social control (Berger and Luckmann, 1967, p. 55). That openness must achieve an institutionalized state in a given social arena is apparent, but how it becomes so is not. The process by which openness is introduced and established is better understood in the case of contemporary behavioural science intervention (Kaplan, 1977) than in the case of historical cases like utopian communes, the Christian church, and Chinese Communist thought reform.

In conclusion, we have established that conditions in society generally do not favour openness. Why this is so raises intriguing fundamental questions about human nature and human civilization that bear significantly on, but lie outside the scope of, this paper.

Summary

The effort in this chapter has been to transcend narrow ideological and technological perspectives on openness in social relationships and to achieve a broad sociological understanding of it as a social phenomenon. With respect to the form it takes, openness is understood to vary on several dimensions, including: considerate vs. abusive, subjective-affective and objective-normative, and contemporaneous vs. historical. With respect to the functions it can assume, openness can be considered to promote *education* of individuals, *regulation* of moral and competent behaviour of system members, and *integration* of people socially and emotionally. Along with its potency as a highly personalized mechanism of social influence, one cannot help but notice the remote reaches of civilization and the special conditions under which openness is known to occur. An analysis of the circumstances supporting its occurrence leads to the conclusion that it is feasible, short of coercion, only when social relations are characterized: (a) by a high level of collective commitment and interpersonal closeness, which in turn is associated with limited competition and minimal hierarchy, and (b) by institutionalization, or the deliberate effort to secure the willing adoption of this atypical social practice. As an integrative device, it is capable of maintaining closeness, or of achieving it in

108

relations with a rich potential for it. But it is inappropriate and virtually useless in disintegrative, competitive, and politicized situations. Because of the need for strong collective identification, openness is viable chiefly within groups. It is irrelevant between groups which are in divisive relation, and it becomes relevant to intergroup relations only when the disparate groups together define themselves as, in some sense, belonging importantly to the same larger group.

Acknowledgement

I would like to thank Clayton Alderfer and John Aram for their critical reading of an earlier draft.

References

Altman, T. (1975) *The Environment and Social Behavior: Privacy, Personal Space, Territory, and Crowding*. Monterey, Cal.: Brooks Cole.
Bach, G. R. and Deutsch, R. M. (1970) *Pairing*. New York: Avon Books.
Bach, G. R. and Wyden, P. (1968) *The Intimate Enemy*. New York: Morrow and Co.
Belgum D. (1969) *Guilt: Where Psychology and Religion Meet*. Minneapolis: Augsberg Publishing.
Berger, B., Hackett, B., and Miller, R. M. (1972) The communal family. In Sussman, M. B. (ed.) *Non-traditional Family Forms in the 1970s*. Minneapolis: National Council on Family Relations.
Berger, P. L. and Luckman, T. (1967) *The Social Construction of Reality*. Garden City, N. Y.: Doubleday.
Durkheim, E. (1893) *The Division of Labor in Society*. New York: Free Press, 1933.
Durkin, H. E. (1964) *The Group in Depth*. New York: International Universities Press.
Frank, J. D. (1963) *Persuasion and Healing*. New York: Schocken.
Freud, S. (1930) *Civilization and its Discontents*. New York: Norton, 1961.
Freud, S. (1950) 'The unconscious.' *Collected Papers*. London: Hogarth Press.
Gamson, W. A. (1968) *Power and Discontent*. Homewood, Ill.: Dorsey.
Goffman, E. (1967) *Interaction Ritual*. Garden City, N.Y.: Doubleday.
Hall, D. T. and Lawler, E. E. (1970) 'Job design and job pressures as facilitators of professional-organization integration.' *Administrative Science Quarterly*, **15**, 271–81.
Hampden-Turner C. (1976) *Sane Asylum*. San Francisco: San Francisco Book Co.
Harrison, R. (1973) 'Role negotiation: a tough-minded approach to team development.' In W. G. Bennis et al., *Interpersonal Dynamics*, Homewood, Ill.: Dorsey.
Henry, J. (1965) *Pathways to Madness*. New York: Random House.
Jourard, S. M. (1964) *The Transparent Self*. New York: Van Nostrand-Reinhold.
Kanter, R. M. (1972) *Commitment and Community: Communes and Utopias in Sociological Perspective*. Cambridge, Mass.: Harvard University Press.
Kaplan, R. E. (1977) 'Maintaining relationships openly: Case study of "total openness" communal organization.' Under editorial review.
Kaplan, R. E. (1977) 'Stages in developing a consulting relation: Case study of a long beginning.' *Journal of Applied Behavioral Science*, (In press).
Koch, S. (1971) 'The image of man implicit in encounter group theory.' In *Psychotherapy 1971*, New York: Aldine Atherton.
Laing, R. D. (1961) *Self and Others*. Baltimore: Penguin Books.

McKinney, J. C. (1963) 'The application of *Gemeinschaft* and *Gesellschaft* as related to other typologies.' In F. Tonnies, *Community and Society* (Loomis, C., ed.), New York: Harper and Row.

Maliver, B. (1973) *The Encounter Game.* New York: Stein and Day.

Mowrer, O. H. (1964) *The New Group Therapy.* New York: Van Nostrand.

Nordhoff, C. (1875) *The Communistic Societies of the United States.* New York, Schocken, 1965.

Noyes, J. H. (1876) *Mutual Criticism.* Oneida, N. Y.: Office of the American Socialist. Republished by Syracuse University Press, 1975.

Schein, E. H. (1964) 'Brainwashing.' In W. G. Bennis, E. H. Schein, D. E. Berlew, and F. I. Steele, *Interpersonal Dynamics*, Homewood, Ill.: Dorsey.

Schutz, A. (1932) *The Phenomenology of the Social World.* Evanston, Ill.: Northwestern University Press, 1967.

Simmel, G. (1950) *The Sociology of Georg Simmel.* K. H. Wolff, ed.) New York: Free Press.

Simmel, G. (1908) 'Conflict.' In Wolff, Kitt, and Bendix (translators), *Conflict and the Web of Group Affiliations.* New York: The Free Press, 1964.

Singer, D. L., Astrachan, B. M., Gould, L. J., and Klein, E. B. (1975) 'Boundary management in psychological work with groups.' *Journal of Applied Behavioral Science*, **II**, 2, 137–76.

Slater, P. E. (1966) *Microcosm: Structural, Psychological and Religious Evolution in Groups.* New York: Wiley.

Stephen, undated. *Hey Beatnik.* Summertown, Tennessee: Book Publishing Co.

Walton, R. E. (1965) 'Two strategies of social change and their dilemmas.' *Journal of Applied Behavioral Science*, 1. no. 2, 167–79.

Zablocki, B. J., 1971. *The Joyful Community: An Account of the Bruderhof, a Communal Movement now in its Third Generation.* Baltimore: Penguin.

Chapter 6

Learning and Lawyering: An Approach to Education for Legal Practice

Lee Bolman

Harvard University, U.S.A.

Law faculty will not teach what they consider unimportant, and cannot teach what they do not know. What they know and consider important depends on the current state of legal research and on the paradigm that informs legal thought and legal education. The paradigm may be viewed as an implicit, intellectual framework that governs how legal scholars view the world, what questions they ask, and what evidence they consider (Kuhn, 1962). The same intellectual model is likely to be shared by practitioners because success in law school requires them to learn how to 'think like a lawyer'. If the paradigm were too much at odds with the demands of the larger society in which the legal system is embedded, it could not survive. But the legal profession is unusually well-insulated by virtue of its control over many of the most powerful institutions in the society. That makes it possible for the system to maintain itself, even if it is not very successful, so long as it remains viable in the eyes of those who are committed to the legal world view.

This chapter reports a pilot effort to explore a series of related questions:

(1) What is the conception of themselves, of their role, and their responsibilities in the legal system that is held by practicing attorneys?

(2) What are some of the elements of the paradigm that governs legal thought and legal education, and what are the limitations or contradictions in that paradigm?

(3) How can educational experiences be designed that enable lawyers to examine and learn from the relationship between their own thought and action?

The pilot effort attempted to combine education and inquiry, using an action-research model. The basic logic of the model involved the following steps:

(1) A group of individuals who were experienced attorneys but inexperienced law teachers participated in a seminar focusing on "clinical" teaching in law.

(2) The participants were asked to provide case examples of lawyer-client relations from their own practice.

(3) Those cases were used to help participants learn about their own lawyering and to explore the implicit theory that informed their practice.

(4) The seminar's teaching process was examined in order to explore the nature of clinical learning and of effective teaching.

An action-theoretical model of education

A lawyer routinely faces a complex, reactive task environment, and cannot make sense of that environment without using some intellectual framework that suggests what variables to attend to, what causal relationships to expect, what information to seek, and what actions to take. In short, the lawyer must have a theory. The regularities in the behaviour of an individual can be conceived to imply a theory of action: a map or programme that informs the individual's behaviour and that can be used to predict what the individual will do. That theory can be conceptualized as including four major components:

(1) *Core value:* basic criteria for making behavioural choices.

(2) *Assumptions:* beliefs or hypotheses about the world, including beliefs about oneself, about one's professional role, about people, about situational contingencies, etc.

(3) *Strategies:* decision-rules that produce recurrent patterns of behaviour.

(4) *Outcomes:* consequences of behaviour, which feed back to influence (confirm, disconfirm, or modify) existing core values, assumptions, and strategies.

Argyris and Schon (1974) distinguish two versions of the theory that informs any action. The *espoused theory* represents an individual's own explanation of his or her behaviour; it is the cognitive 'map' an individual uses to explain and predict his or her own behaviour. The *theory-in-use* is the theory that validly predicts what an individual will do; it is the implicit 'programme' or set of decision rules that guides an individual's choices.

The distinction between map and programme is vital because the two are often discrepant. Individuals' explanations of their own behaviour are always incomplete, in the sense that they do many things that they have never articulated. More troublesome, the espoused theory is often irrelevant to our inconsistent with the theory-in-use. Under those circumstances, individuals are often unaware of important elements of their behaviour, and are unreliable in describing and predicting their behaviour.

When an individual's congnitive map is a poor predictor of the theory-in-use, several consequences commonly ensue:

(1) The individual's behaviour rests on assumptions that are untested or that the individual would view as incorrect;

(2) The theory-in-use in internally inconsistent (the person's behaviour is self-contradictory);

(3) The theory-in-use operates to minimize tests of its own validity and to generate self-fulfilling prophesies.

The distinction between espoused theory and theory-in-use implies an epistemological distinction among four different kinds of knowing. Knowledge is 'intellectual' when it exists in the map but not in the programme—the person can think about it, or talk about it, but cannot do it. Knowledge is 'tacit' when it exists in the programme but not the map—the person can do it, but cannot explain how it is done. Knowledge is 'integrated' when espoused theory and theory-in-use are synchronized—the person can think it and do it. 'Self-knowledge) (or consciousness) consists in knowledge about structure of one's own thought and action (equivalent to an understanding of the paradigm within which one operates).

Most legal education operates in an academic model: students may think and talk about the practice setting, but they are not performing within it. The comparative advantage of such education is in producing intellectual knowledge. But that knowledge may be useless or even harmful when there are significant impediments to applying conceptual learning in the practice environment. That may occur when theory is abstracted at a level that is far removed from practice (as is true of much of the ABA Code of Ethics, for example), when application requires skills that the students do not possess, or when successful application is blocked by the students lack of self-awareness.

In such situations, academic models may produce a change in espoused theory but no corresponding change in the programme informing the student's behaviour. That means that the student, without realizing it, has been helped to become more inconsistent and self-contradictory. A perennial dilemma of education in the humanities is that many persons trained in the humanities *think* much more humanely than they *behave*.

Professional schools often hope that students will learn in practice what they did not learn in school, but the learning students achieve in the field may compound the felony rather than correct it. The practice setting requires students to perform, but not necessarily to reflect on their performance or to articulate its basis. The field is thus an ideal setting for tacit learning. Such tacit learning could actually increase the discrepancies between what a person espouses, and what she or he actually does. In the early phases of practice, the young lawyer is likely to encounter many situations for which she or he received no training, or in which she or he does not know how to apply the training the law school did provide. The student is likely to turn to others in the environment who have more experience (for example, other lawyers, court clerks, administrative and clerical personnel in the law office) in dealing with the safe problems. The experienced others are often willing to share their own theories and thechniques, which unusually serve to simplify and routinize the environment, making it much easier for the young lawyer to function. But they may also function as a form of conservative socialization, and do little to increase the young lawyer's effectiveness or the quality of the service she or he provides. The theories of experienced practitioners often include techniques which do more to make their work easier than to serve their clients, and that include elaborate rationalizations for ineffectiveness that make it easier to externalize failure. If an office is consistently unsuccessful in solving a particular kind of problem, failure may be attributed to excessive pressures from case loads, to unsympathetic judges, to irrational or self-interested bureaucrats, to absurdities in existing law, and even to uncooperative clients. Those theories have a double advantage: they are often partially correct, and they enable practitioners not to feel responsibility for failure to solve the problem.

That suggests that learning in the field setting is often ineffective unless the learner receives help from someone who is effective at bridging theory and practice and who is not locked into the defences, rationalizations and rituals that may be present among practitioners. This paper describes a pilot effort to design an approach to education for lawyers and law teachers that would enable them to integrate intellectual and performance learning, to explore the paradigm that governed their approach to legal practice and to law teaching, and to provide a similar learning experience for their students.

Two models of effectiveness: a dialectic

Research on a variety of adult populations (other than lawyers) indicates that there are consistent differences between the theory that individuals espouse, and the theory that they enact. Those differences correlate with two alternative models of human nature and human effectiveness that constitute a dialectic within our (and probably every) society. One model—for sake of convenience, I will refer to it as the adversarial model—rests on the assumption that many of the most significant resources that humans seek are scarce, and that competition among individuals and groups is inevitably a dominant feature of social reality. The model implies that power-seeking, bargaining and conflict are the central processes in social life, resulting naturally from the pursuit of self-interest by individuals and social systems.

The alternative model—which, for want of a more adequate word, I will refer to as the 'collaborative' model—rests on the assumption that the most significant human 'goods' are not inherently scarce, and that the quality of human life is ultimately dependent not simply on economic goods, but on possibilities for growth, mutuality, trust and love that individuals can create in their lives.

Moral philosophers and religious leaders have generally advocated and emphasized versions of the collaborative model, while pragmatists (for example, business leaders, politicians) have tended to put much of their operating faith in the adversarial model. Research on professionals suggests that it is normative in this society for most individuals to espouse a more collaborative view of society, while enacting a more adversarial one. Argyris and Schon

(1974) found more divergence in espoused theories than in theories-in-use over a large sample of professionals: that is, some professionals espoused a collaborative approach to human interaction, others espoused an adversarial one. But virtually everyone's behaviour mirrored adversarial assumptions. That finding enabled Argyris and Schon (1974) to conceptualize 'Model I' —a generalized theory of human effectiveness that seemed to underlie the behaviour of virtually all the professionals that they studied.

Model I is a theory for action based on the assumption that effective behaviour is unilateral, competitive, protective (of self and others) and private. Under Model I, an actor unilaterally defines goals and strategies, tries to influence others more than they can influence him/her, achieves self-defined goals (at others' expense if necessary) keeps many assumptions and most feelings private, and tries to avoid open conflict and confrontation. The ubiquity of Model I behaviour attests to the possibility of achieving goals while enacting the model's prescriptions, but Argyris and Schon's research also shows that Model I behaviour produces a number of unintended consequences—including minimal learning, defensive and mistrustful relationships, ineffectiveness of relationship and human systems, and long-term deterioration of problem-solving processes.

If that research is correct, and if Model I accurately describes the behaviour prescribed by the adversary system of justice, then such a system should, in the long run, produce increasing self-protectiveness and decreasing freedom, increasing rigidity, decreasing effectiveness and decreasing ability to understand or do anything about the ineffectiveness. There are three basic elements of Model I that lead to long-term ineffectiveness:

(1) Model I suggests that individuals should communicate only that information that will enable them to achieve their own purposes, regardless of the validity or completeness of that information. Model I thus produces a world in which decisions must often be made on the basis of incomplete or inaccurate information.

(2) The Model I emphasis on unilateral protection of self and others encourages a world in which learning is relatively low and occurs largely in areas that are non-threatening. Individuals will rarely be challenged on basic values and assumptions (because such challenge is likely to be experienced as a threat).

(3) A world in which individuals are continually trying to manage and control one another will be one in which individuals experience a low freedom of choice and a restricted range of behavioural options.

In an attempt to find an alternative model of human effectiveness that would not produce the same negative consequences as Model I, Argyris and Schon developed Model II—a model of effective human action based on a more collaborative set of assumptions. Model II posits governing variables of valid information, free choice, and internal commitment. Those governing variables lead to three basic action implications:

(1) Relationships should be jointly managed so that each participant experiences freedom of choice and a high sense of personal causation.

(2) The generation and communication of information should be governed by tests of validity, relevance, and learning. Information should not be distorted or censored in order to achieve one's own purpose or to achieve self-protection.

(3) Because any theory is subject to error and runs the risk of sealing itself off from potential disconfirmation, it is essential that an actor test assumptions publicly, and invite disconfirming evidence.

Several years of research (Argyris and Schon, 1974; Bolman, 1974) indicate that Model II is for many individuals attractive and easy to espouse (because it is so consistent with widely held philosophical and ethical ideals), but is rarely practised. In fact, most individuals cannot produce Model II behaviour, even when they attempt to, and even when they believe they are succeeding.

If the research findings generalize to the legal system and legal practice, there are several implications. Although the Anglo-American legal structure is often labelled as 'the adversary system of justice', that system does not demand or even endorse adversarial behaviour in all of the situations that a lawyer encounters. The norms of the legal profession endorse adversarial behaviour in certain situations (for example, in dealings with opponents), collaborative behaviour in others (for example, in the lawyer–client relationship), and a mixture of adversarial and collaborative behaviours in further situations (such as, in the lawyer's relationship to a court). Such a system is likely to create frequent role conflict and resulting stress, and asks the lawyer to be able to shift back and forth between two very different models of behaviour. The lawyer is likely to experience one of those models—the adversarial one—as easier, safer, quicker, and more effective, and is likely to rely on it much more than on collaborative models (which the lawyer may not know how to implement). Such behaviour is likely to create a number of problems, but the self-sealing qualities of the adversarial model will tend to protect individual lawyers from being aware of their own ineffectiveness, and from seeing their own responsibility for some of the problems they help to create. The result would be legal system in which every actor is aware of problems in the system, but feels no responsibility for those problems, and externalizes responsibility for those problems, and externalizes responsibility on to other individuals or other role groups.

The educational experience described in this paper attempted to create a situation in which a group of practising lawyers could explore their espoused conceptions of effective legal practice, and the conceptions implied by their behaviour. Through that exploration we hoped to achieve a deeper understanding of the paradigm governing legal practice, and of the problem of producing educational experiences that enable lawyers to examine and learn from the relationship between their thought and action.

The seminar context

For several years, two faculty members at a major law school had been teaching 'clinical' courses in which law students worked in field settings with (mostly poor) clients. The clinical courses included lectures, seminars, and field supervision of each student by a practising attorney (some working full-time as law teachers, some working part-time while maintaining a professional practice).

By most measures, the course had been extremely successful, particularly in terms of student evaluations. Many students rated it as the most useful element in their legal education. Yet the faculty was disturbed by several observations:

(1) The faculty felt they still knew little about clinical education: that is, they lacked a systematic conception of the most effective ways to help students learn from their field experiences.

(2) The faculty was particularly concerned that the supervising attorneys had little clarity about their teaching tasks. The attorneys focused mostly on institutional knowledge (such as where the courts were, who the judges were) and rule knowledge (such as the state housing code). Both of those were important to the students' ability to serve clients, but were tangential to the central learning goals of the course (which stressed the student's developing a conception of effective legal practice, and developing the competence to implement that conception).

(3) Mere exposure to the field did not make students into effective lawyers. Indeed, the faculty perceived the standards of legal practice in many offices to be inadequate. If students learned by watching experienced lawyers, they were being conservatively socialized into accepting a low standard of service to clients.

(4) The faculty felt frustrated with their own relationships to the field supervisors, and the field supervisors' relationships with one another. Their hope of creating a group of people who could explore ideas and learn from one another continually foundered on high levels of competitiveness and low levels of listening and risk-taking.

The faculty members invited the author of this paper to work with them in creating a learning experience for field supervisors that would take place prior to the beginning of the academic term, and help the supervisors learn more about how to approach their teaching tasks.

We evolved a seminar design which flowed out of the earlier discussion of theories for action, and proceeded from the assumption that effective clinical education requires simultaneous exploration of thoughts and action (espoused theory, and theory-in-use). In order to explore that relationship with any given individual, the individual needs to provide evidence of both. There are a variety of ways to accomplish this, but an efficient vehicle is a 'personal case experience'. Each participant in the seminar was asked to describe a personal incident involving relations between lawyer and client. There were no other constraints on the choice of a case situation except that the attorneys were asked to select one which they saw as 'challenging' and 'of significant relevance to their own personal and professional development'.

The instruction for writing the case asked the writer to provide the following elements:

(1) A brief description of the context in which the lawyer–client exchange took place.

(2) A description of the lawyer's goals or objectives in the situation.

(3) An indication of major assumptions that were influencing the attorney's approach.

(4) A sample dialogue in the form of a reconstructed script for part of the conversation between lawyer and client. The dialogue was to be accompanied by the underlying thoughts, reactions and feelings that the lawyer might have had during the exchange.

All of the elements except the fourth provide evidence mostly of espoused theory, but the sample dialogue was intended to provide evidence of the lawyer's actual behaviour in working with the client. Previous research (Argyris and Schon, 1974; Bolman, 1974) indicates that such a script does provide reliable evidence of an individual's behaviour (though not necessarily of the other person's behaviour). In effect, the same programme that initially produced the behaviour operates again when individuals try to reconstruct what they did. That is not true when the individual provides an abstract or inferential description of the behaviour. For example, one supervising attorney described a meeting with a student in which he said his strategy was to 'let her talk and just try to draw everything out'. The attorney's reproduction of the conversation showed that he had guided the conversation through a series of leading questions that told the student what to talk about.

The seminar process

The seminar opened with a presentation of the action theoretic conceptual framework discussed earlier in this paper. The seminar leader then suggested that the group progress through discussion of each of the case situations that the participants had written. Three goals were proposed for those discussions:

(1) *Learning about individuals' lawyering.* One purpose of the discussion of each case was to help the case-writer develop a fuller, more systematic understanding of his or her lawyering in that situation.

(2) *Learning about clinical teaching.* As the group discussed each case, participants would be engaged in the process of teaching the case-writer. The

behaviour of group members could be examined in order to clarify the teaching strategies, and to examine the effectiveness of alternative strategies.

(3) *Learning about legal practice and the legal system.* As the group proceeded through a number of cases written by different lawyers, it could begin to search for patterns or generalizations which illuminated the nature of legal practice, the nature of the system within which lawyers work, and alternative models of effective legal practice.

Analysis of individual cases

The espoused norms of the legal profession—including the American Bar Association's Code of Professional Responsibility—imply a lawyer–client relationship based primarily on collaborative assumptions. The lawyer is enjoined to exercise professional judgement 'solely for the benefit of the client and free of compromising inferences and loyalties' (Canon 5), and to 'represent the client zealously' (Canon 7). The code is inexplicit on the question of how the client's benefit is to be determined, but EC 7–7 suggests that the client— not the attorney—has the right to determine what actions ought to be taken to further the client's interests. The Code of Professional Responsibility sets a high standard. If attorneys were actually able to meet such a standard, it would be difficult to explain the low esteem in which lawyers are so often held by the general public (Mindes, 1975). Nor would one expect such a standard to lead to an observation such as Auerbach's (1976) that 'the bar, like the Church, relies upon mysterious procedures to instill reverence and to remove itself from the people'.

Our expectation was that lawyers did not meet such a standard—not even lawyers who were well-trained and sincerely motivated to provide high standards of client service. We anticipated that lawyers' behaviour with their clients would largely reflect adversarial, Model I assumptions. An analysis of eleven cases provided the following evidence relevant to those expectations:

(1) In ten of eleven cases, the lawyer withheld relevant information from the client, or distorted information which she or he gave to the client. (For example, one lawyer did not tell the client he did not really want to take the case. Several did not tell the client that they disbelieved what the client was telling them.)

(2) In ten of the eleven cases, the lawyer controlled and managed the nature and direction of the conversation.

(3) In seven of the cases, the lawyer explicitly rejected the client's preferred option, and pressured or coerced the client to accept the lawyer's definition of a correct decision. (For example, two lawyers pressured clients not to testify even though they wanted to. One lawyer pressured a client to plead guilty despite the client's insistence that he was innocent.)

(4) In seven of the cases, the lawyer behaved in ways that tended to create client mystification and dependence on the attorney.

(5) It was rare for the client to raise questions about the attorney's strategy or judgement. In each of four instances when it did happen, the attorney responded in ways that discouraged or shut off such questioning. (For example, one attorney responded to a suggestion of an alternative course of action by saying, 'That would have been unreasonable. I must be reasonable in my dealings with other attorneys. I have a professional reputation to protect'.)

The participants in the seminar did not espouse adversarial behaviour as optimal behaviour for the lawyer–client relationship; for the most part, they subscribed to the espoused norms of the profession. But their espoused conception of good lawyering did not predict their behaviour very well. We anticipated that the same problem would also occur in the seminar. The task of the seminar asked the participants to focus on learning about their own lawyering, and on helping others to do the same. But our conceptual perspective led to the expectation that the lawyers would behave toward one another as they had toward their clients—by withholding or distorting relevant information, by trying to dominate one another, and by defending themselves from being questioned or challenged.

If the prediction were correct, the participants would be expected to have difficult creating an effective learning environment for one another. The same behaviour would also inhibit their ability to perform effectively as teachers when they began to supervise students. That implied that a major task of the seminar was to help participants become aware of their own teaching behaviour during the seminar process, to explore the consequences of that behaviour, and to consider alternative approaches to teaching.

The first case to be discussed was presented by a lawyer—we will call her Joan—who had represented a client accused of several bank robberies. She described the case situation as follows:

'D. F. had a long criminal record and was facing federal criminal charges on four separate bank robberies. Another lawyer represented him at trial on the first robbery, and he was convicted.

D. F. vehemently asserted his innocence on all charges, claiming the FBI was framing him. He was a difficult, highly emotional, demanding client. . . .

Our investigation of the three pending charges showed a strong alibi defense on one, a mediocre alibi defense on the second, and no viable defense on the third. On each case, the government had eye witness testimony, surveillance films which resembled the defendant, and a handwriting expert. A defense analysis confirmed that D. F. was the author of the demand notes used in the robberies. . . .

When consolidation was discussed with the judge, he indicated that if D. F. would plead guilty to one of the remaining charges, he would not increase the current sentence of 0 to eight years. He made it clear that if D. F. went to trial and was convicted, a substantial additional sentence would be imposed. . . .

I was convinced that D. F. was guilty and would be convicted and sought to persuade him to plead guilty. I stressed the strength of the government's evidence and the weakness of our defenses. I capitalized on his poor health, which made him uncomfortable at the Federal Detention headquarters. I enlisted his wife as an ally in my effort to coerce a plea. In retrospect, I was also influenced by my dislike of D. F. which led me to try to finish with his cases as soon as possible: my reluctance to litigate and lose, and my credibility with prosecutor and judge.

The dialogue [reproduced below] took place after D. F. had agreed to plead guilty on the condition he did not have to admit his guilt (enter an *Alford* plea). Immediately before the time of pleading, the Judge had refused to accept that plea, requiring an admission of guilt from the defendant.'

Joan presented the following dialogue as an illustration of her conversation with D. F. (The left-hand side presents part of Joan's conversation with D. F., while the right-hand side presents her underlying thoughts, reactions, and feelings.)

Dialogue	*Joan's underlying thoughts*
D. F.: No, no way. I'm not going to say I did something I didn't do. I'm going to go to trial. I don't care what happens.	I can't try these cases. The Judge will be angry if the plea falls apart.
Me: But, Don, you can't win. They've got the bank tellers who identify you, the pictures, the handwriting....	
D. F.: They can't prove I did something I didn't do. They can't say it's me if I wasn't there.	
Me: I know, but look what happened at the first trial.	Why does he keep up this ridiculous story?
D. F.: Yeah, but that was Jones [other lawyer]. He sold me out.	That's what he'll say about me if we go to trial. He'll probably sue me for incompetence.
Me: Don, our only chance would be to try all three robberies together, and if we lose you could get up to 60 years on top of the time you've already got.	I know there's no way he could get 60 years, but may be it will scare him. And he really cares about his wife's feelings, and getting out of the jail he's in.
And Mary (D. F.'s wife) doesn't want you to go to trial. If you plead today, you'll be out of [detention centre] in a week.	
D. F.: What would I have to say?	I've got him!
Me: You have to tell the judge you went into the bank, gave the teller the note, and took the money.	

122

D. F.: And you really think that's
what I should do?

Me: Don, if I thought we had any
chance, I'd say fight it. But I really
think this is the only way.

D. F.: (who is crying now) O.K.,   I feel awful. I hate him. I hate my job.
O.K., I'll do it.   Why did I ever get stuck with this
     case?

Joan's case concluded with the following epilogue:

'D. F. pleaded guilty and received concurrent time. A year later, the government revealed that it had discovered evidence establishing his innocence. The convictions were vacated, and he was released.'

The discussion of the case in the workshop was rich and varied—it touched on legal options that Joan might have pursued, the nature of the criminal justice system and the problems it creates for defence attorneys, the role of judges, and the ethical dilemmas lawyers face. If there was one issue that received more attention than any other, it was the nature of lawyers' obligations to their clients: for example, do lawyers ever have the right to coerce a client's plea? What are the implications of the concept of client autonomy?

The discussion was difficult and challenging for Joan. She believed intellectually in the concept of client autonomy, but found it difficult to see anything else she could have done. She did not believe a lawyer has a right to mislead her client, yet acknowledged that she had exaggerated the likely consequences of losing at trial. As she explored those issues, she became clearer about the way in which her own assumptions and feelings influenced the advice she gave the client. Joan realized, for example, that she would have felt responsible and guilty had D. F. gone to trial and lost (even if D.F. had made the choice against her advice). Implicitly, Joan had decided it was better to coerce her client than to allow the client to take a risk that she found intolerable. Joan was able to acknolwledge that if she were the client, she would not want her attorney to take the choice out of her hands; but she had felt that, as a lawyer, she could/should make a decision that was more rational and less emotional than the one her client seemed to be making.

The discussion also illustrated several generalizations which were valid not only for Joan's case, but for virtually all of the cases.

(1) The lawyer was unaware of significant discrepancies between intent and behaviour

Joan, for example, believed in client autonomy, and she had sought to coerce her client. She believed in helping the client make informed decisions, yet withheld significant information (for example, her realistic estimate of the probable sentence; her concern about the judge's becoming angry if the plea fell apart; her fear that D. F. would brame her if he lost at trial). She espoused honesty in lawyer–client relations, yet distorted some of the information that she provided to her client (such as by exaggerating the likely sentence if D. F. were convicted at trial).

(2) The lawyer's behaviour was significantly influenced by assumptions that the lawyer had never tested publicly

Joan's behaviour was influenced by assumptions that her client was lying, that he was not capable of making an informed decision, that he was less able than she to separate feelings from reality, that he would blame her if he lost, and that none of the above could be discussed with the client without impairing the relationship. D. F. was told that there was only one viable choice, but was not told much of the reasoning that led to his lawyer's conclusion.

(3) Lawyers' concerns about their own competence and self-esteem produced self-protective behaviours that, paradoxically, tended to reinforce those concerns

Joan was concerned about losing at trial, about disrupting her relationship with the judge, about feeling responsible if D. F. received a long sentence, about being blamed or sued by D. F. Those concerns produced self-protective behaviours—she kept the concerns private, and attempted to induce the client to behave in the ways that Joan felt would minimize the dangers. Yet she left the exchange feeling 'awful. I hate him. I hate my job. Why did I ever get stuck with a case like this?'

(4) The lawyer's behaviour tended to reinforce a behavioural world in which both lawyer and client experience low freedom of choice, high defensiveness, and limited possibilities for learning or for improving the system

Joan saw herself occupying a role in a legal system that severely restricted the choices available both to her and her client. She resented the fact that the judge gave her only one not-very-good option. Yet she did the same thing to her client. She and other lawyers were largely unaware of the degree to which their own assumptions restricted their behaviour, and their behaviour restricted their clients' freedom. In virtually every case situation, there was evidence of the same paradox—lawyers' unintentionally behaving in ways that mirrored and reinforced the very aspects of the legal system that the lawyers wanted to change.

There were differences among individuals, but most members of the group readily saw elements of ineffectiveness in Joan's behaviour, and could see connections between Model I and problem areas in Joan's relationship with her client. But the group's attempts to help mirrored the same self-protective and adversarial assumptions that governed Joan's behaviour in her case.

The first teaching strategy employed by many participants was seeking additional information. They asked questions that dealt with almost everything except Joan's behaviour—the sequence of events that led to the situation, the client, the judge, the conditions in the detention centre, Joan's experiences in other similar cases, etc. The questions implied that there was significant information that had to be obtained in order to facilitate the teaching process. As the questions continued, more and more information was elicited. But each new bit of information suggested another question that needed to be asked, producing another bit of information and then another question. The cycle continued, producing more confusion and divergence than learning. None of the group members thought to ask Joan whether their teaching was useful to her. When the seminar leader did ask, she indicated that she thought people were trying to be helpful, but she was not sure what she was gaining.

As information-seeking appeared increasingly unsuccessful, some group members began to use an alternative form of questioning: interrogation through a series of leading questions, as if Joan were being cross-examined. The questioners rarely indicated what agenda or set of issues they were hoping to explore, or how the questions were designed to help Joan learn. In some cases, they did not know. In some cases, they were reluctant to make public a hunch that might prove to be wrong. In still other cases, the questioners felt that surfacing their agenda might make Joan less open or more defensive. In any event, cross-examination usually produced frustration for both parties—the questioners became discouraged that they were not getting anywhere, and Joan continued to wonder what she was learning.

As the questioning approach failed, group members turned to more direct approaches, and began to tell Joan what she had done wrong and what she should have done. But the teachings usually came in the form of global, data-free assertions. Joan was told, for example, that, 'It is the lawyer's duty to counteract that emotional response in the client'. But Joan was not told how such a proposition had been derived, how she could test its validity in her situation, nor what she could have done to implement such a proposition (that is, if she accepted such a conception of the lawyer's duty, what are the behaviours that would enable her to counteract a client's emotional response?).

When Joan responded to such teaching with signs of resistance or disagreement, the teachers often became even more directive, telling her that she 'should' or 'must' accept their views on effective lawyering. When, for example, Joan expressed doubt that there was anything else she could have done, she was told, 'You must give the client a choice'. Such a message is self-contradictory and creates a double-bind for the recipient. Joan was being told that she was ineffective with her client for doing what her teacher was now doing to her. Both Joan and the group members were largely unaware of the degree to which much of their teaching was internally contradictory and self-cancelling.

What everyone was aware of was a sense of confusion and frustration. They were trying to help a lawyer learn about a specific piece of lawyering; they were doing the best they knew how to do; they had spent several hours at it; yet no one felt very successful and no one knew what else to do. Some participants responded to their frustration by concluding that the attempt to teach Joan was irrelevant to their future teaching tasks. On several occasions, group members turned to the two members of the law faculty to ask, in effect, 'Can't you just tell us how to teach?' The faculty's answer was, 'We tried that in the past, and it didn't work. Moreover, we are not sure we know enough about how to do clinical teaching'. Many members of the group were reluctant to take no for an answer.

The seminar leader did provide an alternative model of teaching in his inter-actions with Joan, but group members were initially sceptical or negative above his approach. He did not ask questions about the situational context, did not cross-examine her, and did not offer her untestable assertions about what she should have done. He did focus on the evidence in the case about Joan's behaviour and her internal world, and began to surface areas of ineffectiveness and inconsistency revealed by the case.

The leader's behaviour created a dilemma for group members. When he advocated alternative approaches to teaching, he was arguing for behaviours that most group members espoused, but did not behave (such as being honest, able to influenced, testing assumptions, giving clients and students choices). They did not behave them because they feared the consequences, but were largely unaware of the fear and of their own inconsistencies. Anyone who did behave consistently with their espoused values was a threat, because his be-haviour surfaced their inconsistencies. The initial response of many group members was to attack the leader for being too direct, punitive, or inhumane. The leader attempted to respond by inviting feedback and inquiry around his teaching and its effects. The resulting dialogue provided the lawyers with the first example they had experienced of an effective clinical teaching process. When the leader was told, for example, 'If you're going to be an effective teacher, then you have to deal warmly and humanely with what you've done', he invited specific examples of what he had done that was inhumane, and what he might have done differently. He went on to suggest that it was difficult for him to learn from others who offered evaluations and attributions about his motives, but did not provide him with help in exploring what he had done to produce such reactions.

The resulting dialogue began to surface some of the difficulties and con-tradictions the participants were experiencing. They were learning that when individuals—even highly competent attorneys—present evidence of their practice, the evidence is likely to disclose significant examples of lawyers' failure to meet their own standards of good performance. If a teacher diagnoses areas of ineffectiveness, but does not discuss them, then the teacher has diffi-culty testing the diagnosis, and the learner is protected from confronting areas of ineffectiveness. If the teacher does confront those areas, the learner is likely to experience stress. To the extent that the teacher is programmed to protect self and others from such stress, the easier course is to be silent. Risk is minimized, but so is learning.

The participants also began to see that they were not very effective at clinical teaching or learning. The seminar had asked them to create an experiential, learning process, and they reacted with frustration and puzzlement. They had nodded assent to the idea, without realizing that they did not know what it meant. Surprisingly, they were unable to apply one of the basic skills involved in 'thinking like a lawyer'—the ability to infer principles from concrete cases and to test those principles against subsequent cases. If the lawyers participating in the seminar had learned such a skill, they were unable to generalize it to the context of clinical teaching. Their behaviour suggested that they had learned only a part of that skill. They were comfortable applying existing rules, and invited the faculty to provide them with rules for how to teach. But they had little sense of how to discover new insights or to invent new rules or concepts. The participants' legal education had prepared them to be rule-followers more than legal thinkers.

Seminar outcomes

The clinical seminar met intensively for a total of 35 hours over a two-week period, and moved through a discussion of lawyer–client cases presented by each of the twelve participants. In every instance, the case-presenters became aware of elements of their lawyering that they had not recognized, and began to see their were other options they might have considered. But few of the participants left the seminar feeling certain that they could significantly alter their own teaching or lawyering patterns. As a result, the group chose to meet on a voluntary basis, once a month, over the subsequent academic years to discuss experiences they were encountering in working with students.

At one of those meetings, Joan presented a new case, deriving from an experience with one of her students, S. S had been assigned a case involving an inmate in a state penitentiary. While S was interviewing his client, the client became angry and walked out of the meeting. S inferred that the walk-out represented the client's way of firing him, and wrote the following letter to the client:

'I'm very sorry that you resented my questions this afternoon so strongly. If I failed to explain my purpose in asking questions related to your parole having been revoked, and in asking other questions related to your 'nerves,' then certainly you have cause to be angry.

An attorney in order to represent his client effectively must ask basic questions so that he can avoid surprise later in court or in a hearing room. By learning so much, the attorney is able to present the facts in a light most favorable to his client.

I did not mean to pry into your life out of idle curiosity.'

(After further paragraphs explaining why he asked the questions he did):

'I understand your leaving the visitors' room in such haste and anger and disappointment to mean that you no longer wish me or the [university legal assistance project] to represent you any further in this matter.

If you change your mind—or if you would like to talk further—please call me at.... I will be happy to talk further. If you want to talk to someone else, that can easily be arranged. But if I do not hear from you, I will consider your remark, 'Forget it,' to mean you no longer want our assistance.

Again, I am sorry if I failed to explain myself completely to you.

Joan's case presentation was based on a conference she held with the student after receiving a copy of his letter. Joan gave the following description of her intent in the meeting:

'I suspect that what I have been doing with students is telling them what to do, or deciding for them. And I wanted to see if I could really help a student think. If you had talked to me right after the interview with the student, and asked me how I did, I would have said terrific. I thought it was good field supervision—sensitive, aware, tuned, helpful, guiding. When I played the tape back later, it sounded less terrific, but I couldn't think of anything wrong with it. Then I brought it to Bill [another field supervisor] and asked him which parts I should use for case discussion. He reappeared in less than 10 minutes, and said, those pages and those pages. I looked at the two things he picked out, and it was like a light bulb flashed. So one of the dilemmas is how is it going to take less than 20 hours, a typed transcript, and outside assistance before I can begin to see my own behavior.

As she spoke, Joan indicated she was now clear that she was not very satisfied with what she had done, but was not very clear on what the problems were, or on what else she could have done. Part of the dialogue between Joan and the student is represented in the following transcription:

'Joan: "Well, I guess the first question is about your going out there today. Do you feel you want to represent [client] at the hearing?"

S: "Well, I'd like to, but it's just not up to any attorney to impose himself on a person and say, 'Look, you really need representation. It is in your best interest and I know where your best interests are.' "

Joan: "But in terms of an opening line, which is really where we were at, supposing you said something like, 'I came back today because I was really worried about you, and I wonder if we can talk a little bit.' "

S: "It is more sympathetic. Ah, I don't know. (Talks about experience as a volunteer teacher abroad.) One of the things I learned is that if people really aren't motivated on their own to ask for help, really, you get into trouble later on."

Joan: "But he is motivated. He called us, and when you got out there, he practically grapped ahold of you. He was so desperate for help."

S: "Well, he is, but the question is whether he is still motivated. I don't mind driving out there, that's no problem. I just felt the ball was in his court. I'm worried enough to go out there, and see, but in terms of starting from the position of 'I'm worried about you and I wanted to help....' "

Joan: "But it's true, isn't it?"

S: "Well, I am, but I am not worried in that sense. I guess it..."

Joan: "When you told me the story of this guy who was being absolutely f— over by the institution..."

S: "That's right."

Joan: "His hands shake, and he can't work in the furniture shop, and they keep sending him to the furniture shop where his hands would no doubt be caught in machines and fall off and things like that. And they had him like in this Catch-22 situation, right? And that struck you as bad, and you were outraged enough about the case so that you wanted to work on it over the weekend, so that we met late on Friday, and all that kind of stuff. So that it's true that you're worried about him." '

Joan's goal was to stimulate S's thought; her behaviour told S what to think, do and feel. Despite her espoused goals, Joan was actually using the same strategies with the student that she had earlier used with D.F. As she got feedback from the group, Joan was able to see that her behaviour was much less sensitive and more coercive than intended. As she explored more deeply, she began to see that she was manipulating the student to feel guilty about the possibility that the client might be harmed. Joan realized that such guilt feelings had led her to coerce D. F. to plead guilty. She now found that, unintentionally, she was asking S to reproduce behaviours that she did not value in her own practice.

At the beginning of the discussion of Joan's case, the faculty member asked Joan to discuss her evaluation of her performance, and her learning objectives for the discussion. Asking a case-presenter to open the discussion serves several purposes: (1) It encourages individuals to take responsibility for diagnosing their own behaviour, and becoming explicit about their learning goals; (2) it provides information to the group about the kind of help the case-writer is seeking; (3) it also provides the group a sense of the case-writer's current level of understanding of his or her behaviour. Knowing the case-writer's current diagnosis makes it easier for others to confirm or disconfirm.

Joan offered the following summary of what she saw happening in the case:

'Joan: "When I read S's letter [to the client], I was really bothered by it. It was defensive and almost accusatory, and I was convinced that to the client, the letter said, 'Goodbye'. I wanted S to see that he couldn't just shift the responsibility onto the client. What I was not aware of, and didn't help him with, is that I think S was really upset and baffled by the client's walking out. I didn't hear him saying, 'If a client treats me like that, why can't I just walk out and get a new client'. In the second section of the dialogue, I am telling him we are going into federal court, and it is clear that the more I talk about it, the more uncomfortable he is. 'My God, is Joan really expecting me to go into Federal Court? I don't know how to do it.' The other general observation I had was that I was shocked to learn that I did three-quarters of the talking. How can I give him a chance to think for himself if I keep talking all the time." '

After Joan had presented her self-diagnosis, discussion was opened to members of the group, and different individuals began to raise a variety of questions and concerns about the case: Did Joan see parallels between this case and the case she had presented in the autumn? (Joan indicated that she had not thought very much about that possibility.) Was Joan aware of the fact that some of her statements to S had a strongly guilt-inducing quality? (Joan had not realized it at the time, but indicated that part of the motive for guilt-induction was a concern about students' lack of zeal in defending their clients.) Could it be that Joan was having difficulty listening to S's feelings of apprehension because she was finding it difficult to be aware of her own feelings? (Joan found that to be a plausible hypothesis.) Why had Joan never discussed the letter that S had to the client, since it was the letter that had signalled the problem, and it provided the most direct evidence of student performance? (Joan was surprised to realize that she had not discussed the letter directly. As she explored why, she guessed that she feared her negative evaluation of the letter might upset S.)

One example of the quality of the interaction in the seminar comes from the following dialogue between Joan and the seminar leader:

'Leader: "Early in the dialogue, you say to S, 'In terms of an opening line, suppose you say to the client, "I came back today because I was worried about you and wonder if we can talk a little bit." ' One question is, how did you decide that, at that point in the dialogue, you should talk about an opening line, and how did you decide on the particular one you suggested. I imagine that you went through a diagnostic process to get to that statement."

Joan: "Yes, but I haven't stated it."

Leader: "So, as a student, I get a prescription but not the diagnosis that led to the prescription."

Joan: "So that all I have learned, if I am the student, is that Joan seems to know how to think like a lawyer and will give me answers when I have a problem. But I have not learned a thinking process; I've learned a path to Joan's door."

Leader: "Or, at least, I haven't seen a model of her thinking process. It is like your reasoning process is a black box which puts out answers, but it's hard to know what happens inside the box." ' '

Joan was clearer that she had gone through an extensive diagnostic process, and had not shared her diagnosis with S. But she was concerned about what would happen if she did:

'Joan: "I am worried that the next time I talk to S, if I start out by sharing my diagnosis, I may, still do everything else exactly as I did it here." ' '

The statement demonstrates Joan's growing awareness of how difficult it was for her to change her behaviour. As the group moved toward the discussion of alternative strategies that Joan might have used in dealing with S, it was clear that the group members were split on the issue of how direct Joan could or should have been in confronting the parts of S's lawyering that she saw as ineffective. The following excerpt illustrates the discussion around that issue:

'B: "In terms of S's letter, I am not sure how reflective of his personality it is because..."

Leader: "Not his personality, his lawyering."

B: "I'm not even sure of that. He's in a new situation. The prisoner unexpectedly lashed out at him. Given his stage of legal education, and his lack of training—to us it's bad lawyering, but I would be very hard-pressed to tell him it was bad, given where he's coming from."

Leader: "To say 'you are bad' is one thing. The message I would want to raise with S is that it seems to me that when I read this sentence in your letter, it could have the following consequences on the client.

B: "But he would see that as critical."

Leader: "I think he would, and he'd be right. It is critical. Are you saying that you would not want to do that?"

B: "I'm saying I would raise with him, I think, the problems of a letter like that, but discuss it more in the context of 'I don't think this is what one would normally expect of you.' I guess I'm saying there should be more explanation of the circumstances."'

The example illustrates a frequent and important dynamic in the learning process—the faculty member and one of the participants each is offering a theory of how to teach. The role of the faculty member at that point is not to prove that his theory is correct, but to help in the process of clarifying the difference between the two theories, and searching for ways where people who disagree can test their respective points of view.

Joan's case illustrates a number of generalizations that emerged consistently from the clinical learning experience:

(1) A case situation in which a lawyer presents evidence of both intent and behaviour will—almost invariably—reveal areas of ineffectiveness and inconsistency that the lawyer does not recognize.

(2) Many of the basic elements in an adult's behavioural programme are overlearned to the point that the individual cannot choose to behave differently, even though the individual retains the perception of such choice. (Individuals tend to attribute low freedom to external constraints, but internal constraints are often more powerful.)

(3) A lawyer may learn of areas of ineffectiveness and set out to change his or her behaviour, yet continue to be ineffective, and continue to be unaware of the ineffectiveness.

(4) Individuals often believe that their performance has improved when it is unchanged. Self-reports are unreliable as an index of behavioural learning.

(5) An individual may examine his or her behaviour with great care and still not see areas of ineffectiveness which are easily seen by outside observers. That implies that individuals are often not able to learn from their experience and need outside help even to learn that they are not learning.

Those generalizations imply that true clinical education in law can only occur in a learning environment which provides evidence of both espoused theory and theory-in-use. Such evidence can be the basis for an initial learning

phase—the learner's intellectual understanding of current areas of ineffectiveness and inconsistency. By itself, such intellectual learning may lead to
a false sense of optimism, because the learner may believe that it will be relatively easy to change ineffective behaviour. The next phase in learning, then,
is for the learner to find out whether or not he or she knows how to create
alternative strategies, implement them, and test their effectiveness. The abilities to create, implement, and test are the basic skills for 'learning how to
learn'. Many lawyers and law students find that they do not possess those skills
and must learn them before they can improve their effectiveness.

Faculty members in a clinical learning process have a dual task. They must
provide help to individuals with respect to the specific, substantive focus of
the learning context (whether it is law teaching, or lawyering, or something else),
but they must also help people develop the learning skills that they do not
possess. The faculty members carry out that primary task through several
instructional modes as shown below.

Providing theory

Learners cannot learn to integrate theory and practice in an environment in
which there is no theory. If students do not bring conceptual sophistication to
the learning environment, the faculty member must be prepared to provide
the concepts and theories that are missing. Often, it is particularly critical
for faculty members to be able to provide a theory of the learning process.
The lawyers in our pilot project often struggled with questions like: How do
people learn? What is the relationship between intellectual, behavioural,
and emotional learning? What criteria can be used to judge whether or not
a lawyering performance is an effective one? How can a person learn from experience? If the faculty member is able to respond to such questions, students
are helped to develop their own theories.

Providing a model of effective and ineffective teaching

Students who learn that their performances are not effective are likely to feel
impatient to find a solution, and frustrated by the difficulty of developing a
better alternative. At such a point, the faculty member can help by demonstrating alternative behaviours and by discussing the theory underlying those
strategies. It is neither hoped nor expected that participants will become carbon
copies of the teacher, but that the instructor's model will provide new options
and help students to engage in a process of informed experimentation.

Providing analysis and feedback on the seminar process

One of the critical elements in attorneys' effectiveness is the ability to monitor,
learn from the respond to events in real time. The attorneys found that very
difficult in the seminar context. Initially, the clinical learning process was

confusing and frustrating. The participants found it difficult to learn, doubted that they were making progress, and found themselves unable to analyse why the process was frustrating. At such times, the faculty member, who has more experience and a more explicit theory of the learning process, is able to intervene with an analysis of the process. Such interventions are particularly critical when the individual participants are behaving in ways that impede the learning process, but are unable to see their own responsibility for the problems that they create.

Demonstrating a personal commitment to learning

In clinical teaching—perhaps more than in any other form of education—the teacher's openness to learning, willingness to inquire into his or her own effectiveness, and ability to stay in touch with the effects of his or her behaviour are critical determinants of effectiveness. It is common for learners to challenge the teacher's behaviour and theories. The teacher who becomes defensive when confronted provides a model of how not to learn from one's experience, and how to cut off potentially valid information.

Providing psychological support

As Joan's case illustrates, the clinical learning process often asks individuals to confront and to learn from fundamental areas of inconsistency and/or ineffectiveness in their own practice. Such a process is often anxiety-producing and painful, and individuals are unlikely to remain open to learning unless the environment helps them to trust both their own capacity to learn, and the capacity of others in the group to help them learn.

Summary and conclusions

This study reports a pilot, educational effort that was intended to explore three related questions:

(1) What conception of their role and their responsibilities is held by practicing attorneys?

(2) What do attorneys' conceptions of their role imply about the intellectual paradigm that underlines the legal system?

(3) How can more effective, clinical, learning experiences be designed for law students?

A seminar was held for a group of lawyers who were about to become field supervisors for students at a major law school. The primary purpose of the seminar was to help the lawyers develop their skills as teachers. Each of the participating attorneys was asked to generate a case example of a lawyer–client transaction on the basis of his or her own experience as a practitioner.

Those cases showed a number of significant contradictions between the espoused norms of the legal profession, and the lawyers' behaviour. The profession states that the duty of the lawyer is to serve the client's interest zealously and without compromise, and that lawyers ought not to abrogate client's freedom of choice with respect to their legal options. Yet we found that lawyers consistently dominated their clients, restricted their clients' freedom, and substituted their own judgement for the client's in determining what was in the client's best interests.

The espoused norms of the profession suggest that a lawyer's behaviour should appropriately follow an adversarial model in dealing with the client's opponents, but a collaborative one in dealing with the client. The evidence in the seminar was the lawyers followed adversarial models in relating to clients. We had no direct evidence of attorneys' behaviour with other actors in the legal system, but our observations were consistent with Bellow's (1975) finding that attorneys often collude with opposing attorneys so that both lawyers can control their clients and reduce uncertainty.

Lawyers have an exposed obligation to help their clients make informed judgements about legal options. Yet we found repeated instances in which lawyers withheld significant information, provided scanty discussion of legal options, or provided their clients with a distorted picture of the legal situation. The lawyers believed that they were acting in the client's best interest, but had no way of testing the assumption that they could judge better than their client what the client needed. Such behaviour creates a world in which clients feel mystified, powerless, and thankful for whatever favours the lawyer bestows. The attorney attains a position of mystery–mastery through presenting the law as a thicket of arcane knowledge, obscure jargon and quaint latinisms, impenetrable to the uninitiated. Clients' dependence and mystification make it harder for them to judge how well their attorney serves those interests. Lawyers are enabled to get on with the business of doing what they know is right, but cannot be entirely sure whose interests they are furthering (their clients', or their own, or none of the above) because that issue has been rendered largely undiscussable.

Most of the lawyers who participated in the seminar were unaware of the degree to which their practice violated both the espoused norms of the profession and their own standards of good legal work. Most lawyers, in fact, would probably reject the above characterizations of lawyers' behaviour as unfair and distorted. They would reject it because they sincerely believe it to be wrong. But the participants in our seminar would also have rejected it before they began to examine their own practice. It is true that our data comes from a very small, selective group of attorneys. All were relatively young, and primarily experienced in poverty law. All had chosen to become involved in clinical teaching at a law school, often at a significant financial sacrifice. We cannot be certain that the same results would hold for a more representative group of attorneys, but they are consistent with available evidence. Rosenthal's (1974) study of negligent attorneys led to the conclusion that case law treated the client as an informed and responsible decision-maker, but that the legal profession denied the client the information needed to fill that role. Rosenthal also argued that there was a fundamental, economic conflict of interest between attorneys and clients, but that clients had little opportunity to be aware of or protect themselves from such conflict of interest between attorneys and clients. Finally, Rosenthal found that it was precisely those clients who participated most actively in the conduct of their legal affairs (that is, the clients who were least willing to accept the passive, dependent role into which attorneys tend to thrust their clients) who attained the most successful legal outcomes.

If lawyers adopt largely adversarial models of behaviour in transactions with clients, to the detriment of their clients and the legal system, why does that occur? It would be easy to attribute the problem to human venality, but such a diagnosis—even if partially accurate—leads nowhere. The experience in the seminar suggests two alternative diagnoses—one at the level of legal education and the competencies it produces in individual attorneys, another at the level of the intellectual paradigm underlying the legal system.

At the first level, legal education is mostly intellectual in content and competitive in format. Thus, it produces relatively few performance skills, and the skills that are learned are likely to facilitate adversarial rather than collaborative performances. Additionally, the seminar experience suggests that lawyers may learn a truncated version of the ability to 'think like a lawyer'. That skill requires both inductive and deductive skills, but our experience suggests that lawyers' ability to follow rules is much better developed than their capacity to reflect on experience, develop insights, and form new generalizations. Our research leads us to the belief that legal education is critically deficient in helping lawyers learn how to engage in effective collaboration, and how to learn from their own experience.

But the problem goes deeper than adding a few new courses to the legal curriculum (for example, Collaboration I; Advanced Learning from Experience). The contradictions in lawyers' practice suggest contradictions in the legal system and its underlying intellectual framework. Freedman (1975) defends the adversary system on the grounds that it achieves an extraordinary balance between the values of truth-seeking and protection of individual rights:

'In summary, the Constitution has committed us to an adversary system for the administration of criminal justice. The essentially humanitarian reason for such a system is that it preserves the dignity of the individual, even though that may occasionally require significant frustration of the search for truth and the will of the state. An essential element of that system is the right to counsel, a right that would be meaningless if the defendant were not able to communicate fully and freely with the attorney (Freedman, 1975, p. 8)

Freedman elaborates his conception of the role of the lawyer in such a system with an approving comment on Lord Brougham's argument (in defence of the Queen in *Queen Caroline's Case*) that the advocate's 'first and only duty' is 'to save that client by all means and expedients, and at all hazards and costs to other persons, among them himself'. Freedman adds:

Let justice be done—that is, for my client let justice be done—even though the heavens may fall. That is the kind of advocacy that I would want as a client and that I feel bound to provide as an advocate. The rest of the picture, however, should not be ignored. The adversary system ensures an advocate on the other side, and an impartial judge over both. Despite the advocate's argument therefore, the heavens do not really have to fall— not unless justice requires that they do (Freedman, 1975, p. 9)

But Freedman's picture is still incomplete. His argument rests on the assumption that lawyers know how to determine and represent their clients' interests (even at cost to themselves), and that the legal system permits them to do so. Our research suggests that both assumptions are often incorrect. Lawyers are unskilled at learning their clients' interest and blind to the degree to which they confuse clients' needs with their own. Moreover, we found that lawyers chronically felt frustrated and entrapped by a legal system that, in their view, severely restricted their options and their ability to serve their clients. Yet they were unaware of the degree to which their behaviour tended to restrict their clients' options and inhibit the client's capacity to know or to act on his or her interests.

We reported an educational experience designed to help lawyers explore questions like those, so that they in turn could provide the same kind of learning experience for their students. We discovered that it is possible to create a learning environment in which lawyers can explore the discrepancies between their purposes and their practice, and began to explore alternative approaches to lawyering. We also discovered that, once lawyers had learned of discrepancies in their lawyering, it was difficult for them to alter their behaviour, because of their own personal programming, and because of the legal system in which they functioned. The pilot experience points the direction toward more effective clinical education in law schools, and toward research on the legal system that explores the contradictions in the American legal paradigm and seeks ultimately to provide answers to the most difficult question of all: can those contradictions be resolved through the redesign of the legal system and legal education?

References

Argyris, C. and Schon, D. A. (1974) *Theory in Practice: Improving Professional Effectiveness*. San Francisco: Jossey-Bass.
Auerbach, J. S. (1976) 'A plague of lawyers,' *Harper's*, **December**, 37–44.
Bellow, G. (1975) *Memorandum to Law School Faculty*. Cambridge, Mass.: Harvard Law School.
Bolman, L. (1974) 'The client as theorist,' in J. D. Adams (ed.), *Theory and Method in Organization Development*. Washington: NTL Institute.
Freedman, M. H. (1975) *Lawyers' Ethics in an Adversary System*. Indianapolis: Bobbs-Merrill.
Kuhn, T. S. (1962) *The Structure of Scientific Revolutions*. Chicago: University of Chicago Press.
Mindes, M. W. (1975) 'Forcing an identity crisis on law students,' in *Learning and the Law*, 2, No. 3.
Rosenthal, D. E. (1974) *Lawyer and Client: Who's in Charge?* New York: Russell Sage Foundation.

Chapter 7

Peer Consultation for School Improvement

Richard A. Schmuck

University of Oregon, U.S.A.

Much of the consultation in schools today is carried out by professionals with specialized training, advanced degrees, and formal credentials. The social–psychological relationship between the consultant and the teachers or administrators is structured hierarchically and is legitimized by a shared expectation in support of expertise. This chapter describes an innovative sort of educational consultation, entitled peer consultation, that is structured through collegial interactions and is legitimized by norms is support of professional cooperation and responsibility.

Consultation in schools

Three types of consultation are particularly popular among contemporary educators: (1) Expect technical assistance delivered by outsiders to the school district; (2) curriculum expertise offered by specialists within the school district; and (3) process consultation offered within the district but mostly on an *ad hoc* basis.

Expert technical assisters from outside the district are employed temporarily to fills a temporary vacancy in a classroom. For instance, an educational psychologist could be hired to develop a new programme for testing, or an architect could be employed to design a new physical plant, or a professional musician might be hired part-time to lead the chorus at the graduation ceremonies.

Curriculum expertise offered by personnel within the district aims at training teachers and administrators in a substantive area so they can perform their respective functions more capably. Training in a content area is provided to increase intellectual understandings, feelings of ownership, and commitment to changed procedures. The most frequently used mechanism of this strategy is the in-service course or workshop. In these specially designed events an expert trains teachers in a substantive area such as reading, mathematics, or social studies. Other examples include the school psychologist who trains teachers in a new testing battery, or the mental health specialist who trains early elementary teachers in concepts of child development.

Process consultation offered within the district aims to improve the interpersonal procedures used by the school personnel to reach their educational objectives. It focuses on the *how* of interpersonal interactions rather than on the *what* of their content. Process consultants deal with such phenomena as the patterns of communication, leadership attempts, underlying group tensions, and problem-solving and decision-making procedures. Examples include counsellors who meet within a team of teachers to offer constructive feedback on the group procedures used by the team, the administrator who acts as a third party mediator between an angry parent and an uneasy teacher, and the curriculum specialist who observes a classroom in operation and gives feedback to the class and teacher about their interaction patterns. The emphasis in all these examples is on operational procedures; process consultants do not deal directly with the subject matter of the interactions. Such consultation for individuals or small groups appears to be gradually reaching a position of increased parity in relation to expert technical assistance and curriculum expertise. Most of it, however, has been focused upon the solo professional as the target of improvement. Only recently have educators begun to take note of the importance and relevance of consultation for classroom groups as groups and for larger social systems such as entire faculties.

Organizational development (OD), a sort of process consultation, is a planned and sustained effort to apply behavioural science for *system* improvement, using reflexive, self-analytic methods (see Schmuck and Miles, 1971, for elaboration of this definition). It is distinguished from other kinds of process consultation in its emphasis on *the system* as the target of change. System can refer to an entire organization such as a school site, or to subsystems such as academic departments, teams of teachers, or classroom units. OD involves system members themselves in the assessment, diagnosis, and transformation of their own interdependent task groups.

Research findings on school OD

In 1967, Philip Runkel and I commenced a series of interrelated research and development projects to test the efficacy of various approaches to consultation in OD for schools. Our central purposes were to develop both a theory and a technology of structural and cultural change within elementary and secondary schools. To pursue these purposes, we collected evidence regarding alternative organizational procedures and structures a school can use, and we empirically tested the effectiveness of many consultative techniques for helping a school move into an innovative manner of functioning. Our basic value position has been that schools function best when teachers, administrators, and students are participating enthusiastically in growth-producing ways, and when they, as a body, have the coordinated abilities to respond flexibly and constructively to changes from without and within.

The results of our field experiments (Schmuck and Runkel, 1970; Schmuck and Miles, 1971; Schmuck et al., 1972; Schmuck and Schmuck, 1974, Schmuck et al., 1975; Runkel, Wyant, and Bell, 1975; and Schmuck et al., 1977) have shown a myriad of ways in which OD consultation can improve the organizational functioning of schools. For example, OD consultation has helped faculty members become more open and skilful in interpersonal communication, more collaborative with one another, and more willing to take risks in trying new ideas. While OD consultation acts as a vehicle for improving faculty meetings, it has also been shown to increase the number of useful instructional innovations attempted within a school and within particular classrooms. A few studies have indicated that OD consultation can lead to modifications in patterns of teacher–student interaction and that these changes do produce more favourable classroom climates. Because of OD consultation teachers have adopted instructional designs that encourage more student initiative which in turn, lead students to adopt more favourable attitudes toward school. Moreover, as a result of OD consultation, teachers have come to better understandings of their principal's suggestions, although they have not always agreed with them, and have indicated increased interest in participating more in collaborative problem-solving and decision-making about school-wide issues.

Our evidence indicates that three factors are related to a school's potential for successfully implementing a program of OD: *readiness, duration of effort,* and *first phase activities.* The readiness to benefit from OD is related to the support of the district administration, the acceptance to try OD by the principal of the school site, and staff members' interests in increased collaboration with colleagues, willingness to undergo some extra effort, and tolerance for individual differences within the faculty. Our data indicate that when these readiness conditions are high, as little as from 40 to 80 hours of OD consultation strategically dispersed over a two-year period can have very beneficial effects. In contrast, a school with only a small degree of readiness for organizational change can expect to make modifications in its structure, while improving its ability to use its own resources, after a few years during which between 80 and 160 hours of staff time are spent in a sustained OD effort.

The matter of time spent in consultation is crucial. After studying a large number of faculties that had received differing amounts of OD consultation, for example, Wyant (1974) found that staffs receiving less than 24 hours of OD consultation subsequently *declined* in communicative adequacy. A mere two or three days of process consultation in communication and problem-solving can have detrimental effects when there is no follow-up training in the use of the new skills. Perhaps the new communication skills and increased openness function in destructive rather than constructive ways when there is insufficient time for action planning and implementation; 24 hours appears to be a dangerously low number of hours of OD consultation. On the other hand, a newly established school receiving 46 hours of OD spread over two years continued to exhibit very strong self-renewing characteristics even two years *after* the consultation terminated.

Our research also has indicated that the seeds of success or failure often are planted during the very first phase of the consultation. At start-up, it appears crucial for the OD consultant to establish clear, supportive, and collaborative relationships with the key authorities of the school. Introductory demonstrations and contract-building meetings should occur with all participants before the formal workshops and consultative meetings are launched. Topics concerned with the essence of the OD effort, such as communication, goal-setting, problem-solving, decision-making, and the duration of the macro-design for the consultation, should be communicated using graphic and ex-periential procedures during the start-up. We also found that effective start-ups are featured by the consultants and the clients reflecting on their interpersonal perceptions and feelings about working together. Indeed, the possibilities of a successful OD effort are enhanced when the consultants believe they are able to help and when the clients recognize their own needs are willing to be helped to improve their situation. Unfortunately such mutual understanding between consultants and clients has been rare, especially when the consultants have been experts from universities.

Dilemmas in professionalizing OD consultation

OD consultation has become an increasingly popular strategy for system im-provement, especially in industry and government, since our beginnings in 1967. With its increased popularity there has also arisen a considerable interest in the professionalization of consultation in OD. As has occurred before, during the early developmental stages of other kinds of professional helping, the OD consultant has not been expected to have completed specialized professional training; however, OD consultation is coming of age and OD consultants are expected more and more to have received special training, earned advanced degrees, and to have qualified for formal credentials. While the surge of in-terest in OD has not yet arrived in the schools, as it has in industrial organi-zations and governmental agencies, we may expect that similar pressures for professionalization shall occur there, especially given the history of certification in education. Thus, we should anticipate that more and more school OD will be carried out within the traditional context of a hierarchical relationship between the consultant and the client and that this relationship will be ligiti-mized by a social norm in support of expertise.

While professionalization of the OD consultant's role seems inevitable, we must consider also the counter-pressures of expense and distrust of the outsider that are working on behalf of the deprofessionalization of new spe-cialists in education. Hiring expert OD consultants is typically too costly for school districts, especially since the present professionals within the districts are struggling to maintain their own budgets. And, although outside experts might bring the weight of their professional expertise to the district, their non-membership makes them suspect and even distrusted. Indeed, penetrating questions are being asked nowadays about the motives and skills of our con-temporary experts and consultants, especially by the younger generations of students in professional training programmes. Cynicism about outside technical experts, curriculum specialists, counsellors, school psychologists and the like is accompanied by a profound disillusionment with the plans for innovative professional roles in community action that were designed during the 1960s to reduce the problems of poverty and racism. Moreover, the Vietnam war, as well as Watergate, have made it clear to many in the western world that 'expert' judgements about 'system improvement' should not be uncritically accepted. OD consultants, like other professionals, face the dilemma of a distrusting clientele even when trust and collaboration between consultant and client must be the very building blocks of effective process consultation.

The unfortunate escalation of interpersonal distrust and social distance between consultants and practitioners in education could easily generalize to process consultation over the next few years and could become a major stumbling block to efforts at using OD consultation to facilitate school improvement. Already there are many illustrative mismatches between consultants and practitioners to make us wary of the fate of OD efforts. For example, architects are hired by school districts to design new school sites but typically they work very little, if at all, with the teachers, parents, and students of that community. Reading specialists at district offices might issue synopses of articles about new reading curricula, occasionally run a brief workshop on reading, but typically do not visit classrooms, do not act in a way that is viewed as helpful by teachers, and seldom work directly with students. School psychologists carry out psychometric testing, offering the scores to teachers, but the scores are typically given at a time and in a form that do not help the teacher make use of them. Counsellors typically remain behind closed doors much of the day meeting with a small number of troubled students who do not wish to be in class; teachers often view such counselling activities at best as 'bandaid' treatments and at worst as undermining their efforts at classroom discipline. In each of these illustrations the consultant's credibility with teachers is virtually non-existent and a breakdown of interpersonal trust has combined in a cyclical fashion with insufficient opportunities for cooperative action toward mutually shared goals.

If consultation in OD is to facilitate school improvement, it must break out of the mould of the traditional, hierarchical, expert relationship and move to reduce social distance between consultants and professional educators. One promising strategy for the dissemination of OD in schools that we have successfully tested involves practising educators themselves taking on formal and legitimate consultative functions in relation to one another. Such peer consultation can be structured through horizontal interactions among organizational cousins (those who hold jobs within the same school district but who are not members of the same interdependent task unit). Thus, in contrast to placing normative emphasis on expertise, peer consultation becomes legitimized by norms in support of collegial responsibility. OD cadres made up of peer-colleagues offer an alternative to the traditional professional–client helping relationship.

Peer cadres of OD specialists

We have established peer cadres of OD specialists within two school districts of the Pacific Northwest (for details see Arends and Phelps, 1973; Runkel, Wyant, and Bell, 1975; Schmuck et al., 1977). The cadre in Kent, Washington commenced operations in 1969 and was disbanded in 1975. The second cadre has been operating and flourishing in Eugene, Oregon since 1971. Other peer cadres of OD specialists have been tried in a tri-country area of central California, in school districts near Denver, and in the province of Manitoba, Canada.

Members entering these cadres are regular district personnel such as teachers, principals, counsellors, curriculum specialists, and assistant superintendents; each performing only part-time in the role of OD specialist while carrying out full-time teaching, administrative, or coordinating responsibilities. The specialists use their understandings and skills as facilitators to help their peers clarify communication, assess progress toward educational goals, cope with interdependence and conflict in a productive way, systematically solve problems, reach out to use relevant resources, and make decisions collaboratively.

The Kent and Eugene cadres have helped their colleagues create ways of working together to reach their own goals. The cadres have focused their consultations on intact work groups, such as school staffs, teaching teams, and administrative departments, helping them to identify and overcome interpersonal and organizational constraints to productive collaboration. By offering training in interpersonal skills, group teachniques, and organizational procedures, the cadres attempt to build a capacity for continual problem solving into the key subsystems of the district.

The overall sequence of an OD intervention by cadre members includes an initial period of entry, start-up, and contract-building, followed by diagnosis and design. These activities are followed by a series of sequential consultative sessions that are interspersed with data collections for formative evaluation. The evaluative data serve as springboards for redesign and more consultative sessions until the cadre and the clients share the belief that the necessary structures and procedures for self-renewal have been built into the client group. Finally, data often are collected for purposes of summative evaluation and offered to policy-makers.

The social-phychological dynamics involved in this OD sequence can be understood in terms of four distinct, but interrelated, phases. During the first phase, emphasis is on the development of interpersonal openness and trust, both within the client group and between the OD specialists and the clients. Clients learn such skills as paraphrasing, describing behaviour, describing own feelings, checking impressions of the feelings of others, and giving and receiving feedback. In the second phase, focus is on increasing the awareness of interdependence among the clients. By exploring and identifying common goals and the group procedures that will enhance movement toward those goals, the clients discover how to build a smoothly functioning, task-achieving team. During the third phase, the clients clarify their common expectations and attempt to create formal group agreements for the future. Typically, they establish explicit norms that encourage the management of conflict, systematic problem-solving, and participatory decision-making. In the fourth phase, the roles, procedures, and structures to be employed by the clients are designed, clarified, and put into action. Although most OD consultations progress sequentially through these four phases, the issues involved in each phase are enduring and are therefore cyclically encountered.

The cadre's repertoire

The activities carried out by OD specialists can be categorized in the following six ways.

(1) Cadre members provide training to improve *communication* throughout the district, by teaching particular communication skills to district's employees, students, and parents. In Eugene, for example, over two-thirds of the district's 1000 employees and over 400 parents received communication training in school-site consultations, in-service courses or special seminars between 1971 and 1976. Cadre members do not merely present communication skills as abstract concepts; they encourage clients to practise the skills and to gain appreciation of two-way oral communication through structured activities and learning games (see Chapter 3 of Schmuck et al., 1977). Cadre members observe the clients using the skills, and provide feedback as the clients practise the skills during regular work-time. While the lion's share of time is spent on improving interpersonal communication within intact work-groups, the specialists also help improve the quality of intergroup communication within the district.

(2) Cadres help groups in the district develop effective and systematic procedures for *solving problems*. They teach problem-solving skills to intact groups first through simulation and second by addressing actual problems. Cadre members work with their client groups for sufficient time to build the norms and structures that are required to support systematic problem-solving as a sustained feature of the clients' work. For example, in Eugene, more than two-thirds of the district's employees, more than 120 parents, and about 75 students received training in problem-solving skills between 1971 and 1976.

(3) Cadres help groups develop new ways of *assessing progress* toward goals, by involving the clients in three sorts of activities. Initially, the OD specialists assist clients in defining goals clearly. By helping clients to collaborate in writing behavioural descriptions of where they are and where they want to be, the OD specialists help them to define the present situation clearly and to get a shared picture of what would be better. Next the cadre helps clients reach agreement on what their most preferred goals are. By teaching such group skills as asking all member for their opinions before making decisions, brains forming new idea creatively when solving problems, and making sure that all members get a chance to contribute, the specialists help clients share their individual targets so that they can gradually identify their common and shared goals. Next, the specialists teach clients to use simple, systematic procedures for

obtaining important information. For example, clients can learn how to survey group members' opinions and feelings in meetings, how to use questionnaires, interviews, and observations for collecting information, how to interpret the information collected, and how to share the information in useful ways. By learning to collect and use information, client groups create a solid foundation for problem-solving and decision-making.

(4) Cadres help groups to use flexible methods for *decision-making*. Cadre members typically teach that decisions can be made in various ways and that participation is not appropriate for all decisions. Consensual decisions are most appropriate when broad understanding and commitment are required. Cadre members help groups define the decision-making responsibilities of individuals and subgroups for other kinds of decisions. The specialists strive to disperse involvement in decision-making so that decisions are made on the basis of access to information and stake in the outcome rather than simply official authority. At the same time, OD specialists realize that some decisions are best made by individuals or by representatives; the important target being to match the style of decision-making to the issues functionally. Comprehensive research on cadre involvement in several multi-unit schools indicated that OD methods were effective in dispersing participation in decision-making (Schmuck et al., 1975).

(5) Cadres provide a source of innovative ideas about *organizational procedures and structures*. For example, meetings of groups such as faculties, committees, and parents typically are chaired by administrators and are featured by one-way communication, non-participation of group members, and loose reliance on formal rules of order. The OD specialists teach groups alternative procedures such as developing an agenda through group participation, using fishbowl seating arrangements and buzz group discussions to increase participation, rotating the convener role throughout the group, and using methods such as brainstroming, surveys, and communication skills. The specialists also can help clients build new group structures such as leadership teams, *ad hoc* committees for problem-solving, Likert's link-pin structures for decision-making and other formations that allow them to make better use of the available human resources. By helping clients to clarify and to negotiate new role relationships, cadre members help their peer-colleagues develop creative solutions to the organizational problems they face.

(6) Cadres help groups convert innovative ideas into *realities*. The specialists design ways of putting together the five activities discussed above so that new procedures actually begin to take shape within their client groups. Examples from Kent and Eugene show the sorts of innovations that the cadres have facilitated. In one elementary school, for example, in which staff and many parents participated together in an OD intervention, the structure and procedures of the PTA were revised after the proposals of problem-solving groups were adopted. In another elementary school, a staff was aided during one academic

year to create a differentiated staffing pattern. A junior high was helped to establish interdisciplinary teaching teams. Several senior highs were helped to involve students in building an innovative peer counselling and tutoring service. Another elementary staff designed and implemented a plan to provide more information about school programmes to community members. Our research on both Kent and Eugene indicates that through long-term consultation, peer OD cadres can help their colleagues to initiate and follow through on innovative programme that become owned psychologically by those responsible for implementing them. Moreover, our follow-up evaluations of the Eugene cadre this past year showed that those clients who had experienced long-term consultation felt highly favourable about the help they had received (Burr and Bell, 1976).

The cadre's values

The collegial relationships between the specialists and their potential clients embody several distinctive values.

(1) The specialists collaborate with their clients in designing and carrying out the key activities of the OD sequence. They attempt to domonstrate that as OD specialists they value democratic and humanistic relationships by modelling, in their own interactions with clients, interdependence, collaboration, openness and the use of rational inquiry as bases for organizing and getting work accomplished. During each step of a consultation, the specialists strive to remain open to feedback concerning their own performance and degrees of helpfulness or unhelpfulness.

(2) The specialists try not to intrude upon the work of groups without invitation nor do they attempt to convince their clients that they need help when they do not wish it. Thus, the cadre responds to requests from clients who believe that their working relationships could have greater promise of success with outside help. Cadre members believe that coercion would be contradictory to the collaborative values inherent in collegial relationships, and they see little chance that their colleagues would profit much unless they are committed to expend the necessary time and energy to undergo a change process.

(3) The specialists value taking the initiative in introducing a variety of methods for helping potential clients to become aware of what OD is, how it works, and of the special functions performed by cadre members. The Kent cadre has, for example, used a brief brochure to describe the services of OD specialists (See Arends and Phelps, 1973), while the Eugene cadre produced an audioslide show explaining what it does and how interested groups can obtain further information and assistance. Another audio-slide presentation, along with a booklet explaining OD, have been developed and marketed by our R and D team at CEPM and have been used in over 40 school districts to explain the goals and functions of an OD cadre (See Arends et al., 1973; and Arends,

Phelps, and Schmuck, 1973). Along with these resources, cadre members arrange for introductory demonstrations about OD at faculty meetings and other formal gatherings, using these opportunities to answer questions and to clear up misunderstandings.

(4) Perhaps the most important point: cadre members show their value for helpfulness by being available in their proximal positions as organizational cousins over an extended period of time and on a continual, at-the-elbow basis. Organizational problems are, of course, continuing aspects of school life and it is rare, perhaps impossible, for important issues to be dealt with successfully in one brief workshop. Since important organizational changes take time, continued assistance from an OD specialist is necessary in most schools for the change process to come to some fruition. The cadre's help usually takes the form of an initial cluster of workshops followed by a series of process observation and feedback sessions that are interspersed with a few training sessions to reactivate skills or to provide further direction in problem-solving and decision-making.

Typical client groups

Cadre members provide skill training at OD consultation to intact task-oriented groups within the school district. The Kent and Eugene cadres have spent consultative time with the following clients.

(i) *School staffs.* While both cadres have focused a large part of their energy on working with school staffs, the Eugene specialists have consulted with staff more frequently than their Kent counterparts. The Eugene cadre has consulted with 20 school staffs during four years, while the Kent cadre consulted with only five school staffs over the same period. In both districts, the cadres have worked mainly with elementary and junior high staffs, but the Eugene cadre recently commenced work with a senior high that it starting an innovative, interdisciplinary teaching team.

Some school staffs request unspecified assistance in improving their human relations or their problem-solving effectiveness, but most invite the specialists to help in more specific ways, such as opening up communication with parents, getting started in a brand new school plant, helping a staff launch a new school year, or facilitating movement toward some new organizational structure, such as team teaching or differentiated staffing. Regardless of the nature of the specific request, however, most cadre interventions with school staff involve skill training in communication, goal-setting, problem-solving, decision-making, and evaluating progress toward goals. While there usually is a balance between simulations and working on the actual problems of a particular staff, the specialists in both districts have often employed some form of data feedback in launching their efforts. Typically, they have conducted interviews or collected questionnaire data from group members and have combined these data into a single report for the whole staff. After some discussion, the data are used as a springboard for goal-setting, problem-solving, planning and decision-making (for details, see Schmuck, 1973).

Initial workshops with school staffs are often three days long and are held during August just before the new school year begins. In Eugene, the first days of training have sometimes occurred on work days provided by the district at the end of each grading period. The initial training events typically are followed by an equal number of hours of consultation which is constituted of process observation and feedback of staff meetings during the school year.

(ii) *District-wide committees.* The Kent specialists put a considerable part of their energy into working with district-wide committees. They have planned and facilitated meetings of the Social Studies Advisory Committee, the Foreign Language Committee, the Teacher Representative Council, the Superintendent's cabinet and the Executive Board of the Kent Education Association. In Eugene, the cadre has consulted with the district's nurses and health clerks, all junior high department heads and their principals, and a committee of high school principals. In both districts, most of three interventions involved training in communication skills and problem-solving techniques followed by process observation and feedback.

(iii) *District office groups.* As was noted above the Kent cadre provided consultation to the superintendent's cabinet. This team-building design led to opening the previously closed cabinet meetings to representatives of several special interest groups within the district. Kent cadre members also worked with the entire staff of the Curriculum Development Division and with subgroups within the business office. Eugene specialists have worked with curriculum coordinators, a minority relations team, and most recently with the superintendent's cabinet. In some of these sessions, the Eugene cadre has used video tape for giving and receiving feedback and for later evaluation of their consultative efforts.

(iv) *Students and parents.* The Kent specialists have initiated and coordinated a multiethnic camp for area high school students, working with about 450 students over a four-year period. They also conducted several workshops to promote cooperation among PTA presidents and school principals, facilitated a seminar during which the superintendent and citizens discussed a projected budget, and facilitated meetings and provided communication training for the area's PTA council, League of Women Voters, and the Model Cities Council of Tacoma.

Eugene cadre members taught communication skills to a senior high English class and a junior high home room group, clarified norms concerning classroom behaviour within a sixth-grade class, taught problem-solving to the student council of an elementary school, and helped a high school choir to better understand the dynamics of interdependence and cooperation. Recently, several Eugene specialists have been collaborating with educators at the

University of Oregon on the development of a mini-course for senior high students on organizational psychology. Eugene specialists also assisted the teachers of three elementary schools in conducting seminars for parents by introducing communication skills and by serving as conveners for the parent–teacher discussions. One of the most ambitious interventions in the history of the Eugene cadre was carried out when the principal of an elementary school requested help in bringing staff and parents into closer communication and better working relationships. The results which were beneficial are discussed in Phelps and Arends (1973) and in Schmuck et al, (1977).

(v) *In-service course for individuals*. Although the cadres in both districts have focused attention on intact groups, each has also provided some courses for individuals. In-service courses have been offered to acquaint large numbers of personnel with the goals and methods of OD, to give the specialists oppor-tunities to practise and develop their training skills, and to provide training for future specialists. For example, Kent specialists offered a four-phase sequence of courses on the topics of communication techniques, group proces-ses, social dynamics of the classroom, and organization consultation, while in Eugene three separate courses consisting of ten three-hour sessions have been offered. The first Eugene course on interpersonal communication in-cluded such topics as communication skills, interpersonal openness, freeing and binding behaviours, and the effects of competition and cooperation. The second course on group and organizational processes included such topics as norms, task and maintenance functions, leadership behaviours, and group decision-making. And the third Eugene course on organizational theory and OD strategies has included such topics as starting up a consultation, diagnosis, design, training, data feedback, confrontation, observation, and evaluation.

Establishing OD cadres

Our research has shown that to establish an OD cadre of peers within a school district careful attention must be given to legitimation, coordination, selection, and training.

Legitimizing the Cadre

In theory, peer cadres of OD specialists can represent an effective avenue for providing continuous and readily available process consultation to intact groups within the district. It is crucial for the spirit of this theory to be accepted to some degree by the formal authorities such as the superintendent, some of the assistant superintendents and some of the principals. Our experiences in Kent and Eugene indicated that the superintendent need not be enthusiastic about OD for it to go, but the superintendent must provide minimal support and speak of it as a legitimate and worthwhile activity for the district. The superintendent must not veto the idea of continuous process facilitation by peers if the cadre is to flourish. Our experiences also indicated that some assistant superintendents and some principals must both understand the history of OD and strongly support the peer cadre idea.

Beyond support by the official authorities the means of legitimizing the cadre will differ from place to place. For example, in Eugene the cadre was brought up initially by two curriculum coordinators and an assistant superintendent to help several elementary schools move toward differentiated staffing and multiunit structures. The principals and teachers who became involved believed that OD consultation could help build effective teaching teams, thus facilitating implementation of innovative-staffing patterns. In Kent, external OD consultants for our Center were brought in to help the superintendent's cabinet to clarify roles and to improve communication between itself and the principals and teachers within the schools. Several teachers, a counsellor, a curriculum coordinator, and the external consultants later commenced a cadre of OD specialists to assure continuous process consultation within the district after the external consultants left. The successes of the cadres in working in several schools and in their in-service courses led to their eventual legitimation in a few years.

In a recent follow-up study of the Eugene cadre, Burr and Bell (1976) presented data attesting to the high legitimacy of the OD specialists. They state:

'During the five years of the Cadre's tenure, the 35 to 40 people who have been members (approximately 2 per cent of district employees) have exerted a surprising amount of influence on the total district of 2000. The results of the study show a sizeable amount of knowledge exists about the cadre and its functions. Of the 895 respondents, 76.9 per cent have heard of the cadre, and 66.7 per cent of their knowledge is accurate. Attitudes toward the cadre are substantially more favorable than unfavorable, particularly in schools where cadre interventions have taken place.'

There are of course many ways for a district to launch and legitimize a peer OD cadre. For example, the desire to involve more parents in decision-making and school management, or attempts to build new, more pluralistic school structure and alternative schools represent several prime reasons for a cadre. Help in increasing student involvement in secondary schools is another. Whatever the contemporary change target is, however, district personnel interested in an OD cadre should seek to establish a firm rationale for why they are advocating an internal OD cadre. And they must stand behind the work of the cadre even if at times some district personnel are threatened by OD processes. Our research indicates some additional variables that are related to making an OD cadre legitimate.

(1) The support of the superintendent and especially some key assistant superintendents and principals is critical from the beginning. Like other innovative programmes, a cadre requires both financial resources and institutional legitimacy that only the top administrators can provide at the outset. The cadre's primary purposes, how it fits into the district's organization, and

its channels of access to the decision-makers should be agreed upon by some of the top administration. Ample circulars and announcements about the cadre's services should be equally available to all parts of the district. Perhaps most important the cadre should *not* be viewed as an extension of the district's traditional managerial functions. While the cadre must have support from top administrators, it also should be viewed as independent of line decisions and functions.

We found that the school staffs, teaching teams, and administrative committee most likely to benefit from OD consultation are those experiencing a moderate degree of stress. These groups must be relatively free to make decisions without undue pressure from the traditional decision-makers. Districts with moderate stress levels also will constitute the most fertile grounds for an OD cadre. If the district's personnel are completely satisfied, or are totally unaware that problems exist, there will be very little impetus for change. Contrastingly, in districts that are experiencing a profound and pervasive crisis, it will be difficult for the key administrators and potential cadre members to sort out the immediate crisis from the longer-range vision required to launch an OD cadre, and only external experts will be viewed as potentially helpful.

(3) While it is critical for several of the key district administrators to understand fully the processes and the potential benefits of OD consultation, there should be at least a handful of district personnel who wish to be trained as OD specialists as well as some ripe situations for OD consultation. For example, when the Eugene cadre was launched, top-level administrative support for OD was very strong and some district personnel were aware of the benefits of OD consultation. Just prior to launching the OD cadre, three staffs and subgroups of two others had participated in one week of OD consultation as part of the district's multiunit project with CEPM (Schmuck et al., 1975). A few other groups within the district had participated in a two-day demonstration about OD sponsored by CEPM. In summary there was a handful of district subsystems and individuals which knew about and valued OD.

Finally, the community's relationship to the school is an important feature. The Eugene district's organization and its relationship with the community were not marked by serious or sustained tension when the OD cadre was launched. The district was composed of four senior high schools (grades 10–12), eight junior highs (grades 7–9), and 32 elementary schools. Most of the 20,000 students were white, lower middle class, and scored above the national norms on achievement tests. While support for the annual operating budged had gradually diminished over the previous eight years, there had been no revolt on the part of the community. When serious school community tension did arise recently, the cadre was firmly established and in a position to offer assistance.

These sociological characteristics were also present in Kent when the cadre of OD specialists was being recruited. The project had received approval of the district's administrators, the school board, the principals, and the teachers' association. Since CEPM consultants had provided OD consultation for administrative groups and several staffs prior to the start-up of the cadre, some awareness and appreciation of OD did exist in Kent; and although recent growth of the community had created new pressures for change, there was particularly antagonistic.

Selecting a cadre coordinator

After the key administrators have legitimized and approved the idea of an OD cadre, a cadre coordinator should be selected to help in building awareness and support for recruiting potential specialists and clients. Our experiences in Kent and Eugene attest to how crucial an effective coordinator is for the viability of an OD cadre. The coordinator manages the projects of the cadre and links the specialists with outside consultants, others in the district, and one another. The coordinator must understand what OD is and how it works, have experiences as a consultant, be familiar with the organizational processes of school districts, and have skills to manage the efforts of diverse individuals and groups.

In both Kent and Eugene, cadre coordinators were selected from personnel within the districts. Their skills as leaders of adults had already been shown in other settings; one had run many workshops in language arts for teachers, the other had consulted with social studies departments on their curricula and instructional strategies and had chaired a district-wide committee on differentiated staffing. Both commanded a high degree of trust and respect from their peers and were recognized for their tactfulness and high tolerance for ambiguities. Neither had been involved in many OD projects, but both were quick to understand the basic concepts and techniques of OD; and more importantly both understood their district's bureaucratic arrangements. While they were clearly peers to their colleagues, they were also considered as very competent experts in education.

Recruiting cadre members

We found it was important to inform all district personnel about the cadre through circulars and face-to-face meetings to assure that potential members had ample opportunity for asking questions to ascertain their own interest. Question and answer discussions are crucial because many teachers and administrators will not be clear about OD nor will they understand how OD specialists are likely to function. Some may perceive participation in the cadre's training as an opportunity for their own personal development and lack commitment to serve as an active cadre member after training. Others might view the OD project as another effort to bring about a particular change in curriculum or administration.

In Kent, recruitment commenced by circulating a brief description of OD goals and techniques along with application forms for potential cadre members.

In Eugene, the cadre project was announced within the district's annual catalogue of special projects and summer workshops and was mailed to all certified staff. In both districts a meeting was held for those persons expressing interest in becoming cadre members at which the newly chosen coordinator, along with a CEPM consultant, explained how OD works and the functions of a cadre of OD specialists.

Our experience has indicated that certain attributes of the recruits are important to keep in mind: (1) Cadre members should represent a composite of the key roles in the district and a balance of such attributes as sex, race, age, years of professional experience and membership in professional organizations; (2) some knowledge, skill, and previous experience with laboratory education are important; (3) individual motivation to take on cadre duties in addition to regular district jobs should be high; and (4) visibility, trust, and respect with colleagues within the district are crucial.

The initial recruits in Kent included five central office administrators along with a total of 18 teachers, counsellors, and administrators from eight of the district's 22 schools. In Eugene, 26 educators, selected from an initial pool of 51 serious applicants, included two elementary administrators, two elementary counsellors, seven elementary teachers, three secondary administrators, one secondary counsellor, four secondary teachers, three central office administrators, and four coordinators. These persons represented 14 of the district's 44 schools.

Training the cadre

The following four objectives guided the designs for the initial training received by the recruits in both cadres: (1) The cadre was to develop into a cohesive subsystem with clear goals, roles, norms, and procedures both for internal functioning and for delivering consultation within the district; (2) the neophyte specialists were to feel animated about their tasks and for their won potential influence as consultants; (3) they were to learn about OD theory, intervention designs, and techniques; and (4) they were to develop skills in data collection, communication, problem-solving, convening meetings, managing conflict, and to convert these skills into strategies and designs for helping others.

To implement these goals in Kent, the overall period of training went from June 1969 to March 1970. The major event, a two-week workshop, was followed by several short seminars and a substantial amount of at-the-elbow consultative help. Cadre members collaborated with CEPM consultants in carrying out some initial consultations with an assortment of client groups. In Eugene, the training design called for a sequence of four stages that lasted from June 1971 to April 1972. Stage 1 involved a two-week workshop in early June that emphasized team-building, and the theroy and techniques of OD. The second stage was composed of a one-week workshop in August to design possible OD interventions. During the third stage, subgroups of cadre members collaborated with CEPM consultants to deliver OD consultation to selected district groups. The fourth stage was composed of a series of seminars during the school year to discuss the interventions in the district that were being carried out in concert with CEPM consultants.

Results of these training designs for the cadres revealed some important lessons. (1) Cadre members initially learned about OD by discussing how they were communicating with one another during their own team-building sessions in the here and now; (2) lecturettes and readings were designed to increase cognitive understandings, while practice and experiential learning were used to teach behavioural skills; (3) most workshop activities encouraged the trainees to be self-analytic, self-reflexive, and self-directed; (4) structured activities such as games, simulations, and role-playing were used in the early days of training, but were gradually replaced by realistic procedures and skills that were more useful for accomplishing actual tasks; and (5) cadre members worked in several different groups, allowing them to become well enough acquainted with one another to build functional interdependence and cohesiveness.

The Kent cadre had some difficulty in disassociating itself from encounter grouping and sensitivity training which were popular when the cadre was established. During its first year of operation, it highlighted the system focus of OD by using structured learning-games, realistic problem-solving, and consultation for actual decisions that had to be made. The Kent and Eugene cadre had to explain repeatedly that OD consultation was based on a strategy of working primarily with intact subsystems. It was a unique effort since only a few groups in the two districts had ever had in-service money released for total staff development rather than for individuals being trained. Although staffs of new schools had been granted funds, they were usually for materials, scheduling, and preparing the curriculum. Training a total staff was an alien idea to most district personnel in both Kent and Eugene, and it still is a foreign concept in many school districts today.

Because of the geographical proximity of the CEPM staff to the Eugene cadre, the follow-up training for that cadre was more substantial than it was in Kent. In Eugene, after the initial design and field experiences were completed in September, the CEPM consultants continued to serve as members of some intervention teams. However, as the year progressed, they gradually decreased their giving of direction by assuming responsibilities that were similar to those assumed by the cadre members. This gradual shift on the part of the CEPM staff away from authority and toward collegiality continued throughout the 1971–72 school year. The initial plan to cease CEPM involvement altogether in April was modified only slightly after the cadre received a request to consult with a conflict-laden group of parents and staff at an elementary school. After that consultation, however, CEPM consultants have assisted the Eugene cadre only occasionally and always at the request of the cadre.

Institutionalizing OD cadres

In both Kent and Eugene, cadre members were divided into small intervention teams to provide OD consultation. The specialists usually chose the team to which they wanted to belong using criteria such as willingness to work closely with the others on the team, belief that a balanced team with regard to district jobs had to be created, and significant interest in the particular tasks to be performed. They formed into new intervention teams after completing their designs with the client groups and when new clients were identified. The coordinator plus representatives from each of the intervention teams formed a steering committee to direct the overall cadre effort.

Considerable emphasis was placed on building strong temporary teams for delivering the consultation. By understanding and supporting one another, the OD specialists could more validly diagnose the organizational problem of their clients and design more effective interventions. Moreover cadre members who felt comfortable working together learned from one another during the team planning and consultations. While specialists in both cadres occasionally worked alone, their solo tasks typically had been identified and planned by a team. It was fairly typical, however, for individual specialists to focus their energies on particular functions such as designing interview schedules, training for large client groups, serving as process consultants for small subsystems of the client groups, or coaching individual client group members. All team members regardless of speciality shared in providing one another with helpful feedback and in carrying out continual evaluation as the interventions moved along.

No specialist was allowed to participate as a member of an intervention team that was providing consultation to his or her 'family group', for example, a cadre member who taught in a particular school was not allowed to join the team that was working with his or her staff. This limitation was thought by both cadres to be important for several reasons: (1) As a member of the client group, the OD specialist could be directly involved in any problem or plan of action for change designed during the intervention and therefore would have to be free to devote full energies and attention to that task; (2) cadre members who participated as clients in training events could give constructive feedback cadre members who were acting as their consultants; (3) the use of OD specialists who worked in other schools set a useful example of interschool cooperation; and (4) the failure of specialists to participate as clients might be perceived as a lack of faith in what the consultation was intended to accomplish.

The steering committee was composed of persons who represented their intervention teams; it assured its own continuity by replacing a portion of the representatives at regular intervals. Its members served as communication links between the intervention teams and the coordinator, meeting on a regular basis to deal with such tasks as preparing the budget and allocating resources, planning self-renewal events for the cadre, deciding which groups requesting OD help would be given priority, making contacts with potential clients to obtain information to insure smooth start-ups, and identifying and planning for the training of new cadre members.

Our impressions of how the two cadres progressed and regressed over the four years we studied each of them were that the viability of the cadre organizations depended *most* on the skills of the coordinators. The coordinators managed the activities of all intervention teams and convened all meetings of the steering committee. They also worked on a few of the intervention teams as active members, provided introductory demonstrations to potential clients, guided start-up and contract-building for most of the interventions, explained the work of the cadre to interested persons in the community, joined the cadres with district administrators especially in relation to the budget, arranged for outside consultants when these were required, or desired, and linked the cadre to groups outside the district such as local universities, the state department of education, and research and development centres.

Cadre membership

Experiences in Kent and Eugene suggested that cadre members could be district employees with full-time jobs in addition to their roles as OD specialists as long as they were provided released time or other compensation for the additional duties. The part-time specialist role did, however, occasionally create role conflict for several cadre members. The most acute problem arose when a specialist used up time away from his regular teaching job to do cadre work despite his supervisor's concern about the quality of his work in the school. However, conflicts of this sort were rare; most OD specialists kept up an open dialogue about their work with both site and district administrators and most were already excellent teachers, administrators, and curriculum coordinators.

It was also important for the cadres to deal with time and energy demands. The Eugene cadre found it necessary, for example, to define several categories of membership according to the amount of time a specialist could devote to OD consultation. The 'active' category was reserved for specialists currently working on teams and participating in most self-renewal events or meetings of the cadre. The 'support' category included specialists who could attend self-renewal events only occasionally and otherwise contribute to maintaining the cadre's viability. Specialists in the 'inactive' category had stopped all OD work for a limited time-period.

We are convinced that an OD cadre of colleagues should be representative of the various reference groups within the district, both to display to potential clients that the specialists (as colleagues) are knowledgeable about and available to all district groups and to show that they do not represent nor do they advocate a particular cluster of special interests. The original recruits to both the Kent and the Eugene cadres were selected to insure representation of a variety of district job and reference groups. However, a few years after the original selections were made, turnover in membership of both groups did occur; some members resigned while others, particularly those in jobs for whom substitutes could not be readily provided, took supportive or inactive roles. New members were added to both cadres every year to replace those who had dropped out.

The most noticeable change in both cadres over a four-year period has been a drop in the percentage of central office administrators and a corresponding increase in the percentage of classroom teachers taking on active status. These shifts did not undermine the linking activities of either cadre because the assistant superintendents assumed supportive roles rather than resigning. While it appears extremely important to provide initial training to central office administrators to gain their support and to create vital link-pin positions between the superintendent and the cadre, it is also equally as important to recognize that classroom teachers are more likely to provide services on a regular basis.

Cadre self-renewal

The cadre's effectiveness over time requires that the members upgrade their skills continually and remain receptive to new ideas as they come along. This is especially challenging for people working in school districts because they are often removed from the sources of new research and development. The Kent specialists used occasional seminars and an annual summer retreat for their self-renewal. The Eugene specialists have used monthly evening sessions, summer workshops, a small group seminar, and an annual spring retreat. In addition to providing for developing new skills, these meetings allowed for some problem solving about the teamwork of the cadre itself.

Outside consultants, hired several times in both Kent and Eugene, provided the specialists with new theory and intervention activities to help them improve their skills and collaborative working arrangements. The Kent specialists called on a consultant from the Washington Education Association several times, while the Eugene specialists hired two professional OD consultants to help them with their annual retreats. Topics such as dealing with conflict, organizational diagnosis, and formative evaluation were themes at the Eugene retreats.

Besides upgrading the skills of specialists, the cadres also planned ways to insure that there would be a reservoir of trained personnel to call upon to replace those who would resign or become inactive. In Kent, each cadre member agreed to recruit at least one potential neophyte each year, while the Eugene strategy called for identifying potential recruits out of the pool of persons who had completed the three-term sequence of in-service courses offered by the cadre. Also, in Eugene, a general invitation was extended through bulletins sent to all schools in the district. Once the interested parties were identified, they were encouraged to take the three courses and to apply for cadre membership afterwards. By insisting that all potential neophytes take the three courses, the Eugene cadre successfully avoided pernicious 'in-group' designations that would have alienated them from many of their potential clients.

Maintaining financial support

Maintaining strong OD cadres in Kent and Eugene did not require a major outlay of money, but a small budget was necessary. In Kent, the average yearly allocation was a miniscule $8,000, while in Eugene approximately $20,000 was spent for cadre activities during each of the first few years and about $40,000 per year more recently. Most of the money in Eugene went to the coordinator's salary, released time for specialists, self-renewal events, office operation and materials, outside consultants, travel, and research and evaluation. On a few occasions, the Eugene district has also provided funds for salaries of staffs that chose to work with the specialists during summer workshops, just as it has given extended contracts to other district employees for other special events.

Our experiences in both districts indicated that cadres must become part of the political struggle to obtain regular district funds. In addition, cadre coordinators must be prepared to negotiate for support and as a consequence to handle any resentments from others who believe that the cadre's share of resources are too high. But even more severe than money will be issues related to insufficient time for getting away from regular duties. Substitutes for busy specialists are only part of the solution since the specialists who were teachers in both districts had to attend to many teaching details anyway even when they were not in the classroom. The Kent cadre did not work out their budget difficulties well enough; they disbanded in 1975. While the Eugene cadre hesitated to create full-time specialist jobs, they did hire a full-time coordinator and rotated several half-time positions among other specialists on a yearly basis. This core of Eugene cadre members has managed most of the introductory demonstrations, the diagnostic interviews, and the follow-up consultations requiring work during regular school hours. They are critical for the viability of the Eugene cadre.

Conclusion

Reflections beyond these data and analyses lead us to conclude, at least temporarily, that peer consultation is particularly appropriate for North American schools for four reasons. (1) A strong social norm in support of local control puts emphasis on endogenous, evolutionary change, and encourages a wariness about the motives of outside experts and the effectiveness of imported solutions. (2) The ordeal of changing the educational bureaucracy calls for continual at-the-elbow assistance in contrast to the *ad hoc* availability of outside experts. (3) The budgetary constraints on publicly supported institutions, along with a tradition of paying very little money for advice, makes it inappropriate to hire high-priced OD consultants. (4) An ambivalence about using outside resources people is pervasive among educators. While outside experts may be stimulating, fascinating, and prestigious, they are not likely to appreciate or to empathize with the organizational life faced every day in the school, nor are they likely to be there when you need them.

Ten years of research and development on OD in schools have convinced us that peer consultation carried out by professional colleagues can overcome

158

these obstacles. Our intensive experiences in two school districts, along with more casual observations in several others, have shown that cadres of OD specialists can act as strong support structures for school renewal. They have helped members of school staffs become more skilful in interpersonal communication, more collaborative with one another, and more willing to take risks in trying out innovative practices. A few analyses have shown that cadres can have favourable impact on teacher–student interaction. However, even after ten years, a great deal is yet to be researched about how peer cadres compare in effectiveness with outside exports, about the impact of peer cadres, and about ways of establishing them to ensure their effectiveness. We simply have too few cases. We know little about their impact on raising the achievement levels of students, or about their effectiveness in closing the professional— citizen gap that exists in so many school communities. We do not know much about the career lines of part-time specialists and about how they might relate to others for professional recognition. What about the practicality and effectiveness of student or parent cadres? And what about its diffusion to other cultures? For how, we shall continue to observe very closely the diffusion of the idea of peer consultation along with other means of making OD a regular function in schools.

References

Arends, R. I. and Phelps, J. H. (1973) *Establishing Organizational Specialists Within School Districts*. Eugene, Oregon: Center for Educational Policy and Management, 65 pages.

Arends, R. I., Phelps, J. H., Harris, M., and Schmuck, R. A. (1973) *Organization Development in Schools: An Audio-slide Presentation*. Eugene, Oregon: Center for Educational Policy and Management.

Arends, R. I., Phelps, J. H., and Schmuck, R. A. (1973) *Organization Development: Building Human Systems in Schools*. Eugene, Oregon: Center for Educational Policy and Management, 50 pages.

Burr, A. M. and Bell, W. E. (1976) *The Eugene Cadre: Their Impact on a School District*. Eugene, Oregon: Center for Educational Policy and Management, 13 pages.

Phelps, J. H. and Arends, R. I. (1973) *Helping Parents and Educators to Solve School Problems Together: An Application of Organization Development*. Eugene, Oregon: Center for Educational Policy and Management, 130 pages.

Runkel, P. J., Wyant, S. H., and Bell, W. E. (1975) *Organizational Specialists in a School District: Four Years of Innovation*. Eugene, Oregon: Center for Education Policy and Management, 4 vols.

Schmuck, R. A. and Miles, M. B. (eds.) (1971) *Organization Development in Schools*. La Jolla, Cal.: University Associates, 264 pages.

Schmuck, R. A. and Runkel, P. J. (1970) *Organizational Training for a School Faculty*. Eugene, Oregon: Center for Educational Policy and Management, 191 pages.

Schmuck, R. A., Runkel, P. J., Saturen, S. L., Martell, R. T., and C. Brooklyn Derr (1972) *Handbook of Organization Development in Schools*. Palo Alto, Cal.: Mayfield Publishing Co., 436 pages.

Schmuck, R. A. (1973) *Incorporating Survey Feedback into OD Interventions*. Eugene, Oregon: Center for Educational Policy and Management, 14 pages.

Schmuck, R. A. and Schmuck, P. A. (1974) *A Humanistic Psychology of Education: Making the School Everybody's House*. Palo Alto, Cal.: Mayfield Publishing Co., 388 pages.

Schmuck, R. A., Murray, D. Smith, M. A., Schwartz, M., and Runkel, M. (1975) *Consultation for Innovative Schools: OD for Multiunit Structure.* Eugene, Oregon: Center for Educational Policy and Management, 382 pages.

Schmuck, R. A., Runkel, P. J., Arends, J. H., and Arends, P. I. (1977) *Second Handbook of Organization Development in Schools.* Palo Alto, Cal.: Mayfield Publishing Co.

Wyant, S. H. (1974) 'The effects of organization development training on communications in elementary schools.' Unpublished doctoral dissertation, University of Oregon.

Chapter 8

Toward a Theory of Power and Intergroup Relations

L. David Brown

Case Western Reserve University, U.S.A.

Catholics in Northern Ireland revolt against majority rule by Protestants, setting off years of fratricidal conflicts. Third party efforts to resolve the conflict fail miserably. 'Line-crossers' who seek to promote peaceful resolution of differences are maimed or murdered by militants on both sides, and women from both groups who seek an end to the bloodshed are denounced by their neighbours as traitors.

A tiny minority of whites in the Union of South Africa control a vastly larger population of blacks. The technological and organizational superiority of the whites apparently permits relatively stable maintenance of apartheid, in spite of worldwide disapproval, active efforts at subversion by various external agents, and internal tensions.

A large manufacturing concern is plagued by stormy relations with a local independent union. After a bitter strike—accompanied by fights, bombings, and sabotage—the comparatively weak local is replaced by a powerful international union, with vastly greater resources for conflicts with management. Management and workers promptly settle into comparatively peaceful negotiations.

These three cases are all examples of vertical intergroup relations, in which relations between groups are complicated by power asymmetries. Many of the most violent and intractable conflicts in the world today are characterized by the combination of group differences and power differences. But vertical intergroup relations have not been widely studied, in spite of their importance in organizations and societies increasingly characterized by differentiation and hierarchy. Behavioural scientists have examined group relations and power differences in some detail as separate topics, but comparatively little attention has been paid to their combination (van den Berghe, 1972; Converse, 1968, p. 531). Even less is known about how third parties may intervene constructively in those relations.

In this chapter I will examine two behavioural simulations to develop hypothesis about the effects of power differences on intergroup relations. I have two related theoretical objectives: (1) to develop the rudiments of a theory for understanding the structure and dynamics of vertical intergroup relations; and (2) to develop a preliminary theoretical basis for third party intervention in such relations.

I am trying to develop a perspective on and understanding of powerful social forces that I have encountered both as a primary party and as a third party concerned with improving intergroup relations. I am not objective, however desirable that might be. Although I will try to avoid being blinded by my biases, some information about those biases may be useful to readers. For example, I do *not* believe that power asymmetries, group differences, and the conflicts of interest they generate will cease to exist in any human social system I can presently imagine. I *do* believe that there are a number of options for handling differences and conflicts and that some options emphasize the constructive potential of differences more than others. I want to live in a society that allows (and even encourages) the existence of many diverse groups without being forced to accept mutually destructive conflict or oppression of some groups by others as the price for that diversity. I believe that better understanding of power and group relations can be of use in creating such a society, and this paper is intended to contribute to that understanding.

Theoretical background

Although little research directly examines vertical intergroup relations, much attention has been paid to horizontal (equal power) intergroup relations. I will summarize some important findings of research on horizontal intergroup relations as a prelude to investigating the impacts of power differences on them. On the basis of those findings, I will pose some questions to be examined in the context of the simulations.

(A) The effects of horizontal intergroup relations

Groups may be differentiated on dimensions that are not related to power: Religions may vary widely without being differently powerful, nations may differ and still be equally powerful. Such groups may cooperate, complete, or withdraw—and any of those relations may be constructive, neutral, or destructive, depending on the situation. Probably the most dramatic, and certainly the most studied relation is conflict.

Intergroup conflict may have dramatic effects on *intragroup* structure and dynamics. What was a loosely organized or even unidentifiable group is likely to be 'mobilized' by conflict. Mobilization involves pulling the group together into an aroused state appropriate to attack and defence. Boundaries between the group and its environment become better defined and less permeable; it becomes more important to distinguish between members and non-members and to regulate the flow of energy and information to and from the group (Coser, 1956; Janis, 1972). Cohesion among group members and conformity to group norms increases; militant leadership that holds members in a united front and inspires them with common purpose is common (Sherif, 1966).

Over time, the mobilized group develops an ideology and a world view that provides an organizing premise for their mobilization and justification for their actions against their opponent. (Janis, 1972; Deutsch, 1973). In short, intragroup mobilization involves boundary definition and regulation; internal cohesion, conformity, and militance; and the development of world views and ideologies.

Horizontal intergroup conflict also influences *intergroup* structure and dynamics. Conflict between groups produces mutual negative stereotyping, as group perceptions of each other become increasingly unfavourable (Sherif, 1966). Those stereotypes contribute over time to losing sight of similarities and interdependencies between the groups, and to an emphasis on their differences and conflicts of interest (Deutsch, 1973). As group boundaries become less permeable to information inputs and outputs, the amount of communication between groups decreases and the extent to which those communications are received with distrust or distortion increases (Blake and Mouton, 1961; Sherif, 1966). Distorted communications and negative stereotypes promote the use of militant representatives (Blake and Mouton, 1961), and aggressive actions against the other group (Deutsch, 1973). These ingredients in interaction have a self-reinforcing quality: Aggressive behaviour by one group confirms the distrust and stereotypes of the other, and legitimates their counteraggression, which in turn justifies counter-counteraggression in a vicious cycle (Deutsch, 1973).

Horizontal intergroup conflict might be much more frequently intense but for a variety of *extragroup* or environmental factors. For example, conflict between subsystems of a highly organized supersystem tend to be reduced when there are clear interdependencies among the parties (Sherif, 1966; Alderfer, 1975a). Cross-cutting allegiances of group members who share some group memberships but not others may help to moderate conflict (Coser, 1956; Blau, 1974). Mutual recognition of each other as a legitimate party can retard the escalation of conflict (Gamson, 1975; Dahrendorf, 1959). Ultimately, third parties affected by the escalation of conflict between groups may be drawn in to help control it (Thomas, 1976; Dahrendorf, 1959).

(B) The effects of power differences: some questions

What effect may differences in power between the groups involved have on their interaction? Power refers to access to and control over resources (such as physical force, information, rewards, legitimate authority) by one group that can be used to influence the other's behaviour (cf. Gamson, 1968 chapter 4). Upper groups are able to exert more influence over lower groups than the latter can exert on the former. The addition of such power differences to intergroup relations raises several questions that will be the focus of the rest of this paper.

Q. 1: Do power differences between the groups have any impact on intragroup developments within lower and upper groups?

Are the perceptions and behaviours of members of lower groups systematically different from those of upper groups? If there are differences, how do they effect internal group structure and dynamics? Do power differences have any impacts on the phenomenon of mobilization? Are those effects, if any, similar for upper and lower groups?

Q. 2: Do power differences between the groups have any impact on intergroup *developments between upper and lower groups?*

Do upper and lower groups interact in ways that are similar to equal group interaction? Is conflict as likely when upper and lower groups are involved? Do different degrees of power asymmetry make a difference? If conflict does occur, is it as likely to be self-reinforcing as that between equal groups?

Q. 3: Do power differences influence the impact of extragroup *factors on intergroup relations?*

Does the addition of power differences tend to exacerbate intergroup conflicts by reducing cross-cutting allegiances? Do external factors reduce escalation between upper and lower groups as much as they do between equal groups? What roles do third parties play between upper and lower groups?
These questions will be examined in the context of the two behavioural simulations described below.

Simulations of vertical intergroup relations

The simulations described below were designed from quite different perspectives, though they each produced clear cases of vertical intergroup relations. Behavioural simulations offer easily observable development of behaviour over a short term within a carefully bounded environment. The underlying structure and causes of behaviour may be much more visible in a carefully designed simulation than they could ever be in the chaotic complexity of the field, and such confounding field factors are previous history or individual predispositions may be systematically ruled out of simulation dynamics. No simulation is a perfect recreation of the field reality, of course, and a variety of alternative explanations for simulation behaviour may exist (see, for example, Banuazizi and Movahedi, 1975). But where the simulations, like the two below, produce behaviours closely similar to those observed in both laboratory experiments (see Kipnis, 1972) and covert participant observation (see Rosenhan, 1973), it seems reasonable to conclude that their results are worth further examination.

(A) Prisoners and guards in a simulated prison

Extreme power differences are quite common in institutions charged with completely caring for and in some way changing individuals (such as prisons, mental hospitals, boarding schools). Poor relations between unequally powerful groups in such settings have often been explained as the result of the personality types (for example, sadistic prison guards, brutal prisoners) that select themselves into the roles. Zimbardo and several colleagues designed a simulation to test this 'dispositional hypothesis' against the alternative explanation that the structure of the prison situation *creates* the behaviour of prisoners and guards (Zimbardo et al., 1973; Haney, Banks, and Zimbardo, 1973).

The investigators took great pains to obtain a sample of normal, college-age, male participants in the simulation, and then randomly assigned them to either the prisoner or guard roles—vitiating the 'dispositional hypothesis' as an explanation of subsequent behaviour. Guards were charged with maintaining law and order in the prison (realistically constructed in the basement of the Stanford Psychology Buildings), but were explicitly forbidden to use physical coercion. Except for this rule, they were largely allowed to work out their own means of managing the prisoners. The 'prisoners' were arrested at their homes by the Palo Alto police at the start of the experiment and formally inducted into the prison by the guards. The study was expected to run for two weeks.

The first day passed without incident. Guards mustered prisoners for brief 'counts' during each eight-hour guard shift. Early on the second day, the prisoners revolted: they barricaded themselves in their cells and heaped verbal abuse on the guards. The latter called in reinforcements (two standby guards and another shift), and crushed the uprising:

'(The guards) got a fire extinguisher that shot a stream of skin-chilling carbon dioxide and forced the prisoners away from the doors; they broke into each cell, stripped the prisoners naked, took the beds out, forced the prisoners who were the ringleaders into solitary confinement and generally began to harass and intimidate the prisoners.' (Zimbardo et al., 1973, p. 42–44)

The guards then created a 'good prisoner's cell with extra comforts to reward cooperative inmates, and subsequently mixed the 'good prisoners' with potential ringleaders of future revolts—'the prisoners never again acted in unity against the system'. (Zimbardo et al., 1973, p. 44).

As time passed, the guards increasingly made use of their power in arbitrary and unpredictable ways. They: '. . . insulted the prisons, threatened them, were physically aggressive, used instruments (night sticks, fire extinguishers, etc.) to keep the prisoners in line and referred to them in impersonal, anonymous, deprecating ways' (Zimbardo et al., 1973, p. 48–49).

The experience of such power was heady: 'All of the mock guards at one time or another . . . behaved sadistically toward the prisoners. Many of them reported . . . being delighted in the new-found power and control they exercised and sorry to see it relinquished at the end of the study' (Zimbardo et al., 1973, p. 49).

The prisoners, on the other hand, became increasingly passive and docile.

166

Less than 36 hours after the start of the simulation, one prisoner was released because of 'extreme depression, disorganized thinking, uncontrollable crying and fits of rage' (Zimbardo et al., 1973, p. 48). Within the next three days, four more prisoners had to be released because of signs of severe emotional disturbance. The prisoners who remained could be distinguished from those who were left only in that they were more authoritarian. By the sixth day, the deterioration of the remaining prisoners had progressed to the point where the investigators called a halt to the simulation, to the delight of the prisoners and the disgust of the guards.

The investigators concluded that the study did not support the 'dispositional hypothesis' for explaining prisoner-guard relations.

'The pathology observed in this study cannot be reasonably attributed to pre-existing personality differences of the subjects, that option being eliminated by our selection procedures and random assignment. Rather, the subjects' abnormal social and personal reactions are best seen as a product of their transaction with an environment that supported behavior that would be pathological in other settings, but was "appropriate" in this prison.' (Zimbardo et. al., 1973, pp. 56–58)

(B) Elites, Ins, and Outs in a simulated society

Extreme power differences also exist in the larger society, albeit in less confining circumstances than institutions like prisons. Oshry and his colleagues have developed a 'Power and Systems Laboratory' experience that creates a three-tiered miniature society over several days (Oshry, 1972; Smith, 1974). Different groups in the simulation have different degrees of access to and control over the society's resources (such as food, transportation, lodgings, entertainment, personal belongings of its members): the Elites control and have easy access to all resources (including the identification, money and clothes of all the other groups); the Ins have access to many (but not all) of those resources, but control over few; the Outs have neither access to nor control over those resources. The simulation was designed to explore the effects of power and power discrepancies, and to allow participants to learn about their own reactions to and skills in influencing power and system dynamics. Laboratory staff act as 'anthropologists' who observe events and as 'special resources' charged with helping the various groups work effectively. All the staff contribute to participant learning during a day and a half of debriefing after the four-day simulation.

The simulation described below took place in 1973, and has been described in detail by one of the observing anthropologists (Smith, 1974). My own perceptions of events may be substantially coloured by my participation in the simulation as an Out.[1]

The simulation took place at an isolated vacation resort during the off-season. Twenty-two participants were divided into demographically (race, sex, age) balanced groups: four Elites, nine Ins and nine Outs. The physical facilities included a dilapidated five-person house for the nine Outs, a more elaborate and roomy five-person house for seven Ins and a luxurious eleven-person house in which the four Elites and two of the Ins stayed (until the latter were evicted toward the end of the lab).

The Elites arrived half a day before anyone else to develop a plan for managing the society. They chose to preserve the three classes, to deal only with the Ins, and to plant several spies within the Ins to keep them from becoming too well organized. The constant absence of the spies, who did not return fully to the Elite until more than halfway through the simulation, made it difficult for them to continue to plan coherently and cohesively. The group as a whole never did develop much cohesion, though in the closing hours of the simulation they were united by common fear of the other groups.

The Ins found it extraordinarily difficult to work together as a decision-making group. The social pressures inherent in their middle position between Outs and Elites tended to fragment them, and that fragmentation was reinforced by constant tension between the Elite spies and two Ins who recognized the spies almost from the outset but were unable to get the other Ins to eject them. Almost simultaneously, after two days, the two Elites declared themselves and joined the Elite group, and one of their In opponents gave up and joined the Outs.

The Outs, who arrived at the site the day after the other two groups, almost immediately recognized their status and began to discuss their potential for a united front against the rest of the system. There were disagreements among individuals as to desirability of 'working with' or 'fighting' the system, but those disagreements never become a serious threat to the Outs' unity. On the second day of the laboratory when the Outs were feeling apathetic ('What the hell! We can stand on our hands for the next two days; Let's just go down to the beach and lie around'), they suddenly found they were to be deprived of their lunch. Galvanized, the Outs invaded the dining room ahead of the other two groups and ate the lunch of both the Ins and the Elites. This adventure cemented both their internal cohesion and their antagonism to the 'system'.

Relations among the various groups evolved rapidly. The Elite charged the Ins with the task of implementing various schemes to get the Outs to work for the society. But many of these schemes were based on little or no information about the Outs or their concerns, and they all failed. The Elites became increasingly contemptuous and abusive of the Ins, and increasingly fearful of the potential for violence among the Outs. Ultimately they became so disgusted with the 'society' and so fearful of the Outs that they left the site entirely for the last afternoon and evening of the simulation.

The Ins were hampered from the start by internal dissension, but they tried hard to hold the society together by providing a linkage between the Elites and the Outs. Under pressure from the Elites, they tried everything from cancelling meals to returning luggage to engage the Outs in productive activity under their management. But ultimately their efforts were abusively belittled by the Elites, while the Outs engaged in hours of superficially earnest negotiations that were largely aimed at misdirection and deception.

The radical and moderate elements of the Outs were welded together by the lunch takeover, but that split continued to influence the group's behaviour. Recognition of those differences (aided by a third party 'special resource' from the workshop staff) resulted in the gradual evolution of a two-pronged strategy designed to harass the Elites and enlist the support of the Ins. Negotiations with the Ins after the lunch takeover (and no supper) were publicly designed as cooperation and privately designed to harass the Elites by keeping them up all night. But that plan backfired (from the Outs' point of view) when the In go-betweens, exhausted, went to bed after being rewarded with their luggage by the Elites for bringing the Outs to negotiations. Stung, the Outs demanded the return of their own luggage from the Ins the next morning as a sign of 'good faith', while planning a more explicit 'entrepreneur-guerilla' strategy that called for overt cooperation with the Ins and covert sabotage of the Elites (such as, immobilizing their cars, constant subtle threats). They pursued this strategy with great abandon through the morning, contributing to the further deterioration of In–Elite relations.

Finally, the Elites had had enough. Unable to control the Outs, and increasingly fearful of them, they surreptitiously left the site (pushing their car). They left instructions with the kitchen to provide only suppers at the Ins' table that evening. The Outs, as usual early to the table, promptly ate all the food and then ridiculed the tardy and hungry Ins. The Ins, betrayed by both Outs and Elites, gave up their fruitless efforts to hold the society together and retreated to look after themselves for a change. The Outs enthusiastically burglarized the Elites' mansion. Taking away everything moveable.

As the simulation drew to a close, the Outs laboured to entice the Ins into an alliance against the Elites. The Ins, jealous of their newly found cohesion and not eager to join their erstwhile betrayers, finally agreed to participate in a 'new society', granted assurances that their separate identity would be preserved. When the Elites finally returned, they were greeted by a united front that wanted to try them for their 'crimes against humanity', though it was also agreed there should be some place for them in the 'new society'. The revolution was complete.

Discussion: some hypotheses

The two simulations created power differences between groups in the context of an organization and a society, though they varied in the size and the quality of the power differences created. The Elites controlled desirable resources, like money, identification, food, transportation, and housing. But they did not monopolize coercion—indeed, the balance of physical power lay with the Outs or the Ins, since each of those groups was double the size of the Elites. The Elites had little control over the physical setting or the movements of the other groups. If the other groups chose to reject the Elites' resources (as the Outs explicitly did) or to use physical coercion (as the Outs threatened), the Elites were not in a powerful position. The guards, on the other hand, controlled many of the same resources and privileges available to the prisoners. They also had more coercive power than the prisoners as long as the latter were locked three in a cell and the guards could call in reinforcements (at the counts, of course, it was nine to three for the prisoners). The guards also maintained constant surveillance of the prisoners and held close control over the physical setting. The guards were also probably accorded more legitimacy by the prisoners than the Outs conceded to the Elites. In short, the distribution of power in the simulations favoured the guards more than the Elites.

Superficially, the simulations also differed in the number of groups involved, since there was an obvious middle group in the society but not in the simulation. But it can be argued[2] that the prison simulation also involved three groups, in that the guards were in reality a middle group between the prisoners and the wardens (who held the real power in the situation and demonstrated it by ultimately calling off the simulation). In this interrelation, the two middle groups found spectacularly different solutions to the conflicts engendered by their position. The analysis that follows will focus primarily on the relations between upper and lower groups, but the role of middle groups may also bear more attention.

The outcomes of the simulations were drastically different. Power differences became a bone of contention in the society, and the Outs mobilized. The ensuing power struggle culminated in a revolution and an overturn of the relations between the Elites and the Outs. In the prison, in contrast, the initial effort to revolt by the prisoners brought on a reign of terror by the guards that created such oppression and prisoner deterioration that the simulation was stopped.

The following sections are organized around the questions posed earlier. Examination of the simulations suggests some tentative conclusions about the effects of power differences in intergroup relations that I have articulated below as hypotheses. Each hypothesis is followed by a brief description of the data on which it is based and some of its possible implications.

(A) Intragroup effects of power differences

Hypothesis (A)1. Power differences create perceptions, concerns, and attitudes in upper and lower groups that (a) support their power positions, and (b) undercut efforts to mobilize lower groups.

The experience of being powerful or powerless in itself seems to influence the perceptions and behaviour of upper and lower groups. Upper groups, for example, were concerned about system-wide issues. Guards worried about long-term management of the prisoners and the possibilities of invasion from outside; Elites spent hours planning for the society as a whole. Lower groups, on the other hand, worried about immediate and concrete issues. Prisoners talked a lot about food, and Outs were obsessed with food and entertainment. Upper groups were optimistic and active, and lower groups—at least initially—

tended to be pessimistic and apathetic. Upper groups were likely to over-estimate and lower groups to underestimate their control over events. Neither upper nor lower groups were very aware of the impact of their power position on their perceptions, attitudes, or concerns.

The differences between upper groups and lower groups created by power distribution in the simulation are very similar to the differences found in a variety of investigations of power (see Collins, 1975; Nord, 1976). Such power differences are often explained by variants of the 'dispositional hypothesis', in other words, some people are more able to think strategically, be active, and be optimistic, and so they gain power. It seems clear from this analysis that power asymmetry may *create* as well as *be created by* individual differences. In reality, structural position and individual personalities probably interact, with power differences reinforcing individual differences and vice versa. This interaction can maintain or exacerbate initial differences in the distribution of power—and make mobilization of lower groups very difficult since their members are likely to be trained and selected for relative passivity. In this light it seems likely that the society simulation was loaded for conflict, since the Out group was composed of individuals socialized to be active Elites and Ins and so poorly trained to adapt quietly to their Out position.

Hypothesis (A)2. Groups caught between upper and lower groups experience internal conflicts that may result in (a) internal dissention and decisional paralysis, (b) extreme identification with one of the other two groups, or (c) rejection of the middle position to preserve internal unity.

Middle groups that are pressed to mediate between upper and lower groups may be fragmented by the pressure of dealing with both. Thus the Ins found it extremely difficult to make decisions and commit themselves to a single policy even after the Elite spies and the more radical In left. The latter became a relatively radical member of the Outs, immediately joining (though not highly trusted by) the guerilla faction. In contrast to the Ins, the guards adopted an extreme view of their roles as protectors and managers of prison life—under-taking to carry out the wishes of the 'wardens' to an extent that finally provoked the wardens to stop the simulation. A third alternative for middle groups is to step out of the middle position, as the Ins did when they gave up both the Elite and the Outs as untrustworthy and began to look after their own needs—finally developing some internal cohesion in the process.

Middle groups are potential buffers to conflict between upper and lower helping to keep the parties in contact and working out differences (Blau, 1974). But this analysis suggests that the middle position can be highly conflicted, and that some alternatives to remaining in a highly conflicted position may result in escalation of the vertical intergroup conflict. Thus the overidentification alternative can result least two kinds of escalation: (1) middle-group radicals who are more determined than the Outs with whom they identify to 'pull the system down', or (2) middle-group reactionaries who are prepared to countenance acts to 'preserve the system' at which the Elite would baulk. The withdrawal from the middle position alternative brings together the upper and lower groups without a buffer—an outcome that may preserve the middle group but may also contribute to escalation between the other two parties.

Hypothesis (A)3. Power differences create a threat that (a) *increases* the likelihood of *attempted* mobilization, initially by the lower group, and (b) *decreases* the likelihood of *successful* lower group mobilization.

Comparison of the two simulations suggests that power differences can effect mobilization. In both simulations, lower groups attempted to mobilize before upper groups, in contrast to the simultaneous mobilizations of both groups in horizontal intergroup relations. The prisoners' attempted revolt created a crisis for the guards, and they responded by calling in all hands (the off-duty shift remained voluntarily) to quell the rebellion. The Outs grappled very early with problems of group unity, and were welded together by the threatened loss of lunch. The Elites, in contrast, never became as thoroughly mobilized as the Outs, though the eventual threat of Out attack brought them closer together. The existence of serious power differences between groups constitutes a threat to the lower group that encourages them to mobilize in self-defence.

But pressures for mobilization do not ensure success. Power differences may hamstring attempts by lower groups to pull themselves together. The guards had sufficient coercive power to crush the prisoners' initial efforts to mobilize, and their control over information, the physical setting, and subsequent prisoner contacts made it impossible for the prisoners to establish a boundary around their group or to regulate it—an early and necessary step in mobilization. The Elites, in contrast, were not able to control Out associations and interaction. Some minimal control over group boundaries with respect to membership, territory, and information is a prerequisite to mobilization. Power discrepancies that prevent such minimal control can be used to prevent successful mobilization.

Thus the relationship between power differences and mobilization may be curvilinear, as presented in Figure 1. The groups in the simulations are located at points that represent their degree of mobilization and the level of threat at different times in the simulations. The two lower groups—prisoners and Outs—were more mobilized than the upper groups early in the simulations because of the threat inherent in having less power. The guards, mobilized by the relatively small threat of the prisoner revolt, so dominated the prisoners that further prisoner mobilization was unlikely. The Elites, on the other hand, threatened the Outs enough to provoke intense mobilization, which later produced even more serious threats to the Elites themselves.

Hypotheses (A)4. Lower groups are subjected to (a) *overmobilization*, characterized by strong group identification, high energy, and projected

172

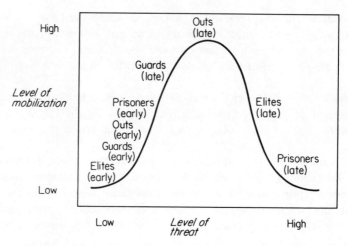

Figure 1 The relationship between threat and mobilization

hostility, and (b) *demobilization*, characterized by no group identification, passivity, and introjected hostility.

Mobilization had dramatic effects on intragroup structure and dynamics. The prisoners and the Outs represented the extremes on the mobilization scale in Figure 1, and their evolution as groups was quite different. The prisoners, after the annihilation of their rebellion, became a demobilized non-group. Prisoners chose individualistic rather than group-oriented strategies for managing their situation; they became very apathetic and passive; they tended to focus hostile feelings on each other rather than on the guards. The Outs, in contrast, clearly resolved the dilemma of the individual and the collective in favour of the group; they derived social support and energy from their interaction; they argued internally but focused almost all their aggressive feelings on the Elites and the Ins.

The pattern of developments associated with mobilization is familiar from studies of horizontal intergroup conflict (Sherif, 1966; Blake and Mouton, 1961), though it seems to be extreme in vertical intergroup relations. It has been less clear that severe power differences may encourage *demobilization* with consequent destruction of group identity. The effects of demobilization may combine with the effects of being powerless (cf. Hypothesis (A)1) to reproduce a long-term, self-reinforcing cycle of powerlessness (Nord, 1976).

(B) Intergroup effects of power differences

Hypothesis (B)1. Small initial differences in power asymmetry that influence early intergroup interactions have disproportionate effects on long-term outcomes.

Power differences in intergroup relations are likely to have complex rather

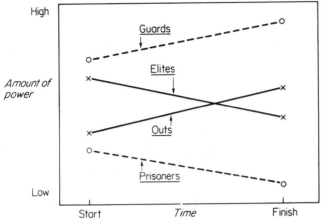

Figure 2 Power differences over time

than simple effects. Power was very important to upper and lower groups in both simulations, though their outcomes were very different. Prisoner–guard relations rapidly became an ascending spiral of dominance and submission, with increasingly sadistic and capricious guards lording it over increasingly submissive and apathetic prisoners. Out–Elite relations, in contrast, became a series of conflicts that resulted in increased power for the Outs and decreased power for the Elites. Although lower groups in both, simulations potentially had more coercive power than the upper groups (such as, three guards 'counting' nine prisoners, or four Elites facing nine Outs), that physical advantage was never the threat to the guards it became to the Elites. The guards' early victory over the prisoners and their subsequent activities apparently aborted the potential physical threat.

The guards did have somewhat more control over the prisoners than the Elites did over the Outs: Information about the lower group was more available to the guards than to the Elites, and the freedom of movement available to the prisoners was less than that available to the Outs. But that initial asymmetry was not comparable to the inequality that developed over the course of the simulation, as pictured in Figure 2. Power differences between guards and prisoners widened over time, while the gap between Elites and Outs narrowed and then flipped over so that the Outs were on top. There may be a critical band of power asymmetry, within which the differences promote conflict and convergence, and beyond which the differences promote oppression and divergence.

Hypothesis (B)2. Power differences contribute to self-reinforcing cycles in intergroup relations that produce (a) increasingly intense conflict between upper and lower groups, or (b) increasingly severe oppression of lower by upper groups.

Power differences influence the process of interaction between upper and lower groups in ways that heighten the level of tension and increase the likelihood of explosive outbursts of conflict. Lower groups protect themselves by not communicating freely about their dissatisfactions to upper groups. The prisoners expressed their discontent before they were able to protect themselves from guard retaliation, with devastating results. The Outs, in contrast, carefully controlled information transmission to the Elites and the Ins, and so were able to manipulate In–Elite interaction and sabotage their cooperation. Valid information about events may become as precious to upper groups as ability to influence those events is to lower groups. Without credible information upper groups must plan on the basis of attributions about the lower groups, like the Elites and Ins planning no lunch for the Outs. Ignorant upper groups may overreact to 'irrational' and 'unreasonable' eruptions of long-suppressed discontent from lower groups. Such overreactions serve to confirm lower group suspicions, thus fuelling escalating conflict. Sensitive intergroup relations around information and influence created by power differences are exacerbated by perception and attitude differences associated with membership in upper and lower groups.

These escalating cycles are not endless. Conflict that continues to escalate eventually culminates in decisive victory for one party or exhaustion for both. Oppression may also have limits—though the prisoners in the simulation seemed to be continuing to deteriorate, it is clear that not all real prisoners become to apathetic and passive (see Jackson, 1970 & Anonymous, 1973). There may be a 'nothing to lose' effect that operates in some oppressive situations. That effect could be expected to promote escalating conflict rather than cooperation, however, since it would be expressed in intense reactions to upper group influence. In general, this analysis suggests that power differences tend to exacerbate rather than retard the self-reinforcing, escalative quality of intergroup interaction, whether the mode of interaction is conflict or oppression.

(C) Extragroup effects of power differences

Hypothesis (C)1. Power differences undermine the moderating effects of extragroup influences on the escalation of interaction between upper and lower groups.

The simulations offer limited (but provocative) information about the effects of extragroup factors, since they were bounded off from the external environment in many ways. For example, cross-cutting allegiances or cross-group social mobility (with the exception of one In who became an Out), that might retard the escalation of interaction, did not exist in the simulations. Power differences undercut the influence of other environmental factors. Thus the common supersystems of the groups ('the prison', 'the Society') made them somewhat interdependent, but appeals to that interdependence were not very persuasive to lower groups that felt no stake in the larger system. Although upper and lower groups may have had legitimate claims that deserved recognition, the power differences made it difficult for them to recognize those claims once they had become threats to each other. Norms against violence existed at the outset in both situations (for example, physical coercion was forbidden to guards, society participants accepted explicit responsibility for physical or personal damage they inflicted), but those norms became 'inoperative' rapidly as threats to group positions were mounted: guards used physical force to subdue and humiliate prisoners, and Outs vandalized Elite cars and burgled their house.

At a minimum, power differences add another dimension of differentiation to whatever dimensions separate the groups in the first place. But power differences tend to affect a variety of extragroup factors. It has been suggested that when a society is characterized by many verical intergroup relations—in other words, that parameters of social differentiation (such as race, power) are highly correlated (for example, whites have power, blacks have none)—that those social differentiations tend to become rigid and impermeable. Societies with rigid concentrations of power and wealth are unable to adapt flexibly to change, and ultimately may require violent revolutions to cope with a changing world (Blau, 1974). This societal analysis is disturbingly consistent with the dynamics of the two simulations.

Hypothesis (C)2. Although the likelihood of third party intervention increases as intergroup interaction escalates and has extragroup effects, the existence of power differences between the parties makes gaining access to and preserving credibility with both groups difficult.

The boundary that guarded the simulations from interventions by external third parties was largely impermeable. But extreme escalation of intergroup conflict or oppression tended to invoke third party attention despite the boundaries. In the prison, for instance, the guards and the researchers became very worried that the first prisoner to be released might return with friends to liberate the others, and created all sorts of contingency plans to deal with the anticipated invasion (which never materialized). Visits by outsiders highlighted the potential for external interference, which may have encouraged the decision to end the simulation. In the society, third parties were also drawn into the fray. A 'special resource', radicalized by Elite scapegoating, joined the Outs to burglarize the Elite house. The manager of the convention centre intervened to prevent the use of centre equipment for that burglary, and the Outs seriously considered calling the local police to report their luggage and wallets as stolen by the Elites.

Third party interventions may take a variety of forms, particularly when the interaction has become overt conflict (Thomas, 1976). Third parties may act as advocates or mediators or enforcers of procedural rules (Lau and Cormick, 1972); they may act to empower or depower one or both parties (Brown, in press). But the more serious and encompassing the power asymmetries, the more difficult it is for third parties to establish and maintain some independent power base from which they can credibly mediate between the parties in conflict. Third party intervention is also possible when power differences result in oppression. But escalated oppression may not come to the attention of third parties, since the lower group is unable to raise the issue and the upper group is unlikely to do so. And the remedies for the human consequences of oppression are not well understood. Third party intervention in vertical intergroup relations is problematic; third party intervention to deal with the effects of oppression may be even more difficult.

Implications

I have discussed intergroup relations in the simulations at three levels of analysis: intragroup, intergroup, and extragroup. Table 1 summarizes the most obvious differences' between horizontal and vertical intergroup relations that have emerged from this analysis. The introduction of power differences produces unsynchronized intragroup mobilizations that may result in either overmobilization or demobilization of the lower group. Power differences also encourage the explosive escalation of intergroup interaction, resulting in extremes of either conflict or oppression. The extragroup factors that moderate intergroup conflict between equally powerful groups do not operate as effectively between unequal groups, so allowing escalation to continue unchecked. In short, the introduction of power differences creates relationship problems at all three levels.

The problems at different levels are further complicated by the fact that the levels interact. Macrolevels constrain microlevels: Extragroup factors provide the constraints within which intergroup relations take place, and intergroup developments in turn provide the context for intragroup events. And microlevels influence macrolevels: Intragroup developments affect intergroup relations, and intergroup relations set off extragroup events. The pressures toward extreme and destructive escalation of interaction that are visible at all levels of vertical intergroup relations are likely to support and reinforce each other.

Given that vertical intergroup relations are likely to be destructive, what can be done? Does this analysis offer any implications for constructive third party intervention in intergroup relations complicated by power asymmetries?

The phenomenon of conflict has been analysed in terms of *process*, focusing on the flow of events or conflict dynamics, and in terms of *structure*, focusing on relatively static underlying conditions that influence conflict (Thomas, 1976). The two analytic approaches are complementary, but they suggest different approaches to third party intervention in vertical intergroup relations. Process interventions involve influencing the stream of events, and structure interventions involve changing underlying conditions. In actual practice the two forms of intervention may be less distant, since structure and process may be expected to interact in a specific situation (see, for example, Alderfer and Brown, 1975). But it is valuable to use both perspectives in analysis and in trying to devise interventions.

Table 1 Power and intergroup relations

	Horizontal (equal) intergroup relations	*Vertical (unequal) intergroup relations*
Intragroup developments	*Synchronized* mobilization of both groups that leads to: boundary definition and regulation cohesion, conformity, and militant leadership ideology and organizing premise development	*Unsynchronized mobilization* that leads to either: (A) *Overmobilization* or strong group identification close cohesion and conformity hostility projection or (B) *Demobilization* individualistic identification fragmentation hostility introjected or projected to own group
Intergroup developments	*Symmetrical* interaction that leads to *progressive* escalation, involving: negative stereotyping reduced and distorted communications militant representatives and aggressive behaviour	*Asymmetrical* interaction that leads to *explosive* escalation of either: (A) *Conflict* strong negative stereotypes covert discontent and aggression from lower group overreactions by surprised upper group or (B) *Oppression* suppression of lower group mobilization escalating dominance by upper group escalating submission by lower group
Extragroup developments	Conflict *moderated by* contextual factors, including: supersystem interdependencies social mobility cross-cutting allegiances mutual recognition norms against extreme behaviour third party pressure	Interaction *unmoderated* by contextual factors: no lower group stake in supersystem allegiances and mobility undermined by correlated differences recognition and norms undercut by conflict intensity no access for third parties

At the intragroup level, the phenomenon of mobilization seems crucial. Vertical intergroup relations are characterized by unsynchronized mobilization, in which the parties mobilize at different (potentially incompatible) times. Third parties may have to help demobilized or unmobilized lower groups organize, aiding the creation of external boundaries and internal structures and facilitating the conceptualization of issues and the management of the mobilization process (for example, Alinsky, 1972). Third parties may also help to create structures and processes to counter overmobilization, like Janis's (1972) 'devil's advocate'. Although access to one party often precludes access to ther other in vertical intergroup relations, independently based and unpolarized third parties may be able to coordinate upper and lower group mobilization—for example, integrating an unmobilized lower group and differentiating an overmobilized upper group so the two can cooperate (Brown, in press). Third parties, in short, may be able to influence the intragroup mobilization and demobilization of upper and lower groups.

At the intergroup level, third parties may be concerned with controlling the escalation tendencies of upper and lower group interaction. Structural interventions include the development of temporary or permanent forums within which communications might take place in relative safety (Dahrendorf, 1959). Alderfer (1975b), for example, created a long-term 'communications group' within a large organization in which representatives from many levels and social groups were encouraged to speak frankly about their perceptions and concerns and to plan strategies for dealing with organizational problems. In a more escalated situation, Klein, Thomas, and Bellis (1973) tried to create a temporary workshop setting in which representatives of the black ghetto and the white police force could meet to consider their differences, relatively protected from inflammatory extragroup factors. Process interventions at the intergroup level may involve improving communications among the upper and lower groups through careful management of their interaction and development of their understanding of the dynamics involved (see Doob and Foltz, 1973).

At the extragroup level, more general structural developments, like increasing cross-cutting allegiances and cross-group mobility (Blau, 1974), and increasing the stake of lower groups in the system may reduce escalation. Third parties may emerge to influence even vertical intergroup interaction where the overriding goal is sufficiently important to both parties (for example, the Irish Mothers for Peace seeking to protect their children). Process interventions that encourage mutual recognition of upper and lower group legitimacy and the development and evenhanded enforcement of norms against escalative tactics may also help promote effective extragroup control of escalative interaction.

Conclusion

I began this paper with three examples of vertical intergroup relations: civil war between Protestants and Catholics in Northern Ireland; white oppression of blacks in South Africa; paradoxical shifts in company–union relations with the advent of a stronger union. Those examples may have seemed extreme, pathological flukes selected from a universe of possible cases. I would argue that the analysis of this paper suggests that those cases are not flukes, but straightforward extensions of the possibilities inherent in all vertical intergroup relations. Indeed, the most obvious lesson of the simulations is that few of us are immune. In a shockingly short period of time, the right social conditions produced extraordinarily intense and violent interaction among everyday human beings. Only rudimentary theoretical frameworks exist for analysis of intergroup relations that are compounded by power asymmetries. Our technology for constructive intervention in them is, if anything, even less developed. Can we afford to neglect the area longer?

Acknowledgement

The author wishes to thank Clayton Alderfer, John Aram, David Kolb, and Barry Oshry for their comments on earlier drafts of this chapter.

Note

1. I am indebted to Barry Oshry for pointing out several instances of such bias in an earlier draft of this chapter.
2. Barry Oshry suggested this interpretation. He also argues that the prisoner in fact won the conflict with the wardens by them, by their 'crazy behaviour' to end the simulation early.

References

Alderfer, C. P., (1975a) 'Boundary relations and organizational diagnosis.' *Humanizing Organizational Behavior*. Edited by H. Meltzer and F. R. Wickert, Springfield, Ill.: C. C. Thomas.

Alderfer, C. P. (1975b) 'Improving organizational communication through long-term intergroup intervention.' Presented to the American Psychological Association Convention, Chicago, September.

Alderfer, C. P. and Brown, L. D. (1975) *Changing from Learning: Organizational Diagnosis and Development*, Beverly Hills, Cal.: Sage, Chapter 5, p. 10.

Alinsky, S. D. (1972) *Rules for Radicals*. New York: Vantage Press.

Anonymous. (1973) 'Voice from the real world.' *New York Times Magazine*, **April 8**, 40.

Banuazizi, A. and Movahedi, S. (1975) 'Interpersonal dynamics in a simulated prison,' *American Psychologist*, **30**, 152–60.

Blake, R. R., and Mouton, J. S. (1961) 'Reactions to intergroup competition under win–lose conditions.' *Management Science*, **4**(4).

Blau, P. M. (1974) 'Parameters of Social Structure.' *American Sociological Review*, **39**, 615.

Brown, L. D. (1978) 'Can haves and have-nots cooperate? Two efforts to bridge a social gap.' *Journal of Applied Behavioral Science*, **13** (In press).

Collins, R. (1975) *Conflict Sociology*. New York: Academic Press.

Converse, E. (1968) 'The war of all against all: a review of the *Journal of Conflict Resolution*, 1957–1968.' *Journal of Conflict Resolution*, **12**(4), 471–532.

Coser, L. (1956) *The Functions of Social Conflict.* New York: Free Press.
Dehrendorf, R. (1959) *Class and Class Conflict in Industrial Society.* Stanford, Cal.: Stanford University Press.
Deutsch, M. (1973) *The Revolution of Conflict.* New Haven, Conn.: Yale University Press.
Doob, L. W., and Foltz, J. W. (1973) 'The Belfast workshop: an application of group techniques to a destructive conflict.' *Journal of Conflict Resolution,* **17**(3), 489–512.
Gamson, W. A. (1968) *Power and Discontent.* Homewood, Ill.: Dorsey Press.
Gamson, W. A. (1975) *The Strategy of Social Protest.* Homewood, Ill.: Dorsey Press.
Haney, C., Banks, B., and Zimbardo, P. (1973) 'A study of prisoners and guards in a simulated prison.' *Naval Research Reviews,* **September,** 1–17.
Jackson, G. (1973) *Soledab Brother: The Prison Letters of George Jackson.* New York: Bantam Books.
Janis, I. (1972) *Victims of Groupthink.* Boston, Mass.: Houghton Mifflin.
Kipnis, D. (1972) 'Does power corrupt?' *Journal of Personality and Social Psychology,* **24**(1), 33–41.
Klein, E. B., Thomas, C. S., and Bellis, E. C. (1973) 'When warring groups meet: the use of a group approach in police–black community relations.' *Social Psychiatry,* **6,** 93–99.
Lau, J. H., and Cormick, G. W. (1972) 'The ethics of social intervention: community crisis intervention programs.' *Paper presented to the Conference on the Ethics of Social Intervention, Batelle Institute,* **May 10–12.**
Nord, W. R. (1976) 'Developments in the study of power.' *Concepts and Controversy in Organizational Behavior* (2nd edition). Edited by W. R. Nord. Pacific Palisades, Cal.: Goodyear Publishing, 437–50.
Oshry, B. 'Power and the power lab.' (1972) *Contemporary Organization Development: Conceptual Orientations and Interventions.* Edited by W. Burke. Washington: NTL Institute for Applied Behavioral Science, 242–54.
Rosenhan, D. L. (1973) 'On being sane in insane places.' *Science,* **179,** 250–58.
Sherif, M. (1966) *In Common Predicament.* Boston: Houghton-Mifflin Co.
Smith, K. K. (1974) 'Behavioral consequences of hierarchical structure.' *Unpublished Doctoral Dissertation, Yale University.*
Thomas, K. (1976) 'Conflict and conflict management.' *Handbook of Industrial and Organizational Psychology.* M. D. Dunnette (ed.) New York: McGraw-Hill, 889–935.
van der Berghe, P. (1972) *Intergroup Relations: Sociological Perspectives.* New York: Basic Books, 8.
Zimbardo, P. G., Haney, C., Banks, W. C., and Jaffe, D. (1973) 'A Pirandellian prison: the mind is a formidable jailer.' *New York Times Magazine,* **April 8,** 38–60.

Chapter 9

An Overview of Recent Tavistock Work in the United States

Edward B. Klein

University of Cincinnati, U.S.A.

Clayton Alderfer, an editor of this book, and I, participated in a four-year faculty seminar—which studied NTL and Tavistock approaches to organizational theory and practice. Last year, he invited me to review recent scientific Tavistock work and I informed him that there were not many American experimental studies. We therefore agreed on an expanded definition of this chapter. I mailed out over 80 requests to colleagues in the United States and England for their work (published, in press and in preparation) which would provide the broadest base for an overview of current activities. Based on their responses and a review of the recent literature, this chapter presents a selected picture of the current state of the field. The review is not complete and I have stressed certain issues more than others. For purposes of clarity, the article is organized into a number of discrete (although related) areas: theory; background; empirical studies; comparisons between different group approaches; training; group process and the application of Tavistock theory in clinical, educational, community and systems work. Women in authority is presented last, since it is the most recent development in the area.

Theory

The Tavistock approach has its intellectual roots in the individually focused psychoanalytical work of Melanie Klein (1959) and other British object relations theorists, especially in their emphasis upon the defensive use of projective identification and splitting which originate in the first year of life. This work was used by Wilfred Bion (1961) in developing a model for understanding group psychotherapy. He posited two levels that simultaneously occur in any group. The first is the *work group*, or that aspect of the collectivity which pursues the socially agreed-on task of the group (agenda setting, leadership, and outcome). The second has to do with the emotional aspects of the group or its *basic assumption* life, which is stimulated by anxiety. Bion introduced the concept of valency, a person's natural attraction toward one of the basic assumption. He then explicated three basic assumptions which occur at a group level. These he called dependency (members acting as if the leader had all of the knowledge), fight/flight (feeling as if the group either has to fight or flee from the leader) and pairing (as if some combination of two people will give rise to a magical solution or an idea which will perpetuate the group). The 'as if' quality has to do with certain fantasies, primarily about the leader, operating in the group which make it difficult to test reality. Bion suggested that there might be more than three basic assumptions and Turquet (1974) has introduced another, fusion, the tendency to deny differences or level members, which results in a certain 'mindless' quality in group discussions (such as denial of obvious racial and sexual differences in the group). In addition, the social structure of the setting also stimulates transference and other phenomena which provides a rich field for study and learning.

Klein and Bion's work was utilized by A. K. Rice and other social scientists affiliated with the Tavistock Institute in applying individual and group theory to the working of complex systems. From Bion's work, they used the idea of investigating task performance and how authority is experienced in a group. The primary stress was placed on understanding group behaviour, and the influences of social structure, rather than specific change-oriented approaches, per se. They studied authority and its delegation, leadership, followership, task performance and covert dynamics.

These authors have proposed the idea of a sociotechnical system and suggested the autonomous work group as a constructive, organizational innovation (Trist et al., 1963). They seek congruence between the system tasks and the structure utilized to enable those tasks to be completed. An important aspect of this work is its emphasis on unconscious motivation and hypotheses for relating organizational structures to individual ego defensive processes. For instance, Menzies (1967) studied a nursing setting and found that the organizational structure formed a social defence system which operated to eliminate activities and relationships that evoke anxieties. Jacques (1955) showed that the negotiation of wage rates by management and labour in the Glacier Metal Company was affected by unconscious mechanisms for dealing with paranoid and depressive anxieties.

A major concept is that of the primary task, which is defined as the work that an organization has to do to survive in its environment (Rice, 1963). The Tavistock approach emphasizes the primary task with group level interventions (Trist et al., 1963; Rice, 1958, 1963). In this way of organizing work, employees form autonomous groups to accomplish total tasks. Within groups, workers exchange assignments according to interests and ability. Workers self-select and the group as a whole is paid according to its total production, rather than individual contributions. The literature suggests that there are many desirable results of this approach. Satisfaction and production are often higher and absenteeism is lower. Workers report a heightened sense of cohesion, greater use of skills and abilities and a decrease in intergroup jurisdictional battles.

With regard to leadership, the major focus has been on external boundary management. The leader is seen as 'Janus-like' since he must look both inward and outward and deal with pressure from both directions. The mutual dependency and hostility between leaders and followers is recognized. Leaders fail and frustrate followers and followers withhold support and threaten leaders. Rice's (1965) emphasis upon the hostility residing in followers and leaders, is noteworthy because this issue is often ignored by other organizational approaches. The difference may be due to the level of systems analysis. Tavistock writers focus more on the external boundary management of top leaders, not the needs of workers or middle managers. Rice (1965) noted that a leader makes decisions on behalf of followers with or without their collaboration. He wished to enable leaders to develop insights which would allow them to stand amid the multiple cross-pressures accompanying their role. Rice viewed leaders as managing the work and sentience boundaries of organizations, although the latter distinction is not as well developed in his published papers (Rice, 1970).

The central Tavistock concept is that of *boundaries*, or the region that separates the individual from the group or the group from the rest of the environment. Boundaries have time, spatial and geographic aspects (Miller, 1959). Another concept emphasized by Tavistock writers is that of *role*, in its social psychological sense as a locus for both internal psychological and external social pressures. Other orientations focus on social or demand aspects of role at the expense of ignoring the more psychological components of role performance. Others take a purely intrapsychic view without accounting for social norms (Levinson, 1959).

Trist and Bamforth (1951) studied a British coal mine which used two different work systems. The longwall method minimized close interpersonal and group relations; workers were assigned to specific tasks and paid on an individual basis. This led to low performance, passivity, and high absenteeism. A more social, group approach was introduced (the 'composite longwall' method) leading to higher morale, productivity, attendance and safety (Emery and Trist, 1960; Trist et al., 1963).

Rice (1953, 1955a, 1955b, 1958) utilized similar sociotechnical procedures in an Indian weaving mill. He observed that there was a decline in both the quantity and quality of products with installation of looms and task specialization. Rice then introduced semi-autonomous work groups with a decrease in job levels, and task interchangeability. Two-year follow-up indicated a significant rise in morale, productivity and decline in wastage.

Recently, Miller (1975) reported on a seventeen-year follow-up of Rice's (1953) original Ahmedabad experiment. Rice worked on experimental changes in automatic and non-automatic loom-sheds in an Indian textile mill. In 1970, Miller returned to Ahmedabad and found that in one of the original sites (the non-automatic experimental loom-shed), the work organization and levels of performance had remained virtually unchanged over seventeen years. He reports that group identification was high, members cooperated with one another in their work, and the group leader exercised the boundary function so that supervisors seldom intervened with individual group members. Miller concludes the Rice's original ideas have been largely substantiated and found that the goal of designing systems to minimize the chances of disaster (becoming technologically or economically irrelevant) may be more appropriate to industrial organizations than is generally recognized.

Hill (1971) focused on management philosophy, the development of human resources, and productivity at Shell UK Limited. This consultation started as an attempt to decrease alienation, and succeeded in positively influencing both attitudes and production within the company. A number of Tavistock investigators have been involved in experiments in Norway. The literature (Emery and Trist, 1960; Thorsrud, 1969; Trist, 1970) suggests that these sociotechnical interventions have increased productivity and decreased worker alienation in projects with workers, employers and the Norwegian government.

The major summary work in this area is Miller and Rice's *Systems of Organization* (1967). The first part of the book presents theory and the remainder applications to several organizations. This book offers rich illustration of the dilemmas of task performance, management, authority and its delegation, leadership, followership and the problems involved in being a consultant.

Background

In America, the group relations conference is the best known application of Tavistock theory. The first Tavistock conference was held in 1957 at the University of Leicester in England. Initially, conferences focused on small group behaviour with some application of small group theory to members' organizational settings. Other group events were gradually introduced into the design (intergroup exercises, Higgin and Bridger, 1964) in order to more readily approximate complex social systems. Over the years, conferences have changed with a shift from the study of authority in small groups to an understanding of the conference itself as a temporary social system. A major role in this development was played by the late A. K. Rice who directed all of the Tavistock–Leicester conferences from 1962 to 1968. In 1965, the first Tavistock group relations conference was held in the United States at Mount Holyoke College, sponsored by the Washington School of Psychiatry, Yale University Psychiatry Department, and the Center for Applied Social Research of the Tavistock Institute of Human Relations. At the first American conference, Dr Pierre Turquet introduced formal application groups to aid members in the transition to their back-home work roles.

A major figure in the importation of the Tavistock approach to the United States was Dr Margaret Rioch who has maintained leadership for its continued development. After the death of Dr Rice in November 1969, the A. K. Rice Institute was formed in 1970 to continue Tavistock work in the United States. The Institute is now a confederation of seven affiliated centres located in Connecticut, New York, Washington–Baltimore, Texas, Los Angeles, San Francisco, and the Midwest (Cincinnati, Madison and Minneapolis). In 1975, a *Group Relations Reader* (Colman and Bexton) was published containing some of the major theoretical and applied work. In 1971, a quarterly,

185

Journal of Personality and Social Systems, was published, sponsored by the A. K. Rice Institute.

Empirical studies

After attaining the first American conferences. Yale faculty members started a work group, the interdepartmental seminar on groups (IDSG). This seminar provided opportunities for mental health and social science students to learn about group process, and investigated the effects of such group training. The first research explored members' perceptions of T-group trainers and study group consultants (Harrow et al., 1971). Students perceived trainers as significantly more emotional, flexible, open, pleasant, friendly, close, satisfying and non-authoritarian than consultants. Consultants were seen as more authoritarian and distant, and less emotional, friendly and gratifying than trainers. Kohler, Miller and Klein (1973) studied the effects of intergroup experience on small group phenomena. After the disorganizing effect of an intergroup event, consultants were rated by members as being more sensitive close and less authoritarian and powerful. The small study group began to view itself as a sanctuary against disruption from the rest of the conference, paralleling individual and group behaviour in disasters. Canavan (unpublished) did intensive personal interviews with twelve mental health students who attended a combined NTL–Tavistock conference. Members learned from both experiences, but felt that Tavistock was more useful in their work and NTL more valuable for personal concerns. Joseph, Klein and Astrachan (1975) surveyed the same members as Canavan with a six-week and six-month follow-up. Not unexpectedly, mental health students reported learning mostly about authority and power at work, socially and personally, and less about family issues. In the six-month follow-up, students who voluntarily joined T-groups were lonelier, unmarried, had been in groups previously and were somewhat more likely to be in therapy. Indeed, these students may have become involved in T-groups to obtain what was missing in the conference. The systems analysis employed helps explain the greater learning and lack of psychological distress at such institutionally sponsored conferences since students had role models at work whom they had experienced as leaders in the training events.

Klein (in press), investigated transference phenomena in NTL and Tavistock small groups in two separate studies. As predicted, there was more transference in psychoanalytically oriented study groups than the social psychologically focused T-groups. Transference manifestations were more apparent in the beginning and end than the middle sessions of Tavistock groups. In addition, particular aspects of members' perceptions of the leader having to do with stern 'superego' qualities (authoritarian, inhibited, frank) were more illustrative of transference than other adjectives.

Butkovich et al. (1975) investigated group atmosphere, focal conflict and member reactions toward leaders of study and T-groups by rating audiotapes of sessions. These authors looked at the course in which the group experience was embedded as a social system and analysed a number of group focal conflicts in each of the two approaches. In addition, they investigated interaction in the groups and observed a number of significant differences between study and T-groups. As predicted, there was significantly more member–leader aggressive comments toward consultants than NTL trainers, and more member–member interaction, member–member aggression, discussion of interactions and feelings in T-groups than in Tavistock study groups.

Cytrynbaum (unpublished) did an empirical study of four discussion-oriented classes, two taught by white and the other two by black teachers at Tuskegee Institute. He then factor-analysed tape recordings of class inter-actions. Cytrynbaum concluded that different student-to-teacher patterns supported the general hypothesis that distinct forms of task-related work and disruptive emotionality were associated with different management strategies employed by the black and white teachers.

Empirical studies of group phenomena have been carried out in other settings. Mills (unpublished) and his colleagues at the State University of New York at Buffalo have conducted extensive analyses of self-study groups utilizing videotape procedures, questionnaires and observations. They have come up with a number of tentative and stimulating results from this ongoing research project. There are a number of group characteristics that lead to difficulties in becoming a self-analytic group: a dependent atmosphere; relying primarily upon abstract principles and universalistic standards; and a strong tendency to remain anonymous. In addition, there is some evidence that groups can add systems awareness to their own culture and that this can be done at both the group and individual level. As such groups become more self-conscious, members tend to value versatility and variety. This work is important in that the analysis is based on many groups, from various institutions, and studied by different quantitative methods.

Brown and Ellithorp (1970) have applied a Bionian analysis of attitudes towards followers of Senator Eugene McCarthy in his candidacy for the 1968 presidential nomination. By use of factor analytic methods, he was able to demonstrate some support by various subgroups of followers who could be characterized as demonstrating dependent, fight and pairing attitudes towards the Senator. For instance, a McCarthy follower demonstrating dependency would be one who saw him as a father-figure type, with an image of strength stability and capacity for providing needed reassurance. A follower who demonstrated pairing is one who viewed McCarthy as a genius or messiah. The fight person is full of anger and hate and saw the remote McCarthy as having tendencies to attack the system. What is of particular interest about this paper is the application of analytically derived group concepts to attitudes toward a political leader.

A number of doctoral dissertations done at City College of the City University of New York have systematically studied, at an empirical level, several aspects of social systems. Gertler (1975) investigated a Tavistock intergroup relations weekend training conference held at City College. Based on questionnaire responses of members and observations by trained staff, he concluded that there was a relationship between some of Bion's basic assumptions and group formation and interaction in this intergroup weekend. At a more systemic level, Gertler provides a nodal analysis of the conference demonstrating that the most critical events had to do with member–staff interactions. In essence, he shows that there are developmental stages in intergroup relations which are most parsimoniously understood by the effects of direct contact between staff and members. This study is in keeping with the development of the Institutional Event at A. K. Rice conferences with its focus on the boundary between the total membership as a group and the staff group. Feinstein (1974) studied the impact of a group and drug training experience at a medical school on a number of educators from a local public school system. The analysis, based on observations, interviews, and questionnaires, demonstrates some of the dilemmas of a subgroup with additional training returning to its parent institution in the hope of carrying out social change. This study richly documents systems resistance to change at a variety of levels. Eagle and Newton (unpublished) studied videotape recordings of scapegoating incidents occurring in four study groups within a weekend Tavistock conference. They observed a phenomenon they call *task displacement* in which the group unwittingly shifts its emphasis from task performance to conformity. Allegedly, antiwork behaviour and motivation are projected into one individual who is then controlled through scapegoating.

Paine and Huebner (1973) provide some statistical support for the idea that students should be exposed first to study group and then T-group experiences in order to maximize learning. Bovilsy and Singer (in press) investigated confrontational group treatment of smoking. The most effective treatment was one in which the leader confronted members continually, organized a fight stance against smoking and developed a culture (group pressure, support and encouragement) which reinforced abstinence from smoking. There have been two investigations of members' personal behaviour. Brown (in press) looked at individual member's personality change over time and related them to the roles they palyed in the group. Ryan (unpublished) demonstrated that members in Tavistock groups, in comparison to control subjects, change significantly more from pre-testing to post-testing on the California Psychological Inventory on the dimensions of Social Presence and Intellectual Efficiency. Brown (1976) investigated the effect of seating arrangements on verbal interactions that occur in Tavistock study groups, but obtained ambiguous results.

In general, several of the empirical studies done to date have demonstrated what one might expect—namely, that group leaders of different persuasions are seen in ways that are consistent with their theoretical orientations; members tend to learn about the issues that receive major emphasis in the different group approaches; transference is more apparent in analytical than in social psychologically oriented groups; and that optimal training might best proceed from analytical to T-groups. In addition, larger events in the conference impinge upon the small self-study group; that there may be developmental stages in intergroup as well as in small group events; and that there are measurable, system resistances to social change in small groups and larger organizations. In addition, there is some work suggesting personality changes associated with membership in a Tavistock study group.

Comparisons of different group approaches

The IDSG included faculty members with both Tavistock and NTL orientations. Both empirical studies (Harrow et al., 1971; Joseph, Klein, and Astrachan, 1975) and theoretical works were undertaken. Alderfer (1970) contrasted both small group orientations from an NTL, and Klein and Astrachan (1971) from a Tavistock, orientation; while Bunker (unpublished) described Tavistock from an NTL view. This was a time of collaboration between the two approaches as witness Klein and Astrachan's (1971) conclusion that in order to learn maximally in groups, a theoretical model needs to be developed which combines elements of both T-group and study theories. The authors recommended a model which provides understanding of the groups' reactions to authority (not only with regard to irrational elements but also the realistic one) and the development of pear interactions. They concluded that the two approaches are complementary and that individuals first be exposed to study groups in order to experience the primitive aspects of group life, then T-groups to experience the ways in which collaboration may restructure the group experience with regard to individual growth and cooperation. This suggestion was subsequently empirically supported by Paine and Huebner (1973).

Singer et al. (1975) addressed the issue of boundary management in a variety of groups. They conceptualized group events as temporary institutions in which a variety of tasks or goals are pursued. The role of the group leader was viewed as containing managerial authority and responsibility. A typology of group events was developed based upon the task system and the psychological level at which it is pursued. The authors described six types of groups: interpersonal learning (T-groups); group process learning (Tavistock study groups); personal growth (Schutz, 1967); focus criterion (Alcoholics Anonymous, Synanon, Daytop, Weight Watchers); individually oriented change (Slavson, 1964; Perls, 1969); and group process-oriented change (Yalom, 1970; Whitaker and Lieberman, 1964; Bion, 1961; Foulkes, 1961). Using a social system, organizational perspective, they explored management aspects of work in these six types of groups. The authors suggest that an accurate diagnosis of the members' or organizational needs is necessary for the proper design of the event, and that a clear contract between leader and clients is necessary for optimal outcome. The article is consumer-oriented (reflecting changes in the group movement and political awareness) and provides guidelines so that both member and leader can be clear about the contractual understanding and the roles involved in training and treatment groups.

There have been comparisons between NTL and Tavistock group relations training, but to date no comparisons of organizational research and consultation. Therefore, after the IDSG ended, a smaller group of six investigators representing both approaches studied the same organization simultaneously. Alderfer and Klein (unpublished) looked at three issues that distinguishes the two approaches: assumptions about human behaviour; relations between social structure and social process; and the nature of leadership and power. They studied a large industrial plant in terms of its internal functioning, relationship to national management and community relations. A team of one NTL and one Tavistock consultant investigated each of these three boundaries (internal, management and community) in a plant which prided itself on having a theory-Y philosophy (democratic, with power sharing). Theory-Y behaviour was most viable for secure internal issues. Theory-X (authoritarian and hierarchical) behaviour occurred when any of the following was present: a dual power source (unions, an alternative philosophy, pressure groups); strangers (minorities; a deviant department); people on unclear boundaries (foremen; community relations executive); or an authority group that is external and more powerful (corporate headquarters), that is, whenever there is potential threat to survival. In general, within plant activities which management controls are more positive and Y-like. If communications are external with people whose value base is similar, it will also be Y-oriented. The authors conclude that no single variable (such as management philosophy, structure, process, leadership, group psychology, or expression of affect) explains the complexity of what was observed, but rather a multidimensional analysis is needed to understand X and Y behaviour in the plant, community and corporation. The research approach used in this study contributed to a more differentiated view of Tavistock and NTL theory. The methodological innovation of one NTL and Tavistock researcher at each of the three boundaries (intraplant, plant–corporation and plant–community) aided in developing a balanced view of the phenomena. One observer from each orientation provided correction for tendencies to move in extreme directions.

Training

There are a variety of descriptive articles focused on the training of members of particular disciplines. Most often these involved Tavistock small self-study groups but occasionally they involved more complex training events. The majority of these articles described the training of people in mental health, though recently this has broadened to include other professions. There have been several papers about the training of psychiatric residents (Almond and Astrachan, 1969; Astrachan and Redlich, 1969; O'Connor, 1971; Redlich and Astrachan 1969); group psychotherapists (Shapiro, 1971); historians (Musto and Astrachan, 1968); architects (Bexton, 1975; Colman, 1975); political scientists (Brown, in press); general practitioners (Gosling and Turquet, 1964); mental health ward personnel (Gustafson and Hausman, 1975); psychotherapists (Rioch, Coulter, and Weinberger, 1976); and paraprofessionals (Bunker and Singer, unpublished). Recently, Rioch (1974) has written about the training conference as offering parallels with university training of health professionals.

In general, these descriptive papers focus on learning about authority, leadership, followership, power, and convert group dynamics. The authors usually conclude that members in such groups find it useful, particularly in terms of work issues. These findings are quite consistent with the empirical studies cited before, particularly the work of Joseph, Klein, and Astrachan (1975).

The study of group processes

Early work in this area by Bennis and Shepard (1956) demonstrated the compatability of the two approaches as seen in a group developmental sequence (that is, group struggles first with authority, then peer relations). This article supports the idea of exposing students to study group and then T-group experiences. Work by Mills (1965; 1967) presents a sociology of small groups. Rioch (1970) explicates Bion's (1961) formulation of the work group and basic assumption life in the small group. Rioch's paper is extremely useful for understanding a number of Bion's concepts. Slater (1966) provides a rich overview of self-study groups, focusing particularly on the phenomenon of revolt.

Tuckman (1965) presents an overview of developmental sequences in small groups, regardless of orientation, and concludes that the first phase of group life is dependency. Taking all of the above studies into account, it would seem likely that there are a series of developmental stages in such self-analytic groups. Klein (in press) has suggested that the stages of group development are as follows: (1) becoming a member of the group (leaving traditional roles); (2) dependency (on the leader to provide direction); (3) fusion (making all members equal); (4) fight (the revolt described by Slater), (5) flight; (6) pairing initially in the hope of a magical solution and later in a sophisticated alliance with the leader to understand the group process); and (7) leaving the member role (preparation for taking on the more traditional roles one has at work).

There have also been a number of papers describing intergroup phenomena (Higgin and Bridger, 1964; Astrachan and Flynn, 1976); intermediate size groups (Reed, in press); and large groups (Turquet, 1975). Reed speculates about intermediate (approximately twenty-member groups), while Turquet deals with the threats to identity in the large group. Turquet focuses on the multiple dilemmas faced by an individual who wants to maintain individuality under the threats of conformity. A recent volume on the large group has been published (Kreeger, 1975) bringing together theoretical and applied work.

Rice (1965) has described the major Tavistock group training techniques in terms of structure and process. More recently, Rice (1969) has detailed individual, group, and intergroup processes from a system perspective. Clearly, the area that has been most thoroughly studied, both in training and treatment, is the small group. Dynamics of intermediate, large, and intergroup events are less clearly formulated. Concepts derived from individual, group, and system theory will have to be more fully integrated and explicated for work to proceed in this area. More research is needed to parallel what has already occurred in the study of small groups.

Clinical work

Newton (1971; 1973) compared the family and psychotherapy as social systems. He focuses on the division of authority and labour between father, mother and child in the family and the analyst and patient in therapy. Father and mother respectively manage the external and internal boundaries in the family while the therapist manages both boundaries in psychotherapy. Newton (1971) details systems reasons for abstinence in psychotherapy paralleling mother's role in family, and describes (Newton, 1973) systems similarities which give rise to transference, resistance and change. The last article is particularly useful for social science students since it demystifies transference and demonstrates the social structural aspects of the psychotherapy situation that reactivate early experiences from the family system. Newton's approach makes it more possible for patient and therapist to be clear about the realistic elements (authority and power relationships) in therapy in addition to the transferential aspects, which are stimulated by the structure of psychoanalytic psychotherapy.

Astrachan (1970) presents a social system model of therapeutic groups which is broader than member to leader, group to leader, or member to member, orientations. He argues for an understanding of the group psychotherapist's role as regulator of the external boundaries of the therapy group. This analysis is useful in clarifying the therapist's management role in conducting group treatment.

There have been applications of this approach in various patient groups and institutions; cancer patients (Gustafson et al., unpublished); day hospital treatment (Astrachan, et al., 1970); in—patient work (Lofgren, 1976; Cooper, 1971; 1974) and the use of sociotherapy in the therapeutic community (Edelson, 1970a; 1970b). These principles have also been applied in doing programme evaluation in psychiatric settings (Kohler, in press).

Miller and Gwynne (1972) studied five residential institutions for the disabled. Most of these developed social defence mechanisms, viewing inmates as both physically and emotionally dependent. A smaller number deny dependency and emphasize achievement. The authors describe the former as 'warehouses' and the latter as 'horticultural'. Using an open system model, the authors suggest ways for leaders and staff to move towards, and operate the latter model. This is a very sensitive report focused on the dilemmas of the treatment of chronically ill patients for staff, patient, family and community.

Reid and Marinaccio (unpublished) provide a system analysis of an open line project in Connecticut. They write about how such a telephone emergency line affects clinical service within the agency and in the larger community. Most recently, practitioners have turned toward a system approach to family treatment. Within the Tavistock tradition, there is the work of Shapiro (1971) and Fleck (unpublished). Writers with other types of system approaches to family treatment have also significantly influenced the area, as witness the popularity of Minuchin (1970) and Aponte and Hoffman (1973).

Kernberg (1973; 1974; 1975a; 1975b) has attempted to integrate psycho-analytical object relations theory, group process and administrative perspective. He is working toward an integrated theory of hospital treatment which would encompass these three perspectives.

What the majority of these papers have in common is a multiple focus on individual, group and system analysis. The authors are aware of the fact that hospital dynamics influence group treatment which, in turn, affects individual patients and therapists. This is a more sophisticated view than an exclusively dyadic, doctor–patient focus.

Educational applications

Elizabeth Richardson (1967; 1973; 1975) has written extensively on the use of group work with teachers; the relationship between the teacher, the school and management; and authority and organization in English secondary schools. Eisold and Schachtel (1976) describe the use of a small study group in a course where students investigate how they have been shaped by their family experiences. These authors conclude that there are two useful outcomes; a heightened sense of individualization and a greater understanding of how the educational system tends to promote basic assumption behaviour (particularly dependency) in the service of established social authority.

Greenwood (unpublished) had 400 students in courses with Tavistock, NTL, *Gestalt* and encounter group experiences keep diaries. Preliminary results indicate that NTL methods lead to the most internal dialogue concerning group roles, process, organization, evaluation, and action plans. Tavistock facilitates introspection about the group, task, consultants, members' short and long range goals, and self. Hausman (1976) has described the dilemmas of becoming the head of a psychiatry department in terms of multiple primary tasks; education, service and research. Klein and Gould (1973) used a study group at the Yale Summer High School with lower class black and white underachievers. This approach surfaced many of the larger issues within the Summer High School including its overly 'pseudodemocratic norm', which often denies the larger societal realities concerning race and social class. Braxton (1974) detailed the creation of a new educational model for change with black youth (the teen leadership institute). Singer, Whiton, and Fried (1970) describe consultation activities to a school system using Tavistock group and system concepts. Zegans, Schwartz, and Dumas (1969) used a group approach which helped to understand a variety of racial, class and other issues confronting a metropolitan high school in conflict. Newman

(1967; 1974) described the use of group process in consultation and practice in school systems.

What the above work has in common is the use of a group for explicating, in microcosm, the larger pressures on the educational setting in interaction with its environment.

Community work

Two articles have reported on the use of the Tavistock group approach with police and community groups. Klein, Thomas, and Bellis (1971) described work done in a training event involving police officers and community residents in New Haven. They discussed a number of difficulties confronting both the membership and group leaders. In general, members tended to learn about each other's viewpoints and the importance of black leadership which led to lesser stereotypes. They discussed issues in keeping with the background of the group leader (legal issues with a lawyer, mental health issues with a psychiatrist and community relations with a community-based group leader). This training event was disrupted by larger political issues not under the control of the group leaders (an attempted police arrest of a member and militants occupying the church used for the group meetings) suggesting that they are often called in crisis situations. The authors conclude that leaders should be aware of their limited authority to provide other than consultation to such groups who wanted a temporary ceasefire rather than an end to their 'war'. Rogers (1972) reported on work done with the Washington, DC police department.

Jones and Thomas (1976) have issued a challenge to the A. K. Rice Institute to make their group approach more broad-based. They particularly suggest reaching out to the community by employing consultants from different ethnic groups and modifying some of the language of the theory to make this approach more acceptable to minorities, particularly blacks.

Hammerschlag and Astrachan (1971) offer a group analysis of a potential disaster in an American airport. They describe, from a system viewpoint, what happened when hundreds of people were snowed in for a number of days at Kennedy Airport.

Janis (1972) analysed critical foreign policy decisions made by the United States government over the past 20 years. One of his examples is the Bay of Pigs fiasco. He utilized a Bionian small-group theoretical framework in order to understand the decisions made by the late President Kennedy and his Cabinet. Janis gave some fascinating data; yet it appears that an intergroup analysis is necessary to provide the broadest perspective on this type of faulty decision-making in foreign affairs.

A crisis-focused community intervention consultation took place in Belfast, Northern Ireland. In a series of papers (Alevy et al., 1974; Doob and Foltz, 1973, 1974; Miller, 1976), a combined Tavistock–NTL training event held for 56 community leaders from Belfast is described in detail. The intervention included a planning phase, nine-day training conference in Stirling, Scotland, one-year research follow-up, and a weekend conference for the original participants which took place a year and a half later in Portrush, Northern Ireland. The Stirling conference was held with a membership which varied by religion, sex, age and political affiliation. The only non-represented group was the British government. The consultants were seen by members as the English authorities. Members used the social defences of religion, age and sex in the training conference to deal with the difficulties at home. In general, youth, women and Catholics were most involved and expressive at Stirling. The one-year follow-up (Doob and Foltz, 1974), based on interviews with 40 of the 56 participants, suggested that a great deal was learned, although for a number of participants there was confusion and distress. There was also some implementation of the learning in the back-home community setting, mostly within one's own religiously defined community.

These community-based interventions are more dramatic and occur under less controlled conditions than the usual training conference. Because of the difficulties of maintaining a boundary around such events and the life and death issues dealt with, people have criticized this type of work. These training activities may indeed get out of control because of external reality factors. The articles cited above illustrate some of the difficulties of organization, conduct and research on such training activities. One might conclude that such events are precarious in nature and the outcomes are highly problematic. The Belfast intervention, although useful for individuals both in terms of learning and back-home application, may not have its ultimate payoff until peace develops in Northern Ireland so that the experiences at the conference could more readily be put into practice.

Social system theory and practice

Most of the system work in the United States has been done in mental health settings. Levinson and Klerman (1967) described some of the dilemmas of the clinician-executive. The authors focus on the need to have an integrated social psychological view of the organization; becoming a social system clinician; problems of authority, relations between disciplines and groups outside of the organization; and providing for growth and innovation in achievement of a fuller identity of clinician-executive. Levinson and Astrachan (1974) describe the entry system to a community mental health centre as a boundary region between the community and the centre. They point out that if difficulties arise on intake, the course of treatment, and particularly termination, becomes highly problematic. Newton and Levinson (1973) studied a psychiatric inpatient ward within a biological research centre. They detail some of the dilemmas involved in systems that have competing tasks, in this case, biological research and clinical care. They describe the ways in which the task(s), social structure, culture and social process of the larger organization enter into and shape the character and task performance of the clinical teams. Ambiguity and covert dissention about the respective priorities among multiple, major tasks interferes with adequate service to patients and negatively affects staff morale. Snow and Newton (1976) studied the community mental health centre movement from a social system perspective. They examined task conflict between direct and indirect services and the ambiguity that developed in the activist, late 1960a regarding the true priority of the direct service task.

Dolgoff (1972; 1973; 1975) has written about small group and institutional boundary maintenance difficulties, sociotechnical systems, and power and conflict within mental health organizations. Menninger (1972) describes the experience of his institution's participation in Tavistock group relations training over a period of six years. He concludes that the group relations experience has given the organization more of an 'observing ego', a conceptual framework that has enabled people to grapple more effectively with the problems of organizational life. He feels that it has provided a means of reducing the impact of irrational forces within the organization, freed up time and energy for work and expanded the clinic's educational thrust. This article may appear overly sanguine, but the client-organization is genuinely pleased with the long-range and long-term effects of its participation in Tavistock group relations conferences.

Many of the papers deal with the dilemmas of leadership and clear authority delegation within mental health organizations which have attempted to broaden their viewpoint. Most take account of not just the total organization's impact on service delivery and client but the surrounding community's pressures (resources, political issues, money) as they impact upon the mental health system. All move toward a broader vision of the mental health service system with related components that communicate well with each other. It is of interest that a discipline which is so involved in studying communication, either individually or socially, has only belatedly turned its attention to communication problems on an organization-wide and interorganizational level. Indeed, one would expect that the consumers of mental health services might experience communication difficulties if the organization itself is not clear about its primary task, its authority and leadership structures.

Women in authority

Bayes, Whisnent, and Wilk (in press) discuss a women's group and its relationship to a community mental health centre. The issues raised are likely to arise when one organization is hierarchical and the other is a social movement, an alternative group whose membership is open to those who share its beliefs and values. This type of organizational encounter is not infrequent, as traditional organizations attempt to be responsive to groups within their communities. They describe the dilemmas involved in simultaneously being a member of both groups, as well as being a woman. In many ways, much of the affect was put into women making it very difficult to accomplish their stated task. Bayes and Newton (1976) provide a sociopsychological analysis of women in leadership roles. Based on two-year consultancy-based observation of a single case, they conclude that: women are placed in a difficult position as leaders because of cultural stereotyping and subordinates' tendency to search for the *real* (male) authority. When authority is invested in a female leader, subordinates often make covert challenges which the leader does not recognize or confront. It is difficult for either a male or a female subordinate to get into the number two position with a number one female leader because there have been few previous important experiences with such a social role relationship in adult life. The presence of a female leader appears to stimulate strong dependency needs within the group and leads to the idea that her real task is caretaking and training. When the female leader behaves in a work-oriented fashion, but non-nurturant, she is experienced as profoundly depriving. The authors conclude that women in authority must counteract strong social forces in order to be effective leaders. These include role socialization, fantasies, and other irrational forces in the organization, the work group and in herself, which act to complicate her attempts to exercise authority. An understanding of these sources of difficulty allows a work group and its female leader to confront problems of authority and subordination more effectively.

A number of group dynamics research studies have looked at the effects of gender composition of group and gender of leader. Aries (1976) found that competition, aggression and concern over status were predominant in all male groups, while in all female groups the focus was on intimacy, openness and personal relations. Men also avoided a high degree of intimacy with other men which was not like the responses of all women's groups. In groups that were mixed by gender, the changes were greater for men than women. Men in these groups developed a more personal orientation, increased the amount of interaction and displayed greater self-revelation. They also decreased in aggressive behaviour. Women changed less dramatically decreasing discussion of personal issues and speaking less in mixed settings than in all female groups. It seems that mixed settings have greater benefit for men than women since it makes men more variable while resulting in greater restrictions for women. Wright (1976), Beauvais (1976) and Hisman (1975) generally agree that men leaders were responded to more positively than female leaders. For instance, Beauvais found that male group members receive non-reciprocating male leaders as relatively friendly while both male and female group members view a non-reciprocating female leader as contemptuous. Wright and Gould (in press) reviewed the above findings, and others, and discussed their implications for group psychotherapy. They discussed issues of identification, transference, countertransference and resistance. They specifically comment that a woman therapist may find herself more often the target of negative transference than a male counterpart. As a consequence, they have more negative or distressing countertransferential reactions, for instance, she may find herself often feeling unskilled, incompetent, isolated and ignored. It is therefore important for women in authority in general, and women therapists in particular, to avoid colluding with cultural stereotypes if they are to be effective leaders. This is a pervasive issue clinically since often therapy groups or family therapy cases are led by male/female co-therapists who can be made into two-dimensional objects by the group with little subsequent growth for both therapists and patients. The studies of women are therefore important for understanding relations between the sexes in general.

Summary and conclusions

The Tavistock work in England has been marked by a good deal of organizational consultation and a number of research studies of the effectiveness of sociotechnical interventions. Most of the organizational work has occurred in industrial settings. Investigators affiliated with the Tavistock Institute of Human Relations have worked with labour, management, business and governmental groups for over 30 years. This relationship with the economic sector is reflected in the Leicester conferences where the majority of the membership is usually from business, industry, prison systems, general health organizations and other governmental agencies. In contrast, A. K. Rice Institute conferences have memberships mostly drawn from mental health and educational organizations. This is historically determined by the prominent role played in the first American conferences by the Washington School of Psychiatry and the Yale Department of Psychiatry. Later, the participation of the Menninger Foundation furthered this mental health trend. The research and application in the United States is also in keeping with this early American experience. Most research has been done with small groups used to train mental health and social science students. Similarly, application has taken place primarily in mental health institutions. Not surprisingly, the research and application are most integrated when there are university-based A. K. Rice centres.

Although there is a strong mental health influence in American Tavistock work, more recent developments have expanded applications into other disciplines (architecture, political science, history, law). Social forces within the United States have also raised awareness about consumer rights (Singer et al., 1975), community involvement, racial issues and the changing role of women in society. Tavistock, having been imported from England, now has an American thrust reflecting the dynamics of our particular society. The boundaries around the A. K. Rice Institute have become more permeable as it adjusts to and mirrors the changing culture. Indeed, from an open system view point, it has to continue to do this or it will become an isolated training model with diminishing influence. Recent specialty conferences have focused on conflicts between disciplines, male–female authority relations, racial issues and normal adult development. The most popular conferences over the past few years have been on male–female relations. This can be seen as a direct outgrowth of the women's movement and its influence on training approaches. In the future, other societal issues (energy, regionalization, planning, employment, and ageing) will be reflected and studied at training conferences, applied in organizational settings, and, hopefully, in investigatory activities.

198

References

Alderfer, C. P. (1970) 'Understanding laboratory education: an overview.' *Monthly Labor Review*, 18–27.

Alderfer, C. P. and Klein, E. B. 'Leadership style and affect as functions of organizational boundaries.' (Unpublished paper).

Alevy, D., Bunker, B., Doob, L., Foltz, W., French, N., Klein, E., and Miller, J. (1974) 'Rational, research and role relations in the Stirling workshop.' *Journal of Conflict Resolution*, **18**, 276–84.

Almond, R. and Astrachan, B. M. (1969) 'Social systems training for psychiatric residents.' *Psychiatry*, **32**, 277–91.

Aponte, H. and Hoffman, L. (1973) 'The open door: a structural approach to a family with an anoretic child.' *Family Process*, **12**, 1–44.

Aries, B. (1976) 'Interaction patterns and themes of male, female and mixed groups.' *Small Group Behavior*, **7**, 7–18.

Astrachan, B. M. (1970) 'Towards a social systems model of therapeutic groups.' *Social Psychiatry*, **5**, 110 -19.

Astrachan, B. M. and Flynn, H. R. (1976) 'The intergroup exercise: a paradigm for learning about the development of organizational structure.' In E. Miller (ed.) *Task and Organization*. London: John Wiley & Sons.

Astrachan, B. M., Flynn, H. R., Geller, J. D., and Harvey, H. H. (1970) 'Systems approach to day hospitalization.' *Archives of General Psychiatry*, **22**, 550–59.

Astrachan, B. M. and Redlich, F. C. (1969) 'The effect of leadership ambiguity on resident behavior in study groups.' *International Journal of Group Psychotherapy*, **19**, 487–94.

Bayes, M., Whisnent, L., and Wilk, L. A. 'The mental health center and the women's liberation group: an intergroup encounter.' *Psychiatry* (In press).

Bayes, M. and Newton, P. (1976) 'Women in authority: a sociopsychological analysis.' Presented at the Scientific Meetings of the A. K. Rice Institute.

Beauvais, C. (1976) 'The family and the work group: dilemmas for women in authority.' Unpublished doctoral dissertation, The City University of New York.

Bennis, W. G. and Shepard, H. A. (1956) 'A theory of group development.' *Human Relations*, **4**, 415–37.

Bexton, W. H. (1975) 'Group processes in environmental design: exposing architects and planners to the study of group relations.' In A. D. Colman, and W. H. Bexton, (eds.), *Group Relations Reader*, 251–63.

Bion, W. (1959) *Experiences in groups*. Basic Books. Also Ballentine Books, 1961.

Bovilsky, D. M. and Singer, D. L. 'Confrontational group treatment of smoking; a report of three comparative studies.' *International Journal of Group Psychotherapy* In press).

Braxton, E. T. (1974) 'The creation and disruption of a revolutionary education for change model (The Teen Leadership Institute).' Unpublished doctoral dissertation, Union Graduate School.

Brown, S. R. and Ellithorp, J. D. (1970) 'Emotional experiences in political groups: the case of the McCarthy phenomena. *The American Political Science Review*, **64**, 349–66.

Brown, S. R. 'Psychodynamics and group dynamics.' In J. W. Sweeney, Jr. (ed.), *Psychology and Politics, a Psycho-social Study of Political Power*. New Haven: Yale University Press (In press).

Brown, S. (1976) 'The relationship of seating distance to the sequence of verbal interaction in small face-to-face groups.' Unpublished Master's thesis, The American University.

Bunker, B. B. 'The Tavistock approach to the study of group process: reactions of a private investigator.' State University of New York at Buffalo (unpublished paper).

Bunker, B. B. and Singer, D. L. 'Independent nonprofessionals in a community setting: a case history analysis' (unpublished paper).

Butkovich, P., Carlisle, J., Duncan. R., and Moss, M. (1975) 'Social systems and psychoanalytic approaches to group dynamics: complementary or contradictory?' *International*

199

Journal of Group Psychotherapy, **25**, 3–31.

Canavan, P. 'Reactions of social science and mental health students to a group relations training conference.' Unpublished doctoral dissertation, Yale University.

Colman, A. D. (1975) 'Environmental design: realities and delusions.' In A. D. Colman, and W. H. Bexton, (eds.), *Group Relations Reader*, 329–41.

Colman, A. D. and Bexton, W. H. (1975) *Group Relations Reader*, A. K. Rice Institute.

Cooper, L. (1971) 'Systematic use of groups in an acute psychiatric unit.' *Group Analysis*, **4**, 152–56.

Cooper, L. (1974) 'Application group: broadening the patient experience in a psychiatric organization.' *British Journal of Psychiatry*, **124**, 247–51.

Cytrynbaum, S. 'Multiple task and boundary management in the interracial college classroom.' Yale University, Department of Psychiatry, (unpublished paper).

Dolgoff, T. (1972) 'Power, conflict, and structure in mental health organizations: a general systems analysis.' *Administration and Mental Health*, **1**, 12–21.

Dolgoff, T. (1973) 'Organizations as sociotechnical systems.' *Bulletin of the Menninger Clinic*, **37**, 232–57.

Dolgoff, T. (1975) Small groups and organizations: time, task and sentient boundaries.' *General Systems*, **20**, 135–41.

Doob, L. W. and Foltz, W. J. (1973) 'The Belfast workshop: an application of group techniques to a destructive conflict.' *Journal of Conflict Resolution*, **17**, 489–512.

Doob, L. W. and Foltz, W. J. (1974) 'The impact of a workshop upon grass-roots leaders in Belfast.' *Journal of Conflict Resolution*, **18**, 237–56.

Edelson, M. (1970a) *The Practice of Sociotherapy*. New Haven: Yale University Press.

Edelson, M. (1970b) *Sociotherapy and Psychotherapy*. Chicago: University of Chicago Press.

Eagle, J. and Newton, P. M. 'An organizational study of scapegoating in small groups' (unpublished paper).

Eisold, K. and Schachtel, Z. (1976) 'Application of study group experience to personal histories: aspects of a course on "growing up" ' Paper, Paper, Scientific Meetings, A. K. Rice Institute.

Emery, F. E. and Trist, E. L. (1960) 'Sociotechnical systems', In C. W. Churchman, and M. Verhulst (eds.), *Management Sciences: Models and Techniques*. New York: Pergamon.

Feinstein, W. (1974) 'Boundary events in systems consultation.' Unpublished doctoral dissertation, City College of the City University of New York.

Fleck, S. 'Boundary issues between family and community systems.' Unpublished manuscript, Yale University.

Foulkes, S. H. (1961) 'Group process and the dynamics of the individual in the therapeutic group.' *British Journal of Medical Psychology*, **34**, 23–31.

Gertler, B. V. (1975) 'Open-systems theory and intergroup relations.' Unpublished doctoral dissertation, City University of the City College of New York.

Gosling, R. and Turquet, P. (1964) 'The training of general practitioners: the use of group method.' Paper presented at the Tavistock Institute of Human Relations, London, England.

Greenwood, J. D. 'A comparison of descriptors of self talk as evidenced in NTL, Tavistock, *Gestalt*, and encounter groups.' Unpublished manuscript, University of Cincinnati.

Gustafson, J., Colman, F., Kipperman, A., Whitman, H., and Hankins, R. 'A cancer patient's group—the problems of containment.' Unpublished paper, Madison, Wisconsin.

Gustafson, J. and Hausman, W. (1975) 'The phenomena of splitting in a small psychiatric organization: a case report.' *Social Psychiatry*, **10**, 199–203.

Hammerschlag, C. and Astrachan, B. (1971) 'The Kennedy Airport snow-in: an inquiry into intergroup phenomena.' *Psychiatry*, **34**, 301–308.

Harrow, M., Astrachan, B., Tucker, G., Klein, E. G. and Miller, J. (1971) 'The T-group and study group laboratory experiences.' *Journal of Social Psychology*, **85**, 225–37.

Hausman, W. (1976) 'Reorganization of department of psychiatry.' In E. Miller, (ed.) *Task and Organization*, London: John Wiley.

Higgin, G. and Bridger, H. (1964) 'The psychodynamics of an intergroup experience.' *Human Relations*, 17, 391–446.

Hill, P. (1971) *Towards a New Philosophy of Management*. New York: Barnes and Noble.

Hisman, B. (1975) 'The effects of leader sex and self-disclosure on member self-disclosure in marathon encounter groups.' Unpublished doctoral dissertation, Boston University.

Janis, I. L. (1972) *Victims of Group Think*. Boston: Houghton Mifflin.

Jacques, E. (1955) 'Social systems as a defense against persecutory and depressive anxiety.' In *New Directions in Psychoanalysis*. New York: Basic Books.

Jones, J. E. and Thomas, J. (1976) 'Uses of group relations methods in black communities.' Paper, Scientific Meetings, A. K. Rice Institute.

Joseph, D. I., Klein, E. B., and Astrachan, B. M. (1975) 'Responses of mental health trainees to a group relations conference: understanding from a systems perspective.' *Social Psychiatry*, 10, 79–85.

Kernberg, O. F. (1973) 'Psychoanalytic object-relations theory, group processess and administration.' *The Annual of Psychoanalysis*, 1, 363–88.

Kernberg, O. F. (1975a) 'A systems approach to priority setting of intervention in groups.' *International Journal of Group Psychotherapy*, 25, 251–75.

Kernberg, O. F. (1975b) 'Modern hospital milieu treatment of schizophrenia.' In S. Arieti and G. Chrzanowski (eds.), *New Dimensions in Psychiatry: A World View*. New York: John Wiley.

Kernberg, O. F. (1974) 'Leadership, personality, and organizational functioning.' Paper presented at Thirty-First Annual Conference, American Group Psychotherapy Association, New York.

Klein, E. B. 'Transference in groups.' *Journal of Personality and Social Systems* (In press).

Klein, E. B. and Astrachan, B. M. (1971) 'Learning in groups: a comparison of study groups and T-groups.' *Journal of Applied Behavioral Science*, 7, 659–93.

Klein, E. B. and Gould, L. J. (1973) 'Boundary issues and organizational dynamics: a case study.' *Social Psychiatry*, 4, 204–11.

Klein, E. B., Thomas, C. S., and Bellis, E. (1971) 'When warring groups meet: the use of a group approach in police–Black community relations.' *Social Psychiatry*, 6, 93–99.

Klein, M. (1959) 'Our adult world and its roots in infancy.' *Human Relations*, 12, 291–303.

Kohler, T. 'A social system's approach to program evaluation.' *Journal of Personality and Social Systems* (In press).

Kohler, T., Miller, J. R., and Klein, E. B. (1973) 'Some effects of intergroup experiences on study group phenomena.' *Human Relations*, 26, 293–305.

Kreeger, L. (1975) *The Large Group: Dynamics and Therapy*. Itaska, Ill.: Peacock.

Levinson, D. J. (1959) 'Role, personality, and social structure in the organizational setting.' *Journal of Abnormal and Social Psychology*, 58, 170–80.

Levinson, D. J. and Astrachan, B. M. (1974) 'Organizational boundaries: entry into the mental health center.' *Administration in Mental Health*, 1, 1–12.

Levinson, D. J. and Klerman, G. L. (1967) 'The clinician-executive.' *Psychiatry*, 30, 3–15.

Lofgren, L. B. (1976) 'Organizational design and therapeutic effect.' In E. J. Miller (ed.), *Task and Organizations*. London: John Wiley.

Menninger, R. W. (1972) 'The impact of group relations conferences on organizational growth.' *International Journal of Group Psychotherapy*, 22, 415–30.

Menzies, I. E. P. (1967) 'The functioning of social systems as a defense against anxiety. A report on the study of nursing service of a general hospital.' Tavistock pamphlet No. 3.

Miller, E. J. (1959) 'Technology, territory, and time: the internal differentiation of complex production systems.' *Human Relations*, 12, 243–72.

Miller, E. J. (1975) 'Socio-technical systems in weaving, 1953–1970: a follow-up study.' *Human Relations*, 28, 349–86.

Miller, E. J. and Gwynne, G. V. (1972) *A Life Apart*, London: Tavistock Publications.
Miller, E. J. and Rice, A. K. (1969) *Systems of Organization*. London: Tavistock Publications.
Miller, J. C. (1976) 'The psychology of conflict in Belfast: conference as microcosm.' Paper, Scientific Meetings, A. K. Rice Institute.
Mills, T. M. (1965) *Group Transformation*. Englewood Cliffs, N. J.: Prentice-Hall.
Mills, T. M. (1967) *The Sociology of Small Groups*. Englewood Cliffs, N. J.: Prentice-Hall.
Mills, T. M. 'Working papers in systems awareness.' State University of New York at Buffalo (unpublished paper).
Minuchin, S. (1970) 'Techniques of family therapy: Interventions with the pathologically enmeshed family.' Paper presented at the Institute of Community and Family Psychiatry, Jewish General Hospital, Montreal, Canada.
Musto, D. F., and Astrachan, B. M. (1968) 'Strange encounter: the use of study groups students in history.' *Psychiatry*, **31**, 264–76.
Newman, R. (1967) *Psychological Consultation in the Schools*. New York: Basic Books.
Newman, R. (1974) *Groups in Schools*. New York: Simon and Schuster.
Newton, P. M. (1971) 'Abstinence as a role requirement in psychotherapy.' *Psychiatry*, **34**, 391–400.
Newton, P. M. (1973) 'Social structure and process in psychotherapy: a sociopsychological analysis of transference, resistance, and change.' *International Journal of Psychiatry*, **11**, 480–512.
Newton, P. M. and Levinson, D. J. (1973) 'The work group within the organization: a sociopsychological approach.' *Psychiatry*, **36**, 115–42.
O'Connor, G. (1971) 'The Tavistock method of group study.' *Science and Psychoanalysis*, **18**, 110–15.
Paine, W. S. and Huebner, B. (1973) 'Some order effects when a Tavistock study group analog and a human relations training analog are experienced sequentially in an introductory course.' Paper presented at the American Psychological Association.
Perls, F. (1969) *Gestalt Therapy Verbatim*. Lafayette, Cal.: Real People Press.
Redlich, F. C. and Astrachan, B. M. (1969) 'Group dynamics training.' *American Journal of Psychiatry*, **125**, 1501–7.
Reed, B. (1976) 'Organizational role analysis.' In C. L. Cooper (ed.), *Developing Social Skills in Managers*. London: Macmillan.
Reid, T. A. and Marinaccio, A. D. 'A perspective on organizational development: the open line project.' Hamden Mental Health Service, Hamden, Connecticut (unpublished manuscript).
Rice, A. K. (1953) 'Productivity and social organisation in an Indian weaving shed: an examination of the socio-technical system of an experimental automatic loomshed.' *Human Relations*, **6**, 297–329.
Rice, A. K. (1955a) 'The experimental reorganisation of non-automatic weaving in an Indian mill: a further study of productivity and social organisation.' *Human Relations*, **8**, 199–249.
Rice, A. K. (1955b) 'Productivity and social organisation in an Indian weaving mill, II. A follow-up study of the experimental reorganisation of automatic weaving.' *Human Relations*, **8**, 399–428.
Rice, A. K. (1958) *Productivity and Social Organisation: The Ahmedabad Experiment*. London: Tavistock.
Rice, A. K. (1963) *The Enterprise and its Environment*. London: Tavistock.
Rice, A. K. (1965) *Learning for Leadership*. London: Tavistock.
Rice, A. K. (1969) 'Individual, group and intergroup processes.' *Human Relations*, **22**, 564–84.
Rice, A. K. (1970) *The Modern University*. London: Tavistock.
Richardson, E. (1967) *Group Study for Teachers*. London: Routledge and Kegan Paul.
Richardson, E. (1973) *The Teacher, the School and the Task of Management*. London: Heinemann.

Richardson, E. (1975) *Authority and Organisation in the Secondary School*. London: Macmillan Education.

Rioch, M. J. (1970) 'The work of Wilfred Bion on groups.' *Psychiatry*, **33**, 56–66.

Rioch, M. J. (1974) 'The A. K. Rice conferences as a reflection of society.' Paper delivered to UCLA Department of Psychiatry.

Rioch, M. J., Coulter, W. R., and Weinberger, D. M. (1976) *Dialogues for Therapists*. San Francisco: Jossey-Bass.

Rogers, K. (1972) 'Group processes in police-community relations.' *Bulletin of the Menninger Clinic*, **36**, 515–34.

Ryan, M. A. 'An examination of the effects of the Tavistock model study group using the California Psychological Inventory.' Unpublished M.A. thesis, American University, Washington, D. C.

Schutz, W. (1967) *Joy: Expanding Human Awareness*. New York: Grove Press.

Shapiro, R. L. (1971) 'The study group as training for group psychotherapists.' Paper presented at American Group Psychotherapy Association, Los Angeles.

Singer, D. L., Astrachan, B. M., Gould, L. J., and Klein, E. B. (1975) 'Boundary management in psychological work with groups.' *Journal of Applied Behavioral Science*, **11**, 137–76.

Singer, D., Whiton, M. B., and Fried. M. (1970) 'An alternative to traditional mental health services and consultation in schools: a social systems and group process approach.' *Journal of School Psychology*, **8**, 172–79.

Slater, P. E. (1966) *Microcosm: Structural, Psychological and Religious Evolution in Groups*. New York: John Wiley.

Slavson, S. R. (1964) *A Textbook in Analytic Group Psychotherapy*. New York: International Universities Press.

Snow, D. L. and Newton, P. M. (1976) 'Task, social structure and social process in the community mental health center movement.' *American Psychologist*, **31**, 582–94.

Thorsrud, E. (1969) 'A strategy for research and social change in industry: a report on the industrial democracy project in Norway.' *Social Science Information*, **5**, 65–90.

Trist, E. (1970) 'A socio-technical critique of scientific management.' Presented at Edinburgh Conf. Impact Sci. Technol., Edinburgh University.

Trist, E. L. and Bamforth, K. W. (1951) 'Some social and psychological consequences of the longwall method of coal getting.' *Human Relations*, **4**, 3–38.

Trist, B. L., Higgin, G. W., Murray, H., and Pollack, A. B. (1963) *Organizational Choice: Capabilities of Groups at the Coal Face under Changing Technologies*. London: Tavistock.

Tuckman, B. W. (1965) 'Developmental sequence in small groups.' *Psychology Bulletin*, **63**, 384–99.

Turquet, P. M. (1974) 'Leadership: the individual and the group.' In G. S. Gibbard, J.J. Hartman and R. D. Mann (eds.), *Analysis of Groups*. San Francisco: Jossey-Bass, 337–71.

Turquet, P. M. (1975) 'Threats to identity in the large group.' In L. Kreeger (ed.), *The Large Group: Therapy and Dynamics*, London: Constable, 87–144.

Whitaker, D. S. and Lieberman, M. A. (1964) *Psychotherapy Through the Group Process*. New York: Atherton Press.

Wright, F. (1976) 'The effects of style and sex of consultants and sex of members in self-study groups.' *Small Group Behavior*, **7**, 433–56.

Wright, F., and Gould, L. J. 'Recent research on sex-linked aspects of group behavior: implications for group psychotherapy.' In L. R. Wolberg, and M. L. Aronson (eds.), *Group Therapy 1977: An Overview*. Stratton Intercontinental Medical Book Corporation, New York (In press).

Yalom, I. D. (1970) *The Theory and Practice of Group Psychotherapy*. New York: Basic Books.

Zegans, L., Schwartz, M. and Dumas, R. (1969) 'Mental health centers' response to racial crisis in urban school.' *Psychiatry*, **32**, 252–64.

Chapter **10**

Toward Improving the Quality of Community Life

Eva Schindler-Rainman

Ann Arbor, Michigan, U.S.A.

and

Ronald Lippitt

University of Michigan, U.S.A.

Among many applied behavioural scientists there is an emerging commitment and excitement about the total community as a client-system. There is a growing interest in exploring the relevance of concepts and methods from organizational development, and a growing recognition that some basic differences in diagnostic conceptualization, intervention strategy, and change-agent role are required in collaborating with a community system to develop meaningful planned change efforts.

There is much criticism and puzzlement, by community leaders and citizens, about the lack of vitality and attractiveness of our communities and cities—the wasteful overlapping services, the fragmentation of professional effort, the overloading of a small core of leaders, the non-involvement of the majority, and a lack of clear direction and planning for growth and development.

In our work with communities, and our concern for the vitality and development of democracy, we have become much involved in the overall problems of community life which are so important if we are to improve the quality of life for all of us.

The clearest path to the development of meaningful, rational goals, and the mobilization of community energy is the focusing of community-wide attention and deliberation on images of desired changes in the quality of life, on the process of making decisions about priorities for action, on the mobilizing of collaboration between organizations, agencies and institutions of the community, and on the involving of volunteer interest, wisdom, skills, time, and energy from all sectors of the community.

We have had exciting opportunities to work with some 50 communities of all sizes and complexities during the past five years, trying to discover ways of stimulating and facilitating processes of goal-setting, collaboration development and citizen participation and mobilization. We have become convinced that the many American communities are ready for significant breakthroughs to new levels of problem-solving, vitality, and support for a more satisfying way of life. This readiness for change has most frequently occurred because of some important and challenging current confrontations to communities and community life. These include:

(1) Requirements for collaboration in order to deal with the increasingly complex societal problems; also shrinking funds for human services and the emphasis by private and public funding sources that organizations collaborate in their efforts put a heavy demand for interdependence and collaboration on all people serving groups and institutions.

(2) Polarization of groups such as men and women, blacks and whites, young and old, confront community decision-makers with the need to try to help these groups communicate better.

(3) Increasing numbers of volunteers are available and active, but they are much more demanding about what they want to do, about their rights and about developing meaningful relationships with professionals; also that their volunteer work be recorded and usable as experience that will count if and when applying for paid work.

(4) There is also distrust and lack of confidence by those being planned for— the citizens, clients, consumers—of the technicians, the professionals who are the paid planners and who usually do not involve the to-be-affected persons in their planning.

New leading ways to work with the community

As we have helped communities develop plans and goals, we have found it helpful to approach 'the community' via its functional sectors. These include the following: *public safety* (courts, police, probation parole services), *recreation* (public, private, commercial), *social welfare* (private and public agencies), *education* (public, private and parochial), *health* (physical and mental health services—public and private), *economic community* (business, Industry), *labour*, *political community* (including elected and appointed officials as well as the more informal community influences), *cultural community* (art, music, dance, writing, architecture associations, museums, etc.) and *mass media* (TV, radio, newspapers).

Some key elements to developing a more vital community include:

(1) Developing new designs for community-wide collaboration—and to help the appropriate persons and groups learn the skills required in order to be able to develop collaborative networks.

(2) Developing ways for polarized segments to communicate better and/or more with each other; often this requires workshops to teach selected persons third-party mediation skills.

(3) Finding ways to recruit and mobilize young, middle and older, poor and

handicapped citizens from all sectors of community to participate actively in a wide variety of ways.

(4) Increasing the awareness, sensitivity and skills of professionals to develop opportunities for and be able to work with citizen volunteers.

An illustrative community system intervention

The illustrative case example which we are presenting below is a condensed narrative sequence drawn from our work with our sample of communities. We comment in the end on some variations of this pattern.

(1) The entry process

Typically it starts with a telephone call or a letter from some community group (such as the Junior League, Chamber of Commerce, Community College, Business Council, City Planning Department Voluntary Action Centre) which has a concern about the quality of community life and planning, the desire to stimulate collaboration, and a concern about some issue or issues such as utilization of volunteers, improvement of education, coping with the lack of collaboration between agencies and organizations, or improving the process of long-range planning. The first dialogue involves helping these initiators clarify the idea and explore possibilities of community representation and community involvement, thinking in terms of the sectors of community mentioned above. This involves thinking through who might be used as nominators to help identify the key leadership groups and individuals in the various functional communities and representing racial, ethnic, religious, age, sex and income groupings, as well as representation from the different sectors. The committee is helped to carry out this nomination process to identify typically 100 to 250 key persons who are truly representative of all aspects of community life who will be invited to the community-wide conference. Methods are available to make this an efficient and feasible process for reaching influentials from all parts of the community system.

(2) The invitation process and pre-conference involvement

One great strength of this process is that no particular organization or institution is seen as the dominant, visible sponsoring group. The sponsorship is a representative *ad hoc* planning committee which drafts the invitation letters; these indicate to the invitees that they are being invited because they have been nominated as key community leaders by a nomination process which has indicated that they are seen as key persons to participate in a community conference concerned with the quality of community life, the setting of community goals, and the working out of creative patterns of collaboration between organizations to reduce budgetary waste, programme overlap, unnecessary competition, etc. Everyone who receives an invitation is connected with someone on the planning committee who has handwritten a little note on the invitation urging a positive response. The invitation indicates the purpose of the conference, who is being invited, and what kind of outcomes are hoped for. It is made clear that participation in the conference needs to be a complete commitment for the one or two days because it is an integrated problem-solving process rather than discrete activities, such as speeches, which can be attended part-time. In the typical case which we are presenting here the conference is a two-day event.

(3) Designing and arranging for the community conference

The planning committee divided itself into three teams. One team worked with the consultants on the designing of the actual flow and materials for the conference. The second team worked on all the physical facilities, room arrangements, etc. for the conference. The third team followed through on the invitations and worked with the local newspaper, radio and other media on announcements about the conference, its purpose and the anticipated involvement of the total community in follow-up actions. This team also took responsibility for recruiting the squad of conference facilitators who would participate in a training session the night before the conference and work as members of the conference team during the event itself. Usually there is at least one facilitator for every table group of eight people.

The committee located an excellent conference site in one of the old downtown churches which had a good acoustically treated room large enough for 200 participants to work in table groups of seven or eight. They were able to supply flexible table arrangements from their large supply of card tables. A local newspaper contributed the supply of newsprint which would be needed during the conference; the school system contributed an overhead projector and portable loudspeaker units, and several agencies contributed the needed name-tags and other supplies. The church had the needed ditto machine and the committee planned to purchase the duplicating masters, felt-tip pens, masking tape and other supplies from the conference fee of $15.00. A very modest buffet lunch was planned, and several organizations agreed to contribute 'conference scholarships' if any of the invited participants felt the conference fee might be a hardship.

The Voluntary Action Centre had agreed to have its telephone number used on the invitation letter and the subcommittee provided volunteers to cover the telephone at certain hours each day so that follow-up calls could be made to invitees who had not responded, and inquiries about the conference could be responded to by someone with good information.

The committee was planning on about 200 participants, so facilitators were needed for an estimated 25 tables of eight each, in order to do a thorough job of documenting the products of group thinking, as well as providing facilitative leadership.

The committee decided to recruit teams of two volunteers for each table, a table documenter and a table facilitator. The committee found it remarkably easy to recruit 50 willing helpers, both volunteers and professionals, from the Community College, the junior League, the junior Chamber of Commerce, and the staffs and boards of several local agencies. The image of a significant conference was developing through the grapevine, through the interviews and other brief stories reported by the local media. Because the conference consultants did not live in town, they arranged for several phone conferences with the subcommittee collaborating with them on the design of the conference. After the firist telephone conference of an hour, the consultants prepared a tentative conference design and sent it ot the members of the subcommittee to review so their reactions could be sent in and discussed at a second phone conference. The consultants suggested the purchase of a small plastic phone amplifier (about $15.00) so that the members of the committee could all talk together on the phone with the consultants, utilizing just one telephone.

(4) The day before

The day before the conference the consultants met in the afternoon, at the conference site, with the members of the 'facilities team' to review the physical set up of the space for the small group work design, to pre-test the equipment, and to run off some ditto masters which they had brought with them for use in the evening training session with the facilitators and documenters. The plans for a rapid-service buffet lunch, and for the continuous availability of coffee, tea, and soft drinks during the day were clarified. The chairperson of the local planning group reported with pride that he had been able to get a subsidy of $3000 from a local foundation to support the production and printing of the conference proceedings and to subsidize some additional follow-up days of support from the consultants, if needed.

From 4.0 pm to 6.30 pm that afternoon the consultants conducted a 'micro-conference' with the 50 group facilitators and documenters, and ten alternates, to orient them to the steps and procedures of the conference, and gave them a chance to try out their own roles as table facilitators and conference documenters. High morale and much commitment to the significance of their own roles as table facilitators and conference documenters. High morale and much commitment to the significance of their own roles developed during this session.

The consultants then had dinner with the planning committee to go over last minute details and changes. The conversation was a mixture of anxious anticipation and preconference celebration.

(5) The community conference in action

(a) *Getting started.* As the conference participants arrived they found welcoming coffee, tea, soft drinks and coffee cake (baked by volunteers), a table with their name-tag and a folder. One of the registration helpers explained that the number on the name-tag indicated their table number, and then asked them to put their name at any and all appropriate places on the large chart on the wall. The chart, superimposed on the rough map of the community, indicated the major sectors of community function (that is, economic, political, religious, educational, recreational, cultural, etc.) and the briefing instructions asked participants to fill in their full name in the sector where they spent most of their time, and to jot in their initials in all other sectors where they were active in some way, either professionally or as a volunteer. They were then invited to find their table where their table facilitator would be waiting for them.

As soon as two people had arrived at a table, the facilitator and documenter began a conversation about the nature of each person's activities in the community sectors in which they had located themselves. The documenter kept notes on this information.

The conference had been announced for 9.30. By 9.45, 80 per cent of the 190 participants who had accepted the invitation had arrived.

The conference began with the chairperson of the planning committee introducing the two conference consultants. Proceedings began with a ten-minute interview with a panel of four well-known community leaders from the conference planning committee, discussing the origin of the conference and its purposes.

They then turned to a team of two members of the committee who had been summarizing the data from the sign-up chart in the hall, in order to make a 'who we are' report. As they reported briefly the data on the number of participants related to each aspect of community functioning, one of the consultants wrote the data on the overhead projector transparency so that the total 'who we are' report was visually up for everybody to see. One of the most interesting visible facts was the large numbers of persons who were active in three or more sectors of the community life in addition to their primary home base. The consultants pointed this out as a great 'linkage resource' for the development of communication and collaboration between subparts of the community.

In three or four minutes the conference leaders gave a brief overall overview of the plans for the day, reminded the group that work would be terminated at 4 o'clock, and would be reconvened at 9.30 the next day to carry through until 3.30. The importance of continuous participation was again emphasized.

(b) *Perspective on our past.* By 10.15 participants were ready to launch into the first inquiry event of the day, which was a half-hour exploration of significant highlights, events and trends in the history of the community which might help with the understanding of the nature of the community today. One of the conference consultants stimulated an active dialogue between the head of the County Historical Society and a professor of history at the local Community College. They had both been asked to be prepared to share in an informal way interesting anecdotes and interpretations of major themes of community development, critical turning points and trends and insights that might help us all understand 'why we are the way we are today' as a community. The table groups were then asked to hold brief discussions to formulate any further questions about community history and to offer comments about causes of 'why we are the way we are today'. The table discussions gave off a very active buzz and the question and discussion period was still going strong when it was terminated at 11 o'clock in order to move to the next phase of community diagnosis.

(c) *What we are proud about and sorry about today.*   Using the sensitization to the past as a warm-up and stimulus, the table groups were now asked to use the two pieces of newsprint on their tables to conduct two five-minute brainstorms. They were asked to take the roles of observers of their own community, and in the first brainstorm to list as rapidly as possible all the things about the community and community life which they were proud of, and in the second brainstorm to list all the things about the community and community life which they were sorry about. Before beginning their brainstorms, the conference consultants put on the overhead projector the four key rules of brainstorming and emphasized the importance of using these rules to ensure productivity of the brainstorm activity. The table documenter acted as recorder for the brainstorms at each table. At the end of five minutes time was called to shift to the second brainstorm. At the end of the two brainstorms each table group was asked to spend a few minutes checking the two or three items which were the 'greatest prouds' and the 'sorriest sorries'. Each table group was invited to call out one of its priority items and by a show of hands, other groups indicated whether they had checked the same item. It was obvious there was quite an interesting consensus about what groups were proud about and sorry about in looking at their community. It was announced that the documenters would work as a committee to summarize these brainstorms as part of the conference report, and also during lunch-hour they would be posted on one wall to be available to all the participants as a resource for reading and use during the rest of the conference.

(d) *Projecting images of potential.*   It was now 11.30 and the conference was ready for the third inquiry project, a trip into the future to develop the data needed for prioritizing community goals and exploring areas of consensus and dissensus. The conference consultants explained the nature of the trip into the future, proposing a one-year's-time perspective, and explained that they would be going ahead one year and making observations of what was happening in community life and intergroup cooperation that pleased them with the progress in the community toward an improved quality of life. This was neither a fantasy trip nor a prediction trip, but rather a freeing-up of imagination to observe credible, realistic, usable images of potentiality which they could imagine could come to pass, given the right amount of collaboration and effort. (For rationale and description of this technique see Fox, Lippitt, and Schindler-Rainman, 1973.) To start the trip the conference leaders asked for illustrations from anybody in the group that might be examples of what they would be seeing as they looked down one year from now and observed things that pleased them very much. Two or three illustrations were quickly forthcoming from participants and it was possible to emphasize the importance of concreteness and of talking in the present tense about what they were actually observing from their position a year from today. It was then suggested that each of the participants take a minute or two to rev up their imaginations, jotting down ideas to prepare themselves for pooling their images at their table in order to arrive at a table report on images of life in their community a year hence. In a minute or two pooling of images began at each table, and the facilitators helped the members at their tables to clarify and articulate their images, and the documenter recorded them on a large newsprint sheet. By 12 o'clock each table had produced, tested and clarified a list of images of desired future which they were ready to post on the wall for a conference reading period.

The conference leaders announced that there would be a one-and-a-half hour break for participants to pick up a buffer lunch to eat at their tables and for them to wander and read the future images reports and to check the four or five images which they personally felt were priorities. They were told that their checking would be the basis for generating the interest task forces to be formed in the afternoon, and that all participants would get their first choice of an interest group in which to go to work on plans for community action and improvement.

(a) *Lunching, reading, checking.* The volunteer catering subcommittee, using the budget provided by the conference committee, had set up a simple salad and dessert lunch on a long table in the hall outside the conference room so that participants could pick up their lunch easily and quickly, walking down either side of the table. Some participants began reading future images sheets on the wall and checking them before they ate, and others ate first and then began their reading project. At 1.30 there was a reminder that half an hour remained to finish the very important process of checking priorities, so that interest task groups could be established on the basis of the votes of the total 190 participants.

During this period the two conference consultants and three helpers from the planning committee were scanning the checks on the wall to see which items were definitely selected as interest-group priorities. This involved combining items from different sheets which were very similar. By two o'clock it was quite clear that 12 or 13 images were the most frequently selected ones. Many others had two or three checks. The ones receiving the high priority ratings were:

(1) A senior citizen resource centre
(2) A community talent resource bank
(3) A coordinating council for child and youth development, advocacy and education

(4) A 24-hour 'help for anybody for anything' service
(5) An interagency parent and family life enrichment programme
(6) A community leaders' exchange forum
(7) An arts council (coordinating all art activities)
(8) A teen employment and occupational exploration committee
(9) A women's advisory and career development centre
(10) A community calendar planning group
(11) A community 'ombudsman'
(12) A community closed-circuit TV forum
(13) A low-cost housing advisory group

This listing of interest groups was written on the overhead projector, with table location assignments. Before moving everybody into their first choice interest groups, conference leaders suggested that there might be some participants who felt that a very high priority had been neglected, one which they would like an opportunity to 'sell' before people made their final choices. It was suggested that if any such new interest group could attract at least three or four volunteers, it could certainly form as one of the planning task forces. Two such additional groupings were formed on the basis of effective presentations by advocates. Everyone then stood up and moved to the table location of their chosen interest group. In two cases more than 12 people chose a particular group, so two interest groups were formed on the same topic to make it possible to have a more effective small group process.

(f) *Diagnosis and action plan development.* During the next hour and a half each task force was helped by one of the trained table facilitators, to clarify and flesh out in greater detail their statement of their image of a desirable outcome or goal image. They then did a diagnostic force field analysis of the kinds of resources and supports which would be helpful in movement toward this objective and the major barriers and blocks and inhibitors of such movement. Through this process they identified the most important resources to be mobilized and the most important blocks to be coped with. They were then helped to brainstorm all the alternative possibilities for effective action and to use a planning sheet to formulate first steps of action and who would need to be involved in what ways to help make these steps successful.

During this period each group was introduced to the procedure of a five to ten-minute 'stop session' in which they used a brief evaluation check sheet to look at their satisfaction with their own work process in their interest group, and to share ideas about ways of improving their productivity as they continued to work. During this period of work the final plans and ideas for needed next steps were recorded on ditto masters so they could immediately be produced and made available for the participants in the other groups. The other thing each interest group did, in looking ahead to tomorrow, was to identify three or four persons either in the conference or not in attendance who might be important reactors to and testers to their ideas and plans. It was suggested that such persons might be either resource experts, or policy or budget gatekeepers, or important sanctioners.

During this period the consultants were actively moving from group to group to support the facilitators and to help any group that was having difficulty in its planning process or in making decisions about those they wanted to invite for the review process the next day. Each group was responsible for doing its own inviting of the reaction panel members, either contacting them at another table to make an appointment for the morning, or to plan who would make telephone calls to invite key persons who were not present.

All participants received dittoed one-page summaries of the reports from the other task forces by the end of the afternoon.

(g) *Pulse taking and preparation for tomorrow.* As the participants left they jotted on a prepared feedback sheet their personal reactions about their own participation during the day, their evaluation of the progress and needs of their group, and their hopes for activity and support the next day.

The planning committee met to review the reactions and expressed desires for the next day, discussing needed changes in the design and checking-out plans for Day 2.

(6) The second conference day

(a) *Feasibility test reviews.* The participants were remarkably on time the second day, with many evidences of vitality and eagerness to 'get on with it'. Coffee was picked up and taken to task-force tables as members convened to move ahead on their planning. The conference consultants conducted a brief general session of about 15 minutes, presenting on the overhead projector a series of questions the group might want to consider using in testing the feasibility of their action ideas with the resource persons they had selected. There were about a dozen newcomers who had been recruited by telephone calls to come and help the particular task forces assess the feasibility of their ideas and their planning. Those new participants were welcomed and given a brief perspective on what had happened the day before and on the importance of their particular function. They were invited to stay for the remainder of the conference, but it was also made very legitimate for them to give their input and leave during the course of the morning. Until 10.30 all of the task forces worked actively with their resource persons and with each other on critically testing their action strategies, their goals and their first-step ideas.

(b) *Anticipatory practice.* During the next hour the participants were introduced to the procedure of behavioural simulation or anticipatory skill practice. After a brief demonstration the facilitators helped each task force to identify critical confrontation situations they could anticipate in initiating their first steps of action, for example recruiting new key persons, responding to criticism and resistance, presenting a proposal to a key power group, being challenged by vested interest groups. In each group there was an opportunity to 'dry run' and try out such critical situations and to brainstorm alternatives, strategies and actions for coping more successfully.

(c) *Support for risk taking.* During the buffet lunch the conference planning committee invited several of the key leadership figures of the community, particularly from the political and economic community, to comment on their feelings about the significance of the conference and of the planning activities of the task forces. They were invited to indicate not only their sanction and their support but their readiness to collaborate in concrete ways, for example, providing meeting facilities, helping in the search for needed money, linking to external resources such as county, state and federal.

(d) *Towards transition and continuity.* The final period, starting about 1.30, was essentially a planning conference for each task force to clarify their division of labour for next steps, the time and place of the next meeting, their agenda for their next session, the interim work to be done by various members of the group, steps to be taken in recruiting any additional task force members, needs for continuing consultation, and the preparation of a two- or three-minute report to the total conference on their progress and their plans. At three o'clock the final general session was convened, and each task force made its public report, which was also documented by the conference documenters working with their particular task forces. The conference leadership made a commitment about the preparation and distribution of a conference report. They also welcomed and identified representatives of the media who had been invited in for the afternoon report session. The media were encouraged to interview any of the task force group members after they had heard the several reports, in order to prepare any types of special interest stories they might want to report. A press conference had also been arranged with the conference leaders and several of the other key community figures to provide perspective and information on the total conference process and on the plans for continuity of effort.

A final personal evaluation form was filled out, which gave individuals an opportunity to evaluate the conference, to indicate their personal commitment, and to give guidance to the steering committee as to future needs for support and facilitation.

The conference planning committee had consulted with the elected convenors of each of the task forces and were able to announce a meeting in about a month of the planning committee with all of the task force convenors to assess progress and to clarify needs for future steps of action and coordination.

Some variations of intervention design

The process described above has been remarkably potent in generating sustained continuities of community development and change. Several variations in design have adapted this intervention to the needs, structures, and start-up sponsorship of various communities.

One of the major variables is the time available for the actual conference. Sometimes both time and money budgets limit the process to a one-day conferences. If this happens, the second day activities described above become part of the follow-up action plans for each task force, and follow-up consultation support, and an internal 'support cadre' are even more important.

Sometimes the conference is held around a more specific and narrow theme, such as community-wide recruitment and training of volunteers, improving services for youth, new roles and opportunities for women, etc. In these cases the groups invited to participate are those appropriate to the particular topic.

Pay-offs

Follow-up has been done in many of the communities that have participated in these collaborative community conferences. Here are some typical results of accomplishments.

(1) Task forces to coordinate volunteer activities have helped to establish new voluntary action and information centres.

(2) The need for collaborative action relating to some kind of 24-hour information and referral service has resulted in such services being set up.

(3) Directories of human services, often bilingual, have been prepared with regular updating plans as an integral part of this effort.

(4) Several student employment opportunity centres have been initiated.

(5) New, especially minority, leadership that emerged during the conference has become an important part of the community leadership structure.

(6) New facilities have been found or established for youth offenders.

(7) Coordinated community calendars have emerged, produced cooperatively by the Chamber of Commerce and the volunteer agencies.

(8) Courses on volunteer administration have been established at many community colleges and universities.

(9) Several community coordinating committees have been established with representation from the private and the public sectors.

There are also many examples of mechanisms of continuity of effort emerging from the conferences. They take a variety of paths:

(1) Conference task forces who find a permanent 'roof' or sponsor (for example, the task force on youth employment opportunities gets taken on by the Mayor's Commission on Youth)

(2) Conference task forces who merge with an already established body to

strengthen and often change the direction of that group (for example, several task forces on development of low cost housing have merged with other groups working on this activity)

(3) Sometimes a task force does its initial work (e.g., exploring the establishment of a voluntary action centre) and then the new board of that agency takes over. Often some members of the task force become board members.

(4) Professional trainers and consultants, internal to the community, have been identified and continue to be utilized.

(5) Follow-up meetings and conferences have been planned and held in many places.

Summary comments

Our approach of helping with community goal-setting and action-taking draws much from Douglas McGregor's approach to the process of organizational change and from Kurt Lewin's analysis of the re-educative process in small face-to-face groups. We have found their insights about the integration of system concepts, interpersonal relations concepts, and personal motivation and voluntary involvement very basic to our work with the more complex intergroup systems called communities. Both McGregor and Lewin would have been quick to recognize the key differences between groups, organizations, and communities, and very inventive in adapting to their differences. We believe our values, assumptions, strategies, and designs are in a direction they would have chosen. The total community has certainly been a neglected client-system, and one where some of the greatest needs for development of planned change theory and practice exist today.

Bibliography

Benne, K., Bradford L., Gibb, J., and Lippitt, R. (eds.) (1975) *The Laboratory Method of Changing and Learning*. Palo Alto, Cal.: Addison Wesley.

Bennis, W., Benne, K., and Chin, R., (eds.) (1975) *The Planning of Chance*. New York: Holt, Rinehart and Winston.

Bloomberg, W. and Schmandt, H. (eds.) (1968) *Poverty and Urban Policy*. Beverly Hills, Cal.: Sage Publications, Inc.

Davidoff, P., Gold, L., and Nell, N., (1970) 'Suburban action: advocate planning for an open society.' *Journal of the American Institute of Planners*, **XXXVI, January**.

Fox, R., Lippitt, R., and Schindler-Rainman, E. (1973) *Towards A Humane Society: Images of Potentiality*. Fairfax, Va.: Learning Resources, Inc.

Gardner, J. W. (1971) 'We have learned some rules for effective action.' *Common Cause*, **September**.

Goodman, R. (1971) *After the Planners*. New York: Simon and Schuster.

Kramer, R. (1969) *Participation of the Poor*. Englewood Cliffs, N.J.: Prentice-Hall.

Lippitt, R., Watson, J., and Wesley, B. (1958) *The Dynamics of Planned Change*. New York: Harcourt, Brace.

Mazzlotti, D. F. (1974) 'The underlying assumptions of advocacy planning: pluralism and reform.' *Journal of the American Institute of Planners*, **XXXIX, January**.

Schindler-Rainman, E. (1963) 'Leadership training in underdeveloped neighborhoods.' *Adult Leadership*, **June**.

Schindler-Rainman, E. and Lippitt, R. (1969) 'What we have learned from working with the poor.' *Human Relation Training News*. Va. NTL, **13**, 1–3.

Schindler-Rainman, E. and Lippitt, R. (1972) *Team Training for Community Change*. Riverside, Cal.: Univ. of Calif. Exten. Press.

Schindler-Rainman, E. and Lippitt, R. (1975) *The Volunteer Community: Creative Use of Human Resources. 2nd Edition*. Fairfax, Va: Learning Resources, Inc.

Silberman, C. E. (1969) *Crisis in Black and White*. New York: Random House.

Warren, R. L. (1973) 'Comprehensive planning and coordination: some functional aspects.' *Social Problems*, **Winter**.

Chapter 11

Reflections on These Advances in Experiential Social Processes

Clayton P. Alderfer

Yale University, U.S.A.

The chapters in this volume represent some of the best contemporary intellectual work on experiential social processes. They show how concerns about human values have been elaborated, how the field has become increasingly differentiated in both theory and technique, and how the experiential perspective is having an impact on a widening range of social science problems. The results suggest that after years of being primarily an educational methodology the experiential approach is becoming an increasingly serious force in social research.

Value themes

In its short history the experiential social process movement has encountered value confrontations both from inside and outside its boundaries. Cooper and Levine accept the validity of some of these criticisms and provide a systematic way of understanding how value issues impact education by experiential methods. Taking a frame of reference utilized by several authors in this volume, these writers discuss value issues in experiential education according to the level of analysis where the dilemmas arise. They note five sources from which values may affect T-groups: society at large, organizational context, trainer, members, and the interaction process itself. Despite the fact that human values have played a key part in the development of experiential social processes, few practitioners have the kind of broad-ranging framework for analysing value problems provided by Cooper and Levine. Moreover, few critics of experiential methods recognize the degree to which experiential designs can be moulded to address a vast variety of value questions.

Kaplan calls attention to the wider historical and cultural context in which experiential methods are employed. Although the problem of transferring learning from the laboratory to the 'real world' has been a matter of concern since the discovery of experiential techniques, advocates of these methods have nonetheless often behaved as if society was the 'enemy' standing against a far more desirable utopian community. Kaplan confronts the field with its own ethnocentrism by his analysis of the forms, functions, and feasibility of openness in human affairs. His work also indicates that openness as a value and a behaviour has a history that begins long before the discovery of experiential methods. In fact experiential processes participate in a reasonably well-developed tradition ambivalently promoting openness for individual and collective improvement.

These chapters provide a timely re-examination of the idea of a 'cultural island' in experiential education. While it may be technically sound to separate some experiential activities from the pressures of day-to-day events, it is conceptually unsound to view this intervention as creating a setting that is able to develop its own values without constraints from the wider cultures which surround it. There are more complex value issues in experiential education that was once understood, and it is now possible to reason more completely about the value implications of various experiential social processes. Experiential social processes are less separate from the broader culture than ever before.

Theoretical developments

At the origin experiential methods primarily relied upon inductive thought processes. The T-group was the primary work unit, and feeding back minimally conceptualized observations was the major means of learning. Advances in experiential social processes have broadened the array of intellectual processes available to people in this field. Theory now influences the design of experiential processes. Deductive thinking has a place in the design and execution of laboratory education. Moreover, data from experiential activities are directly provoking theoretical advances. *Theories of intervention* are developed to provide better concepts for practitioners to understand, predict, and control the consequences of their professional behaviour. *Theories of phenomena* are emerging as intellectually oriented practitioners uncover anomalies or discover new phenomena, unaccounted for by existing theories.

Lennung's classification of experiential social processes provides a series of defining dimensions for the field. His work shows the great variety of issues that bear upon simply understanding how this area should be conceptualized. Greater definitional clarity makes more precise interventions possible and sharpens the empirical and theoretical inquiries that may be conducted.

Bolman's chapter gives an example of reasoning from a theoretical position to the design of an experiential intervention. Bolman used a theory of action perspective that called for participants to provide evidence regarding personal theories of action and samples of behaviour during professional work. The theoretical framework predicted discrepancies between theory and action. The intervention method was devised to reduce the discrepancies by changing behaviour without the interventionist's behaviour becoming discrepant from his theory of action. Bolman presented evidence that was consistent with his *a priori* predictions. He was able to show how the theory of action guided his own behaviour as interventionist and helped to explain the responses of his clients.

Brown's work on power differences and intergroup relations demonstrates how new theoretical formulations can be stimulated by data produced in experiential laboratories. Reflecting on the data generated by simulations of relations between groups of vastly unequal power, he was able to develop a series of hypotheses regarding the conditions effecting the mobilization of lower power groups. This work contrasts markedly with most of the experiential work with intergroups, where power is frequently equal, and with social class theory, where lower group mobilization has not been a primary variable to be explained.

As noted in the introduction, the chapters in this volume are roughly organized by level of analysis—from individual to society. They are presented in this order for additional reasons than simply logical convenience. Brown's analysis of intergroup phenomena employs a multilevel analysis; his hypotheses are organized in terms of intragroup, intergroup, and extragroup. Cooper and Levine's value analysis is taken directly from a consideration of how value differences impinge upon T-group functioning from five levels of analysis and their intersection. In both the Brown and Cooper–Levine chapters we see a second order of analysis by level. Brown's focus of attention is intergroup behaviour, and he calls upon other levels of analysis to help explain intergroup behaviour. Cooper and Levine's target is T-group (or small group) behaviour, and they point out the need to account for other levels in designing T-group laboratories.

The design and analysis of experiential methods is significantly aided by an open systems view of human behaviour, which includes major explanatory concepts by level of analysis. While this view is implicitly accepted by a large number of practitioners, the pattern revealed in this series of papers suggests that there will be even greater acceptance of this basic theoretical position as increasingly sophisticated intellectual developments about experiential social processes continue.

Technical advances

The roots of experiential social processes rest with the invention of new social technologies, and the chapters in this volume maintain this tradition. Works by Schmuck and by Schindler-Rainman and Lippitt are particularly good examples of sophisticated practitioners inventing new social technologies to cope with especially complex social system dynamics. Chapters in this volume also show another twist in the proliferation of social technologies—the effects of one class of social technology impacting another. The chapters by Mahrer, Walter, and Klein all deal with the intersection of more than one major social technology.

Schmuck's concept of peer consultation in public schools derives from a social necessity and a value position. Given the size and complexity of urban public school systems, there will never be enough time to train all the applied behavioural science consultants needed to meet the potential demand for service. Further support for the 'peer' model comes from antihierarchy values within the experiential methods movement itself, and perhaps, as Schmuck notes, from the democratic norms of United States' public education. Despite the title, the chapter on peer consultation, in fact, is a discussion of conditions when the development of internal cadres of 'peers' can aid the improvement of public schools in conjunction with consultation by external experts.

Schindler-Rainman and Lippitt write about their experiences with community consultation and the techniques they have developed to deal with this most complex intervention. Their approach relies on bringing together a large number of individuals (100–250 people) from many diverse groups to promote a sense of the total community and to engage in interunit problem-solving. This paper is of special historical interest because Lippitt was among the original inventors (along with Bradford, Benne, and Lewin) of experiential methods in the United States.

Psychotherapy does not qualify as an 'experiential technique', according to the normal use of the term. Nonetheless, there has been a long association between therapists and experiential educators. A substantial number of people are qualified to practise in both fields, and there are a variety of elements common to both therapy and experiential education. As people initially trained as therapists have been attracted to experiential techniques, they have in turn utilized experiential techniques in education of therapists or in the actual conduct of therapy. Mahrer's chapter in this volume is unique in its message and mode of communication. It literally demonstrates what 'experiential psychotherapy' is by treating readers as if they were clients of the writer as psychotherapist. The intersection between experiential education and psychotherapy is thereby vividly communicated.

Psychoanalytical theory originally developed from the treatment of psychotherapy patients. A major step in extension of psychoanalytical technique to experiential education was the development of the Tavistock method of group relations training. Klein's chapter in this volume explains the theoretical roots of the Tavistock method in the United Kingdom and the United States. His work includes a review of empirical research concerning participant reactions to psychoanalytically oriented experiential methods. Tavistock theory and technique have also contributed to the training of psychotherapists and the analysis of psychiatric hospitals and other human service institutions.

Perhaps the boldest effort extending experiential technology to other fields is Walter's chapter forging a link between video tape viewing for behaviour change and television watching for entertainment. This author proposes a single theoretical framework for explaining the different effects of observing human behaviour, which attempts to account for both individual and societal level changes. This effort also demonstrates the press toward multilevel analysis provoked by experiential methods. It also suggests that the intersection of social and engineering technologies may be an important force stimulating theoretical developments in social science.

Taken together the technical advances described in this volume show that social inventiveness continues to characterize the field of experiential social processes and that experiential technologies are influencing the design and interpretation of results from other methods as well.

Conclusion

If one accepts the framework proposed by Thomas Kuhn (1962) in the *Structure of Scientific Revolutions,* then most parts of social science are in a 'pre-paradigm' phase in their development. At this moment in history there is no universally accepted body of theory and method that every writer feels forced to employ and explain. Instead there are a variety of 'schools', which compete with one another without clear resolution with respect to such issues as the definition of crucial variables and the nature of relevant evidence. Kuhn (1962, p. 17) and others have noted that technological developments often play a key part in moving science from pre-paradigm to an initial paradigm. The Leyden jar, discovered independently by at least two investigators in the early 1740s, played such a part in the study of electricity. Perhaps the discovery of experiential methods will play a similar role in the social sciences. The papers in this volume—with their attention to the intersection of values, theory, and technology—and the existence of the series itself, at minimum, testify that a new 'school' in the pre-paradigm social sciences has come into being.

References

Kuhn, T. S. (1962) *The Structure of Scientific Revolutions.* Chicago: University of Chicago Press.

Index